Playwriting for the Puppet Theatre

Jean M. Mattson

The Scarecrow Press, Inc.
Lanham, Md., & London
1997

SCARECROW PRESS, INC.

Published in the United States of America
by Scarecrow Press, Inc.
4720 Boston Way
Lanham, Maryland 20706

4 Pleydell Gardens, Folkestone
Kent CT2O 2DN, England

Copyright © 1997 by Jean M. Mattson

British Library Cataloguing in Publication Information Available

Library of Congress Cataloging-in-Publication Data

Mattson, Jean M., 1925-
    Playwriting for the puppet theatre / Jean M. Mattson.
      p.   cm.
    Includes index.
    ISBN 0-8108-3324-7 (alk. paper)
    1. Puppet plays, American.   2. Puppet plays—Authorship.
   3. Puppet theatre.   I. Title.
PN1980.M38   1997   97-8165
808'.066791—dc2l   CIP

ISBN 0–8108–3324–7 (pbk.: alk. paper)

∞ ™ The paper used in this publication meets the minimum requirements of
American National Standard for Information Sciences—Permanence of
Paper for Printed Library Materials, ANSI Z39.48–1984.
Manufactured in the United States of America.

This book is dedicated to the memory of Paul Nelson, whose talent and love of puppetry provided the foundation for my love affair with puppets, and to Joan King, who has made the last fifteen years a satisfying vocation and a wonderfully exciting romp.

CONTENTS

Part I   PLAYWRITING FOR PUPPET THEATRE

Part II   PLAY SCRIPTS

Two-Person (or more) Scripts

Part I

Playwriting for Puppet Theatre

Introduction

I never understood why I was a "playwright" instead of a "playwriter" until I read somewhere that the word "wright" means worker. It was originally used for those who crafted various items or worked in various occupations. A "wheelwright" was a person who made wheels. A "millwright" was a person who built mills. So playwrights are workers who make plays.

I have been fascinated by theatre and motivated to write plays since I was in grade school. In high school I wrote pep assemblies. In college I wrote sorority programs. My degree was in a completely unrelated field and my jobs did not include dramatics of any kind. Nevertheless, I continued to develop programs and plays, managing to sell a few periodically. I finally went back to school and earned an M.A. in theatre arts. My focus, however, was always on traditional theatre, not puppet theatre.*

I was not formally introduced to puppetry until 1973. At that time I met Paul E. Nelson, a gifted actor who had loved puppets since he was a child, when he did shows for the neighborhood in his back yard. In 1973, Paul and two of his friends were launching a series of Saturday morning puppet shows for children and they needed an extra puppeteer for their Christmas program. I happened to be working with them in a Seattle theatre production of *Dark of the Moon*, so they asked me to join them. It sounded like fun, so I did. It was fun—but anything but a financial success.

The two friends left for more prosperous prosceniums. Paul and I decided to start a puppet company. He had a suitcase full of puppets. I had a tape recorder plus a station wagon, and we worked well together. Thus the Seattle Puppetory Theatre was born.

Before then, my academic and vocational focus had been on live theatre. I soon recognized puppetry as a genuine and appealing branch of legitimate theatre that engaged my energies and added another dimension to my playwriting endeavors.

For a number of years I have been script consultant for the Puppeteers of America, which means that members send their scripts to me for evaluation. In these scripts I have often found weaknesses, but I have also come across sections of genuine feeling, appealing characters, and provocative concepts. The individuals who write plays are almost always highly imaginative and motivated. However, for any person unfamiliar with play structure, character development, and so on, the number of variables involved in the formation of a play can lead to confusion and frustration. I have found that some of these inexperienced playwrights could use a few guideposts to help them through this maze of possibilities.

There are a number of books available on playwriting for traditional theatre, but they do not address the unique aspects of puppet theatre. The books written on puppetry usually focus on the history of puppetry, the various types of puppet construction, staging, and so

---

*The one notable exception (which is probably best forgotten), was a puppet project for the Women's Missionary Society of the First Lutheran Church in Anaconda, Montana, many years ago. Several other women and I, inspired by an article on marionette construction in *Woman's Day* and galvanized by the altruism of our missionary messages, wrote, produced, and performed a series of puppet plays. We were totally oblivious to the fact that we knew nothing about puppetry. Fortunately, what the plays lacked in artistic merit was offset by the postperformance euphoria of the puppeteers and the exceptional charity of the audiences.

on, with perhaps a chapter on developing a script. The script is the backbone of any puppet show, and this book, which focuses exclusively on writing plays for puppet theatre, provides the special attention that scripting deserves. It is a book for teachers who need a play to fit into their curriculum, for librarians who wish to dramatize a story, and for a program chairperson who wants a show with a particular theme. This book is also for professional puppeteers who have not been trained in theatre and who know little about playwriting but end up writing their own scripts because of the dearth of good puppet scripts available.

When referring to playwrights I have used "he," "his," and "him" throughout. I have avoided the awkward "he/she" constructions in order to simplify my writing.

At different times through the years, various talented people who shared an interest in puppetry have also been associated with Seattle Puppetory Theatre. Among them were Betsy Tobin, Naomi Baltuck, Heather Ellis, Selma Johnson, John Bartelt, John Miller, Tam and Bev London, and Jennifer Kulick. I appreciate the assistance of each of these puppeteers who, through our team efforts in mounting countless productions, have helped me immeasurably in developing my playwriting skills. My current partner, Joan King, and I have worked together for fifteen years. She has always been the undisputed technical director of our company. (Unless otherwise noted, the puppets in the photos are her creations.) Her inventive mind and persistent effort have led us into many creative explorations, even international adventures. Almost as important as her vast knowledge of puppet theatre and her unfailing encouragement is her expertise on the computer, which, fortunately for the author of this book, she has always been willing to share.

I am also grateful to those who have helped in the development of the book, especially Jeanine Bartelt, a manager of the Puppetry Book Store, and Bev London, current president of Puppeteers of America, for their invaluable suggestions.

Chapter I

Getting Our Bearings

Puppetry is "theatre," serious, exciting, legitimate! And in puppet theatre, as in any type of drama, there are six basic components. Aristotle recognized them in the third century B.C. and they haven't changed since.

Plot: The organization of the material in the play.

Character: Those people or beings participating in the play.

Thought: The emotions, qualities and ideas of the characters and the underlying themes.

Diction: The words, the dialogue, the expression of the thought.

Sounds: Music, sound effects, and the way in which dialogue is spoken which gives meaning.

Spectacle: The physical action and all the things that make up the stage pictures.

Furthermore, most of the same general principles that govern traditional theatre are intrinsic to puppet theatre. Therefore, some foundation in theatre art is helpful to anyone interested in writing for puppet theatre. Among the many commonalities are the scores of terms familiar to those in traditional theatre that also are used in puppet theatre. For general understanding, I have included here some of the most often encountered, most of which are used later in this book.

Antagonist: The character who stands in the way of the main character. The character who causes the problems.

Backdrop: A piece of scenery, often made of cloth, which is hung at the back of the stage. It can be plain or painted with a scene. Some are changed several times during a play.

Blocking: The pattern of movement of the characters on stage as they act out the scenes of the play.

Climax: The highest point of the play, the final crisis toward which the action has been building.

Conventions: Accepted rules of the theatre and of a particular play. For instance, night scenes are seldom played in the dark because the audience would not be able to see what is going on. Or, it might be established that characters in white are ghosts and those in color are living people. In some hand puppet stages, puppets must enter as if springing up out the ground or the puppeteers are in plain view of the audience. These conventions are set by performers for a particular play and are accepted by the audience.

House lights: Lights in the auditorium or room in which the performance takes place.

Props: Abbreviation for properties. Any of the smaller items an actor or puppet uses on stage during a performance—fans, flowers, books, pipes, cooking utensils, and so on. (Also known as "hand props.")

Proscenium: The open frame in a solid wall, or curtained wall, which forms a playing area. The frame of the stage.

Protagonist: The main character in a play, the hero or heroine.

Resolution: The dénouement. The ending of the play after the climax, when the loose ends are tied and indications of the future are given.

Set: The complete arrangement of the scenery or setting created for a play.

Set pieces: Large pieces of scenery that make up the complete set—furniture, steps, door frames, trees, fences, and so on. (Also called "stage props.")

Stage business: Activity by the puppets on stage, such as watering the flowers, sweeping, sewing, picking up items, and so on.

Stage directions: Stage directions remain the same no matter the type or size of theatre.

Stage Right is always to the actor's right as he faces the audience.

Stage Left is always to the actor's left as he faces the audience.

Downstage is toward the audience.

Upstage is away from the audience.

Wings: Set pieces or curtains at the sides of the stage to mask the backstage areas and the actors and puppets as they exit.

Despite the similarities between puppet theatre and traditional theatre, there are important differences that must be noted and assimilated by anyone who writes for puppets. Several of the most obvious are listed here.

Puppets are not actors (although the puppeteers should be). Most puppets are by their very nature limited as far as facial expressions and body movements are concerned, but have their own unique capabilities. They are extraordinary creatures, existing in their own milieu and offering magical possibilities to the playwright.

Blocking is a problem for all theatre productions, but it possesses special problems for the puppet theatre, because every puppet is in some way attached to its puppeteer. As the playwright moves his puppets through their paces, he must continually remind himself about the puppeteers, who are inevitably over, under, or behind (and sometimes even inside) the puppets.

Staging is also a major consideration. Stages are seldom provided at the various performance locations. The puppeteers usually must furnish their own to fit the type and size of their puppets. Furthermore, because the vast majority of puppet companies tour, this stage and all the equipment must be portable and compact. Likewise, because most teachers and librarians seldom have enough room, they also need equipment that folds and packs easily for storage. Needless to say, these circumstances have a considerable effect on the staging (and, therefore, the scripting) of any show.

This book aims to address the challenge of combining the basic principles of theatre with the fascination and foibles of the puppet.

Preparation for the Job

After the initial exhilarating decision, "I'll write a play!"—what then? At that time, a beginning playwright needs to know just what constitutes a play script. I have found that the easiest way for anyone to understand the playwriting process is to view the script as a recipe.

Imagine a large, luscious chocolate cake. The people who eat it seldom have read the recipe used to make the cake. The cook who wrote the recipe first envisioned the finished delight in his or her mind, how it would look and taste. Then he listed all the **ingredients** needed to create the culinary masterpiece— eggs, sugar, vanilla, chocolate, baking powder, milk, and so on, and the exact amount of each ingredient. Next, the cook figured out just how these ingredients will be combined, the **directions**.

Similarly, the people who see a play seldom have read the script. Just as a detailed account of the baking operation is meant for the cook, not the diners, so the play script is written for those who are producing the play—the director, the puppeteers or actors, the puppet or costume maker, the set designer—not the audience. The playwright must incorporate all the **ingredients** important to the production of his brainchild, including the characters, sets, costumes, props, and lighting. Just as germane are the **directions** on how, where, and when to put these ingredients together.

Many playwrights who write for their own companies do not write detailed play scripts because it is thought to be time-consuming and unnecessary. Their thinking is partially correct. It is time-consuming, but it also is prudent. If a playwright writes a script for others, to make it understood he will be forced to analyze and describe in detail his characters, the blocking, every word of his dialogue, and every stage direction. Such an exercise not only enables any director to produce this same play later but also immediately clarifies and refines the details for the puppeteers and for the playwright himself.

But the written script is no more the end result than the recipe is. Before the recipe can be printed and used or shared, it must be evaluated. Do people ask for a second piece of this cake? Is it what the cook had hoped for? Perhaps it needs brown sugar instead of white, or more baking powder. Or perhaps it wasn't baked quite long enough. Or the eggs should have been separated and beaten first to give it that extra lightness he wanted. Changes must be made in the original recipe. Then it is tried again—and again—until it pleases the consumers and is just what the cook had in mind.

A play script is no different. After a play is finished it must be tested before an audience. Changes usually are required because wonderful ideas envisioned in the playwright's mind often do not translate onto the stage. Characters need development. The climax is weak. The dialogue is stilted. Rehearsal and revision are an essential part of the playwriting process. Only with testing and refinement will the creators see satisfying final results,

whether it be an elegant dessert or a smash hit.

You can combine the six components of drama in countless ways, but there are some basic requirements involved in playwriting which, if they are ignored, will result in a less than successful play. The guidelines noted in this book for creating a successful play are offered from my experiences in writing and producing puppet plays. They are given in reference to the anticipated dynamics between a play's performance and the audience's responses, not from my own personal preferences. Just as the ultimate test of any cake is the way in which it is gobbled up, so, regardless of the playwright's novel ideas or a critic's evaluation, **the ultimate success or failure of a play is the way the audience receives it.**

No doubt, someone will bring up some play that failed dismally on Broadway, only to later be revived to become an audience favorite and an award-winner. Granted, these flukes happen—but seldom. A negative audience response, devastating for the playwright, usually indicates that something is wrong with the play. Of course, a playwright has the prerogative to include anything and everything in his script. "It's my play!" But he runs a serious risk if he carelessly indulges his own whims and fantasies without regard for his audience.

What, then, are the basic requirements for a positive audience response? From my experience as spectator, playwright, and director, I have concluded that the people who come to see a play generally have three basic needs. First, **they need to understand.** Why would a person watch a play if he doesn't understand what's going on? Second, **the audience needs to care**. Why would a person watch a play involving people he cares nothing about? Third, **the audience needs to feel satisfied**. A happy ending is not necessary, but we want to leave the theatre feeling contented, that the time there has been well-spent. Playgoers often sense that something is out of whack, although they may not know what it is.

This book is aimed at those who wish to write for general audiences. It is not for the iconoclast who worships the avant garde and the obtuse, or whose only purpose is to provide visual pleasure, vague emotional responses, or dramatic experiments. Those who consider themselves the impetus behind the latest paridigm shift in the philosophy of the puppet need not read further. However, that is not to eliminate the "absurd" or the "fantastic," for puppets excel in these areas. Such approaches are welcome, as long as they cater to the audience needs as mentioned above.

Any person who writes a play must be a cerebral director of sorts. In order to develop a concept, through words and actions, he must sense the emotions and reasons behind those words and actions. He must know the abilities of the actor or puppeteer who will be speaking his lines. He must visualize the composition of the stage as his drama unfolds, feel the tensions, and imagine the movements. In other words, he must literally direct the whole production in his mind as he sets it down on paper. Though his ideas may shift during rehearsals, and though another director may adjust the details and alter the perspective, the play will reach its highest potential only if the initial vision encompasses the production as a whole.

But before beginning to visualize or write, some things must be clear in the playwright's mind. Although they may seem too obvious, the following questions should be asked, whether the playwright is writing for his own company or for others. The answers to these questions will influence the type of play he chooses and how it is developed.

1. **Toward what age group is this play directed? What type of social background predominates in your audience?** The audience must have some kind of bond with the characters on the stage, must identify with them in some way. A group of four-year olds can hardly identify with an unhappy lawyer and his problems.

On one of our performance tours in Japan, we took two plays, one that involved a wife who leaves her husband in charge of the house and the baby. Disaster results. The show had delighted American audiences, but it did not elicit the same laughter in Osaka. We initially attributed this to Japanese reserve, but later realized it was partially, if not totally, due to cultural differences. Our audiences were mainly housewives and children, who found it difficult to identify with the action. Until very recently, a husband in Japan would never take care of the house or baby-sit. Fortunately, our other play was suitable.

2. **What type of puppets will be used for this play?** Each type of puppet has its own strengths and its weaknesses. The characteristics of each impact the action in the play. Usually, a play written for one type cannot easily incorporate other kinds of puppets. It's best to be specific. Directors can then adapt to suit their own circumstances.

3. **What type of performing area will be used?** The puppets and the action usually dictate the type of stage needed. However, the available stage sometimes dictates the type of puppets and the action. Some hand puppet stages have playboards that are similar to the aprons on a traditional stage. Some require the puppeteers to stand, sit, or kneel. They all have various systems for using scenery. Sometimes, instead of a stage, playing areas are incorporated. It is important for the playwright to first delineate the type of stage for which he is writ-

ing, because it so often impacts his later choices.

4. **How many puppeteers will be available?** Six puppeteers can perform a show designed for two, but two puppeteers cannot perform one designed for six. One, two, three, or a whole class?

5. **How many puppets are available or can be made?**

6. **How long does your play need to be?** The age of the audience or the schedule of the sponsor often dictates the length of a play. The story should fill the time allotted, but should not be padded with superfluous material.

7. **What is your budget ?** Budget is usually more important to the director than to the playwright. However, it would be advantageous for the playwright to know if the production will be produced on a shoestring or is funded by a large grant.

Chapter 2

Getting Ideas

There are various formats for producing shows for audiences. For instance, a series of unrelated acts can be strung together to make a vaudeville-type show. Some dramas amount to mere character studies, while some productions feature historical or thematic threads that cement the various scenes into a meaningful whole. However, the main focus of this book is the play that has a beginning, a middle, and an end—a definite progression of the action—perhaps the most popular type of presentation.

Whatever the format, an initial spark is needed to fire the playwright's imagination. Some playwrights complain that the hardest part of writing a play is formulating the seminal idea. Who knows where ideas come from? Perhaps something tickles the right side of our brains. Perhaps we are born with artistic inclinations. Scientists have not yet determined the nature of "thought". But where the creative thoughts originate doesn't matter, as long as they come—but sometimes they don't! A writer's nightmare!

Many puppeteers develop their plays from folktales or fairy tales, which provide numerous sources of inspiration. (Transposing a story from the literary medium to the dramatic form has special problems that will be addressed in the chapter "Adaptations.") A playwright, however, should not be limited to old favorites but encouraged toward original stories. The germ of an idea can come from almost anywhere: an object (a toy bear or a basket of fish), a person (the funny man selling balloons or Aunt Minnie), an experience (a trip to the pound or a Halloween party), and so on. After finding this little spark, then what? Following are several suggestions for fanning the flames.

Pose a question *that can be answered.*

Pose a question involving your germ of an idea. Who leaves the basket of fish on Granny Baker's doorstep every Friday? What kind of costume can I wear to the Halloween party?

The popular children's picture book *Are You My Mother?* by P. D. Eastman begins with a little bird hatching in a nest high up in a tree. The mother bird has flown off to find her new chick some food. Before she returns, the chick falls out of the nest. Lonesome, he looks for the mother bird. "Are you my mother?" he asks the pig. The rest of the book is a series of pictorial encounters with various animals in which the chick asks the same question. The answer is always "No," until the Snort (the steam shovel), which has also answered "No," picks up the chick and places him back in the nest. When the mother bird returns with a worm, he asks again, "Are you my mother?" She answers, "Yes, I'm your mother." The story ends. The question is answered.

Every mystery or murder thriller is developed along these lines. "Who plunged the fatal knife into the broad, blue-and-gold brocaded back of the count?" "How did the murderer enter the room when the doors were bolted and the only windows were eighty feet above the jagged rocks below?" "What caused Lillibelle to disappear on her wedding day twenty years ago, and what now induced her to return to the church?" These questions usually are asked early, and the rest of the story comprises ways in which the characters endeavor to answer them.

In our play, *Zap Happy*, a question asked by a student was the springboard: "Ohhhh. Whatever can I use for my report on electricity for the assembly?" she wails. She turns to an electrical safety pamphlet for ideas.

GINGER LEE: "Think 'Zap' when you play with electrical appliances, especially near water." Like in the bath tub. Say, that might be a good idea for my presentation. Ohhhhh, no. I don't think I want to take a bath in front of the whole school. *(Thinks, giggles, and shakes her head.)* I'll be the only one who doesn't have a presentation at the assembly. I'll be laughed right out of school. Just think, a wash-up at age ten!

Ginger not only does find a topic, but eventually outshines the other students at the assembly.

In *King Pinch of Oregano*, a folk tale I adapted, the king asks the question, "How much do my three daughters love me?" When one of the girls answers, "As much as salt," he is furious, thinking that she compares him to that "cheap and common stuff." The daughter is ostracized until he realizes that "salt gives joy to eating," and he is as important to her as "salt is to all our meals." The climax here is not her answer to the question but the king's understanding of her answer.

Create a conflict *that must be resolved.*

Conflict, the cause of tension in many a good story, comes in many guises. It can be between two people: The Prince of Orange-

adia vies with the Duke of Persimmonia for the hand of the beautiful Princess Prunella. A clash of hearts and minds and perhaps swords.

Conflict can be between a man and nature: The fur-clad figure struggles against the fierce wind, the blinding cold, and the deep snow. His dogs have run away. His last match goes out. Can he win out over the elements?

Conflict also can be simply a matter of a person trying to decide which direction to take—trying to sort things out in his own mind. "Sorry, I can't. Mom told me to stay in the yard. But, hey, she didn't know you'd come along with coupons for free ice cream at the dairy store. Hmm."

Create a conflict and you will probably have the makings of a play.

Present a problem *that must be solved or a goal to be attained.*

Cinderella had a problem. She was mistreated, overworked, and unloved. The miller's daughter had a problem. She had to spin straw into gold. Robinson Crusoe had a problem. He was shipwrecked and alone. Finding a wife was the goal of the prince in "The Princess and the Pea." Some stories involve a physical goal to be reached, a destination. The play's format, then, becomes "the journey," as in *The Wizard of Oz* by L. Frank Baum.

Whether it's a question to be answered, a conflict to be resolved, or a problem to be solved (or sometimes all three), each of the these possibilities creates suspense in the mind of the viewer. The yearning to know makes the audience stay in their seats to find out what happens next. It makes them wonder how the hero will meet his challenge, how the story will end. In other words, it makes them **care** about your play!

The playwright's attitude toward his material is important.

Writing a play, even a simple play, means immersing oneself in the lives of the characters, feeling what they feel, wanting what they want, fearing what they fear. Such involvement is impossible if you either do not appreciate the personalities in your play or deem the whole idea silly or pointless. A playwright's attitudes somehow permeate his work. He needs to believe in his play, have a positive approach, or his play will suffer.

The theme of the play is important.

Undergirding most plays are central ideas that the plays demonstrate, such as "honesty (or loyalty or goodness) is rewarded." These themes or morals are not always apparent, even to the playwright. He is so busy figuring out plot angles and developing characterizations that he does not see the forest for the trees.

Not long ago, the editors of children's literature finally recognized how many old fairy tales implanted notions of "wicked" stepmothers. "Mothers are good, but stepmothers are not" was an underlying theme. Newer versions don't include the offending suggestions embedded in the old favorites.

Many years ago our company developed a charming little play about Greenie Witch, a young witch who was having trouble getting through witch school. Her main difficulty was the "presto changeo" assignments. With magic words, she was supposed to change a rock into a golden slipper, a bone into a pearl necklace, a branch into a jeweled crown. Though she tried very hard, every time she used the incantations, instead of a slipper or a necklace, she always got a duck. She was upset because, if she could not pass the test, she could never become a real witch. The sorcerer comes to give her the final test; she must change various items into animals.

Greenie knows she won't pass the test. What can she do? She then gets the idea that perhaps the audience can help her. (A wonderful chance for audience participation, we thought.) If the sorcerer wants her to change a

boulder into a herd of cows, will they "moo" like cows? Of course, they would. What fun! If he asks for pigs, will they "oink" like pigs? And so on. The kids in the audience loved it.

It was a successful little show, and we performed it a number of times before realizing the undesirability of the underlying theme. Our sympathetic main character was not only cheating, she was talking the audience into helping her! We were actually trumpeting that it's OK to help someone cheat on his exams!

Admitting how much truth there is in the old adage that children accept the moral values of their heroes, we reluctantly rewrote our play a bit so that the sorcerer was quite wicked, and when the audience helped it was to save Greenie from some unfortunate fate—but not to assist her in immoral pursuits.

At the outset, a playwright must be clear in his own mind about what he is saying on all levels, because these intentions will affect his writing in subtle ways. Since most puppet productions in this country are aimed at children, the effects can be very detrimental. However, subliminal messages can also enhance a play's value far beyond mere entertainment. Puppeteers have a grand opportunity to counteract the harmful messages that continually bombard the younger generation.

The Subject Matter Relative to Your Audience

Playwrights are free to write about anything they like, but it behooves anyone who is developing a script to consider the audiences for whom he writes. Having critiqued many scripts, I know this is not always the case.

Naturally, the general age of the group for whom the play is intended is important. If a playwright is writing for children in the primary grades, he must have some idea of their special interests. He must be aware of their vocabulary limitations. The little folks have yet to understand many concepts that we take for granted. Furthermore, the childhood milieu changes with each generation. Don't assume the sandbox routine and the birthday party mores are still as you remember them. Check with available sources. Teachers, preschool directors, and librarians are usually happy to share information.

Seattle Puppetory Theatre performs often in libraries and among family groups where there are as many parents as there are children. A good children's show should be enjoyed by adults as well. I try to write my puppet scripts on several levels to insure that each age group can appreciate the play in a special way. After all, it is parents who elect to bring their offspring to the performances and adults who pay for our services. (Besides, it always pleases me when a mother comes up after the show and says, "I don't know who liked it more—me or the kids.")

Different age groups respond to different types of humor. When we go to a school and perform one of our all-purpose family shows, first for the primary children, then for the upper grades, I am fascinated by the laugh responses. There are just as many laughs at each performance, but they are often in entirely different places. The age of the audience must be a determining factor as you write your play.

Almost as important as audience age are the attitudes of the sponsors, since most puppet companies perform for sponsor-generated audiences. Most schools in the United States now prohibit programs with Christmas themes. Any story that includes a racial slur or is demeaning to a particular race or culture is unacceptable. Guns, violence, and sex are not approved by most family groups. Various church groups and social organizations have their own standards.

It is amazing how upset some people get about seemingly innocuous material. One woman objected to our play "The Fisherman's Wife" because the wife wanted to be "pope." It seems we were including religious material. Another person complained about our presentation of "The Old Woman Who Swallowed a Fly" because, when she swallowed a horse, "she died, of course." The subject of "death" was not acceptable.

Some playwrights refuse to be restricted or to consider any standards but their own. However, if the number of bookings is important or the goodwill of the sponsor is a priority, it would be prudent for the writer to analyze the contents of his play in view of his prospective audiences. Favorable comments are the best advertising.

Chapter 3

Thinking before Writing

After pondering these practical points, a playwright's imagination may begin to soar and his nebulous ideas to solidify into some semblance of a story. But before he plunges headlong into writing, there are other aspects of puppet theatre to be considered.

Does This Story Idea Lend Itself to the Puppet Theatre?

It is often said that a play that does not use the unique capabilities of the puppet is better suited for dramatization by actors in live theatre. It is true that puppet theatre should exhibit the rare gifts of the puppet whenever possible. For instance, a character that must disappear in a flash before the eyes of the audience can be portrayed stunningly by a hand puppet. Actors obviously have trouble with this type of maneuver. A bird or a cow can come to life much more easily and believably as a puppet than as an actor. It also works the other way: If a character must change clothes several times, especially if it is done in full view of the audience, the puppeteer is in for trouble, while it would be no problem for an actor. Some stories seem tailor-made for puppets. A worthy goal of any puppet playwright is to find such a story or create one. It will charm the audience.

Many a purist, when considering the art of puppetry, would insist that puppets should appear only in plays that are especially suited to them. However, there are practical reasons for using puppets in other plays as well. Economy is always an important issue in theatre endeavors, whether we like it or not. It generally is true that production expenses are much less for puppet theatre than for traditional theatre. For confirmation, one need only compare the cost of brocade for a costumed figure one foot tall to one five or six feet tall. Likewise, tiny props and sets usually cost much less.

Economy in terms of personnel and space is also an important factor for most puppet companies. Fewer technicians are needed for a puppet performance. Often, the puppeteers take care of the backstage business. Furthermore, a few puppeteers can manage an army of puppets, certainly a benefit to any company that pays its puppeteers. Sets and props are proportionately puppet size. The smaller and more compact the sets and props, the better for any group with storage problems or with bookings that require all the equipment and personnel to be stuffed into a van. This economy of personnel and space, and the resulting mobility, increase performance prospects and income possibilities.

Another compelling reason why some plays, appropriate for regular theatre, are still done with puppets: The people involved just happen to love puppets and their charm.

I mention these reasons to defend the writing of puppet plays, even though they may contradict the generally accepted rationale, and even to suggest that the puppet milieu can sometimes, in surprising ways, augment the dramatic effect of a theatre experience.

Limitations of the Puppet

Sometimes a playwright in the creative mode tries to communicate messages beyond the capabilities of the puppet. He must learn that many subtleties and nuances conveyed in the traditional theatre by an actor's brilliance simply cannot be transferred to the theatre via the puppet. The marvelous puppets in *Dark Crystal* and *E.T.,* with their expressive eyes and faces, are exceptions, of course, but the average puppeteer has neither the money nor the technology to manage such creations.

Though the puppet may have limitations (and these are addressed in the following chapters), he also possesses a wonderful freedom. His is a world of fantasy waiting to be explored. In his realm, dreams become possibilities. His being, unfettered by a human nature and fashioned by the limitless imagination of the playwright and the puppeteer, can bring a magical reality to the land of make-believe.

Main Action Scenes

Action is what makes the play go 'round. The audience wants to see and experience what is going on. However, if the fairy godmother changes the pumpkin into a coach offstage; if the prince kills the fire-eating dragon offstage; if somebody only *reports* that the schooner, Hornswoggle, exploded, and Winston, the cabin boy, managed to drag the officers to safety and rescue the strong box with the pearls, the audience will be disappointed and frustrated because they missed out on some of the most important parts of the story. If the main scenes are impossible to create onstage, then the story is a poor choice for the play. The "hows" of production must be seriously considered before the writing is tackled.

What Is the Perspective of This Story?

All right. A story has been decided on—a story that is fit for puppet theatre production. Before the actual writing begins, a playwright must ask another question: "Whose story is this?"

One story can be told in many ways, depending on the point of view taken by the teller. The tale of *Cinderella* will be quite a bit different if told from the perspective of the prince. Imagine the story of the *Three Little Pigs* if told from the wolf's viewpoint!

Once I saw a play in which a conflict between two testy old men was introduced. Each character was well-drawn and appealing. The set was magnificent. The manipulation was excellent. During the course of the play, each man presented his case and argued his points—quite vociferously. Unfortunately, although the conflict was the focus of the play, I found that I wasn't identifying or rooting for either one. I didn't care who won. Nobody else did either. This good production could have been an excellent one! The playwright successfully communicated the two opposing sides, but lost the emotional involvement of the audience and the potentially powerful impact of the play because of a wishy-washy perspective. The play was extremely informative, but not dramatic.

Once a perspective is chosen, it should not switch during the play (unless the playwright has deliberately decided to present the same event from the perspective of the various characters). If a playwright loses sight of his chosen perspective, it causes subtle inconsistencies in the dialogue or the plotting that are not always readily apparent to the audience. Nevertheless, the subliminal effect will lessen their sense of satisfaction and possibly the impact of the play.

How Do You Plot Your Story?

When you have decided on your story, it is time to develop your plot. "Plot" and "story" cannot be used interchangeably. The plot of a story is the way it is put together, the flow of the action, the sequence of the scenes. One story can be plotted in many different ways. For instance, the story *The Three Little Pigs* can begin with a scene in the mother pig's house as she is saying good-bye to her little piggies. Or the initial scene could be along the road after the pigs have left home and are trying to decide what to do. If the playwright has developed the story from the wolf's perspective, it might begin in the wolf's den, where the little cubs are complaining how hungry they are. Some playwrights are partial to flashbacks.

How the playwright plots his story is an important step and deserves to be planned ahead with the perspective in mind, so that the story progresses smoothly, bringing the audience along.

Is It Believable?

Any story, to be satisfying, must be believable. In other words, the solution of a problem must be a natural, even though surprising, development in the story. It has been said that an audience will believe anything initially, but you can't change the ground rules midstream. The hero cannot suddenly be able to live at the bottom of the sea—unless the playwright has established that his grandmother was a Mediterranean mermaid and he was born with the ability to breathe under water as well as on land, or a mighty talented magician is somewhere in the vicinity. Likewise, an ancient manuscript, which saves the museum from ruin, cannot be found in the forgotten Floren-

tine vase at the last minute, unless the reason for its being there in the first place has been addressed.

This business of making events seem natural is referred to as "foreshadowing"—informing the audience of certain facts that are going to be important in the dénouement. If the audience is left unaware, the situation will seem contrived. The audience will not be satisfied, and the play simply will not gel for them. (The exception, of course, is if the wink is in the eye and the tongue is in the cheek.)

Likewise, the puppets, whether they are beautiful, eccentric, whimsical, bizarre, curious, or downright weird in appearance and behavior, must be real in their particular make-believe world, a challenge to the playwright and the puppeteer. Believability is, after all, the essence of puppetry, bringing the inanimate to life.

Now the Scenario

Having thought through all his ideas, a playwright often needs to write a scenario—an outline of his proposed play listing the scenes and what actually happens in each one. This saves time and eliminates many rewrites.

Think about Pantomime

Before going to the typewriter or computer, the playwright should examine his story idea as potential for possible pantomime production. As I have mentioned, theatre is action over dialogue; and the more action the better. Some stories cannot possibly be told without dialogue or lengthy narrative, but those that can provide the essence of puppet theatre.

A pantomime depends on the movements of the puppets to tell the story. This, of course, presents a special challenge to the puppeteers who cannot use words to explain or voices to express passions or sentiments. Music can convey moods and feelings, but seldom the specifics of plot development. The puppet must communicate the tiniest of nuances. The audience must be able to **understand** what is going on, **care** about the characters, and be **satisfied** as in any production. Such a production requires intense effort on the part of all concerned.

Writing a pantomime show is best done by a playwright who has had extensive experience as a puppeteer and understands the potential of the puppet, or in conjunction with the puppeteers and director who will be involved in the production. To write the script, the playwright must think in dramatic terms but write in prose. He must *describe* the actions and thoughts, aspirations, and feelings of the characters and all details pertinent to the performance of this play. Connotations and insinuations, usually expressed in the dialogue, must somehow be defined for easy assimilation by the puppeteers.

Some years ago, Seattle Puppetory Theatre developed and produced *The Return of the Bounce*, the story of a clown who loses his job in the circus because he's too old, he's not funny anymore and he's lost his bounce. With the exception of several sentences at its beginning and end, this show has no dialogue, only continual background music. It can be understood in any language. As a result, we have been invited to perform this show in a number of foreign countries. For Spain, Mexico, and Japan, we taped the few lines of dialogue in Spanish and Japanese. In Pakistan, Korea, and Malaysia, the necessary bits of information were included in the program or announced in the introduction. Our experience proves that a successful pantomime show can be a valuable commodity, as well as an artistic achievement for the company.

Jiggles, without his clown make-up, and one of his fans in *The Return of Bounce*. Puppets by John Bartelt and Joan King.

CHAPTER 4

Developing the Script

A playwright should consider the first few minutes of his play as the introduction. Whether his play begins with a cataclysmic event or a gentle lead-in to its main focus, he needs to communicate some essentials. First, the people in the audience should be made aware of the type of play they are going to see, be it a comedy, a tragedy, a musical, or a satire. A program or an announcement can, of course, broadcast the play's genre. The introductory music certainly gives clues. *Finlandia* and *Pop Goes the Weasel* will communicate totally different messages to the audience about what kind of play is to follow. But in addition to giving his audience the general idea, the playwright must answer some specific questions for them early on.

Who?

Most puppet shows do not include printed programs that list the characters according to the order of their appearance. Nevertheless, puppets that appear must be identified in one way or another. I have seen plays in which puppets have entered, spoken, and engaged in all kinds of activities without making their identities clear. As long as these nameless characters wander about the stage, it is impossible for the audience to become totally involved in the story. Unless the puppet is some kind of generic character, or the playwright has a specific structural reason for keeping the secret, the audience must not be kept in the dark.

Clarification is not difficult. Some characters need nothing more than a costume. Almost everyone would recognize a clown or a ghost. If a character is wearing a white hat with a top puff and is mixing something in a bowl, the audience is safe in assuming that the character is a cook. A puppet with a white beard, a red suit and hat trimmed in white fur needs little introduction. And there would be little question about a figure dressed in white, sporting wings and a halo.

Netak and Sat-se-kub from the Indian legend *The Miser of Mount Rainier.* Puppet heads were made from bark with coconut hair. Clothes were made of fur, suede, and raffia to reflect native American use of natural materials. Puppets by Betsy Tobin and Jean Mattson.

19

But many male and female puppets, both adults and children, may lack visual definition and some clues must be given about their individual personalities. This can be done by a bit of narration. "Long ago, in a land far away, there was a young girl who . . . " The audience knows that the character who then appears is that "young girl " (or certainly should be).

Sometimes puppets even talk to the audience—or to themselves—a popular convention, especially in puppet theatre. "Oh, why did mother make me sign up for that art class anyway. I'll be the only fifth-grade boy there! And besides, I can't even draw a straight line, let alone a basket of fruit!" Or "Hey, folks, I'm a plainclothes policeman. And I have to find out what's going on around here."

The sets or props alone often communicate the message to the audience. A puppet working behind a stall that is loaded with fruit and vegetables would be accepted as a vendor if no further information were given. A puppet pushing a baby carriage would be taken for a mother or a nanny until further notice. Sometimes a sign can identify a character for the audience. If the audience reads "Elementary School" on a building and hears a bell, they will assume that the puppets who run into the building are the students.

In addition to the identity of a specific character, the relationship of characters must be made clear. If two female puppets enter, the audience needs to know that they are sisters, boss and employee, mother and daughter, teacher and pupil, or whatever, in order to understand the ensuing dialogue or action. In most instances, this can be established with a word or two in the introductory dialogue exchanges. "No son of mine is going to sit on any flagpole," says one male puppet as he drags another along. Or "Hester, answer that door. I hired you to be a maid, not a bird watcher!"

Elementary though this business may sound, such details often are overlooked by the playwright who is so immersed in his play that he forgets it is new stuff to the audience.

What?

Stage actions sometimes need to be explained. Many puppets are small and often do not have good arm motion, so a puppeteer cannot communicate what the puppet is doing with his hands. Furthermore, puppet props often are too small to be seen by the back rows. Therefore, if the audience sees a puppet behind a workbench busily working on the project before him, the playwright usually needs to provide further clarification. A narrator's voice can explain, "In a small shop on the edge of a certain village, a shoemaker was hard at work on a pair of lady's slippers." Or perhaps the initial few lines of dialogue could include the essential information: "I know this time I will be able to make a time machine that will work!" Or "Some day I know I'll find a pearl in one of these oysters." Very small clues will smoothly enlighten the audience.

Where?

Seldom are plays so general that they could take place anywhere. Action usually needs to be grounded—at the very least, whether it is inside or outside. But "outside" is often not enough. Sometimes more is needed if, for instance, the action takes place in the jungles of New Guinea or the Sahara desert. Likewise, if the characters are on the moon or in a deep mine, the audience must know about it early on to make sense of what is happening. Awareness of location not only promotes understanding but also creates an emotional atmosphere for the developing action, an added bonus for the playwright.

Again, clues can be given unobtrusively

by set pieces, narrative, or dialogue. Or a bit more can be added to the previously mentioned opening narrative to indicate place: "Long ago, in a land far away, a young girl approached the outer gates of a dark, forbidding castle."

When?

Sometimes it doesn't matter "when" the play takes place. Human nature is such that some stories could be told about people in any year of any century. But if the "when" is essential, such as in a story about cavemen or the early days of the Old West before communication and modes of transportation had been developed, the audience needs to be told. "How" is up to the playwright. Narration can focus the audience: "When civilization was dawning and man lived in caves . . . " If the characters are dressed in fur pieces and carry clubs, the message is clear (unless a costume party is in progress, in which case the first lines of dialogue should clarify.)

So, somehow the playwright must let the audience in on the who, what, where and when. He must do it cleverly and succinctly, aware that exposition can be tedious and boring. When dialogue or narration do not suffice, some playwrights use puppet MC's. The MC can be an actor who becomes an integral part of the whole show.

And so the play begins, the main characters have been defined and are on the road toward accomplishing their goals (or failing in their attempts). Most of the play concerns what happens on that road. How does the character try to answer his question? What frustrations keep him from solving his problems? How can he conquer the opposing forces or outwit the villain? The harder the character struggles, the greater the suspense and the stronger the play.

The climax occurs when the problem is solved and obviously should be close to the end of the play. Any play that goes on and on after the climax is boring. Of course, the loose ends—characters still in limbo, unexplained details, and indications about the future (all these make up the resolution)—should be taken care of satisfactorily—but quickly.

Motivations

The playwright should keep in mind that puppets, like actors, must have reasons for being onstage. The maid cannot just happen to be behind the screen to overhear the villain's plan (unless it is complete farce). There must be a believable explanation for her presence. Likewise, a puppet should not just come in one door and go out the other in order to speak a line of dialogue or position himself for his next entrance. He should be coming from somewhere and going somewhere with good reason. There must be motivation for all actions (unless the convention has been established that, in this play, puppets freely pop in and out, up and down, etc.).

Transitions

To keep the audience informed and involved as the play progresses, it is necessary to pay special attention to the transitions between the scenes. Again, you (hopefully) know exactly where your play is going, and you must make sure your audience knows too.

When the action moves from the wheat field to the throne room of the castle, a set change may be enough to communicate the shift. However, other producers may mount the play with less-than-detailed sets, so it's always safer for the playwright to gently ensure that the audience is in tow. If the audience is wondering what is going on, their involvement will be splintered. If the audience is mainly children, loss of interest can be disastrous.

A bit of narration or a line of dialogue can easily pave the way for what is coming, either at the end of one scene or at the beginning of the next. "Let's go and ask the miller!" "I wish I knew what was going on at the castle." "Did we have to come here to the tower?" Some playwrights even use signs quickly shown: "Along the Road to London" or "The Attic of the Wesley Mansion"; whatever fits the style of the writer and the story.

Whatever the transition, it must be brief. Without action or sound onstage, the play is in danger of losing its momentum. Musical interludes can fill the gap for a moment or two, but if the transition is lengthy, the attention of the audience wanders from the story, and extra dramatic energy is needed to bring them back.

Unity

As the playwright works on his play, he needs to maintain his conceptual focus. He must stay on the course he has set. If he is sidetracked, his audience will be sidetracked. But temptations are many, and diversions have a sly way of sneaking into a script.

Playwrights who develop plays for their own companies are often beguiled into including a wonderful puppet, already constructed, that would add pizzazz to the show. "Let's work Old Lady Strumpet in somehow. She always goes over with a bang." Or "I'll add Toodles in Scene I. We need a little humor and audiences love dogs." It's the playwright's prerogative to include whatever he wishes, but he should be aware that a character unrelated to the action of the play will interrupt the flow and fracture the unity, thereby weakening the play's impact.

Likewise, it may seem fitting to include the appealing little song *Little Miss Muffit, Stuff It* or have some character tell that hilarious joke about the monkey and the bungejumper. But again, the playwright must realize that these insertions divert the attention of the audience. Before making such an addition, he must determine if the appeal of the musical selection or the joke's belly laughs will offset the inevitable decrease in momentum.

A loss of interest can also occur if the playwright becomes enamored of his secondary characters and spends too much time with them. Unless they are part of a bona fide secondary plot, this focus derails the main action of the play. Secondary plots are acceptable, but are not incorporated into most puppet plays because of their need for simplicity and brevity.

The dialogue itself can sometimes jeopardize the involvement of the audience. As a script consultant, I have noticed the tendency of some playwrights to get carried away by realistic dialogue. Exchanges appropriate for this particular occasion or that particular character may be perfectly normal chitchat, but they often are nonfunctional, causing audience attention to waiver and sag. No matter how natural the dialogue is to the situation, if it does not further the action or reveal the personalities of the puppet, it should be excluded.

Dramatic art, like other artistic fields, is not an exact copy of reality. Playwrights select certain words and vocal exchanges that together contribute to the unity and direction of the play. The trick, the art of playwriting, is creating the illusion of reality.

A final warning: Audience participation, as alluring as it sounds, can actually undermine the involvement of the audience. If children are invited to engage in conversation with the puppets or contribute to the outcome of the story, they can become so excited by this interaction that their attention to the performance in general is fragmented. Playwrights must be aware that special skills are needed by the puppeteers who undertake audience participation.

Unity, then, should be the primary focus of the playwright as he revises and refines each draft of his play. Without it the audience will be less than completely satisfied, and the play will not reach its potential.

Chapter 5

Character Development

Although a playwright can envision a full-blown character about whom he then writes, the process is usually the other way around. The story comes first, then the main characters are fleshed out, given life, so that the audience will love them, despise them, tolerate them, distrust them, blame them, and agonize for them—in other words, **care** about them. And just what is it that involves the audience and makes him care about a figure on a stage? Certainly, what is happening to that character can engage a person's interest and sympathy, but the degree of response depends a great deal on the ability of the playwright to create that character.

Know Your Characters

The personality of any character dictates the way in which he speaks and acts. So in order to communicate the essence of a particular puppet, a playwright must be familiar with that puppet's personality. He should have an idea of his history, his family, his job, his goals, and his likes and dislikes. Seems obvious, right? But how many playwrights plunge into writing their plays without a thought about what type of creature their protagonist is, let alone the rest of the cast? "Got the story—so go with it!" This is especially true if you happen to be using an old folktale as a basis for your play. After all, everyone knows about the characters in old folk tales. Right?

Let's look at an old folktale. More often than not, the characters in these tales are two-dimensional. Consider the Norwegian tale,

"The Three Billy Goats Gruff." This simple story describes the three goats only as "little," "middle," and "big." Granted, they have survived in children's literature for hundreds of years as "little," "middle," and "big," but to translate them into dramatic terms—well, they really don't have much going for them. For two-year-olds with two-minute attention spans, little-middle-big may work just fine. But to come excitingly alive on the stage, the goats need more. They need personalities.

In my version of this story, I tried to give each animal individual traits that would contrast with those of the others. As the goats enter, I had them introduce themselves.

FLUFFY (Little): I love to smell the violets and dance among the flowers.
I like to watch the clouds float by to while away the hours.

STUFFY (Middle): They call me Stuffy Gruff because I really like to eat.
I munch and chew and chomp all day on grass that's green and sweet.

TUFFY (Big): I love to jump from crag to crag. It's here that I belong.
So watch it everybody. My head and horns are strong!

Before I arrived at these descriptions, I needed to think about this family of goats. How did they live? What was closest to their little goat hearts? What was their relationship to each other? The descriptions, then, provided some character traits that helped me fashion the dialogue and the actions as each one of these goats tries to cross that bridge. Suggestions are concurrently given to the puppet maker about the appearance of the goats and to the puppeteers on voice and movement.

Many folktales and children's stories present animals as the protagonists. It is then the playwright's job to give those characters human characteristics, to enable the audience to identify and sympathize with them without losing the essence of the animals themselves. We can appreciate a goat who eats grass, gambols on rocky crags, and trip-traps with his little hooves across the bridge, but our hearts are more engaged if he loves to smell violets and dance among the flowers.

As characters develop under the pen of the playwright, they might even alter the story line. Let's play with the character of the troll.

TROLL (Option 1): I am a troll. This is my
                bridge.
                It's mine. I am the boss.
                And I will gobble any-
                one
                Who dares to go across!

TROLL (Option 2): I am a troll. This is my
                bridge.
                My life is misery.
                'Cause I'm more scared
                of people
                Than people are of me.

Seeing the troll as fearful and unhappy instead of aggressive and mean could make a big difference in how the playwright ends his play.

Again, in the story of "Goldilocks and the Three Bears," Goldilocks is simply a little girl. If she is presented as a nice little girl who knows how to behave and who causes no real problems at home, she would then know that she shouldn't go into someone's house without being invited. But then, she is tired and needs to rest, so she rationalizes and enters the house of the bears. When she breaks baby bear's chair, she is appalled. She shouldn't be in the house and here she's broken somebody's chair. She tries to fix it but fails. Oh, dear! When she sees the porridge, she knows she shouldn't help herself without being asked, but after her walk in the woods she is soooo hungry. Before she knows it, Baby Bear's porridge is all gone. She is sorry. And she is also very tired. She should go home, but she (yawn) needs a nap and there are three beds . . .

But think again. Suppose we make Goldilocks a brash, nasty little brat. She comes along the path in the woods and sees the house.

GOLDILOCKS: They'll give me a drink. (*She knocks*.) Well, where are those stupid people anyway? The door is unlocked. Oh, well. (*She enters*) What a dump! At least they've got chairs. (*Sits*) Oh, hard as a rock! (*Sits*) Hey, too soft. Went right to the floor. (*Sits*) Oh-oh. The dumb thing broke right in two. Crud! Wonder if they have something to eat in this place. (*Tastes*) Porridge? Is that all they've got around here? Yuck! Ick! Too hot. Phooey! (*Tastes*) Too cold. (*Tastes*) Hardly enough for a tadpole in that little dish! Oh, a bedroom. I think I'll just take a little nap before I go home.

Maybe she even jumps on the beds to test them out. Obviously, the personality of the girl makes a tremendous difference in what she says and how she behaves! In choosing the second Goldilocks option, you might even decide to change the perspective of the story to that of the three bears.

To write meaningful and credible dialogue, it is imperative that a playwright first develop the character in his mind or, even better, on paper. Then, if he has written a scenario of the action, the dialogue will almost write itself.

Developing the Character within the Script

Most plays are not structured so the characters tell about themselves as the billy goats did. Sometimes a resumé is provided through a printed program, but the majority of puppet shows do not have this luxury. How, then, does a playwright communicate the nature of his characters? Besides the stage directions for the

Cinderella, in Seattle Puppetory Theatre's *Cenerentola,* wears drab, patched clothing and scrubs the floor. Puppet by Nick Lefeuvre.

cast and director, he can provide intrinsic clues within the script itself.

Of course, in actual production, the puppeteers, puppet makers, and the director (they sometimes are one and the same) contribute in great measure to the puppet's personality. The playwright must rely in most cases on their discretion and vision. However, if certain details are significant to the playwright's concept of his play, then he should, by all means, include them in his stage directions.

The details to which I refer are both auditory and visual. It goes almost without saying that the way a puppet looks sends dozens of character messages. **Color** is important. A red sparkley outfit says something entirely different from the statement made by a dull gray robe. A crazy quilt or harlequin **design** says something else again. If the playwright envisions a gauze or a canvas costume, he should probably mention that fact, because such textures connote certain subtleties and contribute to a puppet's movements. You might also want to include some reference to the puppet's **facial expression** or **size,** if these details are significant.

A playwright may even want to comment on the quality or pitch of the various **voices** to enhance his characterizations. But every playwright absolutely needs to comment on the way in which certain lines are spoken, because some lines must be said in a particular way to project the intended meaning.

Take this simple line of dialogue: "I'm going to the castle today." It can be spoken loudly or softly, quickly or slowly, arrogantly or excitedly, in many different ways that denote joy, fear, anger, nervousness, awe, boredom, and so on. It is, therefore, imperative to include the manner in which a speech is made, if it is to be read and/or produced by anyone other than the playwright. It is also a helpful exercise for his own understanding.

Likewise, the puppet's **body language** is as important as that of any human being. The movements of the body help to communicate the character's age, his physical condition, and his mood. A puppet who bounces along sends a far different message than one who, hunched down, drags across the stage. And jerky, erratic movements connote something different from a rhythmic, military bearing. As I have mentioned, the puppeteer and director often make these decisions. But body movement is too important to a character's personality to be totally ignored by the playwright. Even small mannerisms, a recurring twist of the head or the tapping of the chin, can provide individuality and interest.

Furthermore, because puppet creations are unique, they can move in ways an actor's joints could never manage. Free of genetic dictates, characters can sport two heads or six arms. A frog can change into a prince. Some puppets can separate themselves into their various parts. Puppetry, despite its limitations, provides the playwright with a different dimension and endless possibilities for characterization.

Besides the stage directions about voice, appearance, and movement that accompany a script, the playwright gives clues within the script itself, sometimes so subtly that the audience absorbs the information almost without realizing it.

1. The character divulges information about himself.

We've touched on how the personalities of the puppets can affect their dialogue. It follows that through this dialogue, when well-written, the audience begins to comprehend the character the playwright had in mind. The general content of the dialogue is important, of course, but the rhythms, the choice of words and phrases all lend substance to the character the playwright is creating.

Each puppet has his own way of speaking, depending on his origins, his education, how he feels at the moment and who he is—sol-

dier, professor, or stand-up comic. The puppet's speech style is created as much by the playwright as by the voice of the puppeteer. Notice the difference between the following two speeches:

1. "I want to go back to Montana. I liked it there. I miss the mountains. I'm homesick."

2. "I shore do hanker fer Montana country. Yup. I miss livin' outa saddle bags—drinkin' tin can coffee—sleepin' under them stars. I jist ain't myself out here. Nope."

The second speech provides more of a glimpse into the background, feelings, and sensitivity of the character.

Perhaps the character has some word-habits. In my play, *The Bad-Tempered Wife*, the hero, Poova, usually addresses his wife with sweet Norwegian terms of endearment. "My little spritz cookie," " My little ginger snap," "My little krumkaka." Later, when he is disgruntled, he addresses her in a similar vein, "My little lump of curdled cheese." This particular way of speaking to his wife differentiates him from other characters and makes him unique.

Each character should stand apart, be himself. Perhaps he gets his tongue twisted. "Please ceed the fat—ahh, I mean feed the cat." Or perhaps a character often prefaces his remarks with "Somebody once told me . . ." Or maybe the lady has a habit of exclaiming, "Oh, diddely, daddely dud!" Or she takes a big breath before saying anything. A playwright can mold a character with words and actions as carefully as a sculptor molds his figure in clay.

Besides the clues to character inherent in the dialogue, the puppet can sometimes simply tell the audience about himself through his conversation with others. In *The Bad-Tempered Wife*, a troll complains about how this unpleasant woman treated him.

TROLL: "Wash behind your ears," she says. Imagine—a troll washing—anywhere!

"Stop spittin' on the floor," she says. Been spittin' on the floor for 3,000 years. No human's going to tell me to quit. (*Spits*) "Don't pick your nose,"she says. Huh, I'll pick my nose when and if I want to. Us trolls like to pick our noses. See. (*Picks his nose*)

This troll tells us a lot about himself.

2. Other characters talk about him.

Often characters will talk about each other. Imagine listening to the conversation between two villagers who are complaining about their cruel and greedy ruler, King Reuben. "He's raising taxes sky-high." And "His dungeons are full of poor wretches who can't pay the taxes. He strings them up if they complain." When King Reuben enters the scene, the audience already knows he's mean and villainous.

In a scene from a nautical story, the first mate leaves the galley and the cook says to the cabin boy, "I don't trust that bloke. He has eyes like a shark." Certainly a clue to the first mate's dishonesty and potential as a wicked character.

3. The narrator gives clues.

A narrator's introduction can go a long way in communicating important details about the story's personae. Consider the introductory lines, "On a wintry night long ago, a frail, frightened child huddles on the bench outside the empty store." We know something about this character. Our feelings about this character have been aroused. We're beginning to *care*.

4. Names give hints.

The value of nomenclature is sometimes overlooked in puppetry. Most playwrights realize that certain names invariably connote certain ideas, but they seldom capitalize on the fact. Consider your reaction to various characters as you hear their names: Leticia Augusta Edgerthorpe compared to Bubbles McGee; William Mansfield Sussex III or Smitty Brown. As you probably noticed, the name itself invokes responses in the listener's mind. These responses can be of great help to the playwright, immediately imbuing the puppet with certain characteristics. However, they also can work against the playwright, giving erroneous clues to his audience. Because of their suggestive quality, names must be selected with caution.

This "name dynamics" can also be a wonderful source of humor in puppetry. While actors with remarkable names may sometimes seem a bit foolish, audiences will accept puppets with peculiar or outlandish names with no difficulty whatsoever, and be captivated and amused.

In a play about electrical safety commissioned by a power company, our elementary school student characters were named Ginger Lee, Alec Smart, and Noah Lott. The man who thought he knew everything and continually got into electrical trouble because of his ignorance was named Mr. Hazard. His first name was Hap.

Melodramas are notorious for descriptive names and ours followed suit. In my melodrama, *"The Saga of Grime and Glory,"* the villain is named Casius M. Grime. (His middle name is "Money," and they call him "Cash" for short.) On the same plane, the hero is Victor Lovejoy, and his heroine is Glory Goodwill.

In *King Pinch of Oregano* or *The True Value of Salt*, our King's daughters were called Spinachina, Carrotina, and Stringa Beana. The palace cook was Mozzarelli. The audiences have always enjoyed this playfulness.

And speaking of names, a word should be said about titles. A catchy or provocative title can tease the imagination by creating an in-

terest in a main character or the story line. No
playwright or producer wants to miss an opportunity to stimulate preperformance curi-
osity.

A Few Tips on Writing Dialogue

1. It is important when writing dialogue to
read your lines aloud. Sentences that look
great on paper may sound awkward.

2. A character's dialogue (and his behavior) should be consistent throughout the play,
unless the story dictates otherwise. If a frog
changes into a prince, of course, we might expect a difference in his speech, but otherwise
a change in voice pattern is disconcerting and
confusing.

3. Dialogue needs to be terse and to the
point. (This bears repeating.) Puppets who
babble on can be very boring. They should
say only that which is necessary to carry the
action forward or to develop their personalities. And never have your puppets say things
that the audience can see for themselves.

4. Avoid dialogue about action the audience has already seen and understood. However, have your puppets explain what the
audience cannot discern for themselves.

5. When developing characters, it is best
to strive for contrast in their looks, speech,
and behavior. Such contrast not only makes it
easier for the audience to keep the various
puppet characters straight, but also makes a
more interesting show. This differentiation is
especially important if a puppeteer is taking
more than one part and the voices tend to be
similar.

Chapter 6

Props, Sets, Lights, Sound Effects, and Music

The director who has the most to say about the costumes also has final control of the production details: props, sets, music, and sound effects. However, it is important for the playwright to think about them too. Details that are crucial to the embodiment of his vision and to the ultimate impact and success of the play must be included.

Sets

A playwright can provide the merest suggestion of a set, or he can describe his castle scene down to the last parapet, replete with flowing banners, ornate crests, cupolas, moats, and Gothic windows. Detailed descriptions, whether followed or not, can be productive. They will impart a sense of the playwright's dream and help determine the course the future director may take.

The playwright should keep in mind that certain stage effects are especially appealing to an audience. I speak from the experience of being an audience member for hundreds of puppet plays. Somehow, a puppet becomes a more interesting character if it enters through a door or leans out a window. And somehow, a scene is enhanced if a puppet appears in the tower or on the balcony. Interaction with set pieces in this way gives the puppet another dimension of vitality. Even though the playwright knows that such instructions may not

be heeded, he should not be deterred. He should write as he imagines it.

In one of Seattle Puppetory Theatre hand puppet plays, a little girl had to climb up a ladder into the attic. While this would have been no problem for a marionette, it created a definite challenge for this particular little hand puppet girl. It was accomplished by placing the ladder behind a sofa, giving the hand puppet legs and feet and having a second puppeteer ready to pull her through the attic door as the girl went up the ladder and the girl's puppeteer withdrew his hand. The audience really liked that scene and, should I share this script, I would certainly describe that set and operation.

Props

Similarly, the illusion of life is strengthened and enjoyment is increased when puppets actually use and move things. My scripts usually have a substantial prop list. Seattle Puppetory Theatre and their friends are always on the lookout for puppet-sized items that I can include in my scripts. I regularly visit the Salvation Army and other thrift stores. One time I found a beautiful wooden spinning wheel that had once been a lamp. The support for the bulb and shade was gone but the wheel was anchored to a solid foundation. The wheel revolved and was exactly hand puppet size. It cost more than it was worth, but as a prop for a puppet show, it was a rare find. We fitted it with batteries, a small motor, a switch, and a rubber band. Because we now had the spinning wheel that could spin straw into gold, we produced *Rumplestiltskin*.

Travis Ptarmigan rides his recycling machine, made from a child's toy locomotive, in *Once Upon a Ptarmigan*. Puppets by Betsy Tobin and Jean Mattson.

Children's banks offer many ingenious possibilities. We have a globe-of-the-world bank that has had a place in several puppet schoolroom sets. In one thrift shop I found a wonderful black safe with a revolving dial and a door that opened. It sat in my basement for several years before we produced a melodrama for which it was needed and appreciated. Our villain stashed his stock certificates and bags of gold in this safe.

Electrified, old-fashioned street lamps made for Christmas displays were perfect for a park scene. A child's plastic bubble pipe in the shape of a saxophone, when treated with gold paint, became an authentic-looking instrument on which our puppet had no trouble playing *When the Saints Go Marchin' Home*. My basement harbors a collection of gadgets,

toys, and oddities just waiting to hit the limelight. The more of these items I can legitimately incorporate into my plays (not just as padding), the better. Any suggestions I can include on where or how to obtain or construct unusual props are welcomed by others who use my script.

Lights

As much as most puppeteers would like to have complex, sophisticated lighting plans, they are usually thankful if they have lights that work and provide adequate illumination. Unless a company has permanent quarters or is working in a professional theatre space, it cannot afford the time, the money, and the inconvenience of an electrically produced wonderland.

A playwright might envision and wish to mention various effects, such as dimming the lights, spotlighting a character or using colored gels on the stage lights. He might want to suggest a strobe light that produces a pulsating light for slow motion and psychedelic effects. Or he might propose the use of black light and fluorescent paints for a surreal or magical effect. Unless the playwright is also the director, the final decisions are not his, but if he feels strongly about certain lighting effects, he has every right to include his directions in hopes of persuading the director to use them.

Sound Effects and Music

Sound effects are extremely important and should be suggested whenever possible. Besides adding general interest, they offer great opportunities for humor. Because of the fantasy nature of puppets, audiences can believe that their movements generate certain noises or that the puppets themselves can emit strange and unexpected sounds. In our electrical safety show, Nurse Penny Cillan's entrance always was preceded and accompanied by the sound of a bicycle siren horn. After the first time or two, the audience was laughing before they ever caught sight of Penny Cillan.

Nurse Penny Cillan ministers to Hap Hazard in *Zap Happy*. Puppets by Nick LeFeuvre.

Furthermore, sound effects enlarge and enhance certain stage business. Our mill in *Rumplestiltskin* was an uncomplicated, two-dimensional set piece with a rotating mill wheel fastened with a nut and a bolt. Not an imposing setup. But add a few sound effects and the mill becomes a ponderous affair that grudgingly grinds the wheat before it lurches to a grumbling halt. The audience has no doubt that the miller is telling the truth when he complains that "The gears are broken and the mill wheel needs replacing."

Likewise, music creates mood. Besides setting an atmosphere for the whole play, mu-

sic can heighten the emotional impact of a scene and add to the development of a character. Our *Return of the Bounce* is a pantomime show with background music and only a few lines of dialogue at the beginning and the end. Each of our characters has a musical theme, unobtrusive but definitive. The music used for the main character, whose mood shifts from happy to sad, changes in an almost subliminal way from major to minor, accenting the feelings and movement of the puppet.

You can indicate the actual pieces of music that you feel send the appropriate messages to the audience. Or he may wish to simply describe what he has in mind— "soft, ethereal music"or "unobtrusive flute solo." Such suggestions are helpful to a director's understanding of the play and its subtleties. The playwright must keep in mind that, unless the music happens to be old classical music or original compositions, the copyright laws are in effect and permission must be obtained.

Chapter 7

Rhyme Can Be Sublime

Most of us enjoy rhyming verse in one way or another, whether it be a book of Emily Dickinson poems, a clever advertising jingle on TV, or a greeting card.

Why do we like them? Somehow, rhythm is, and always has been, pleasant to the ear. And somehow, each rhyme manages to elicit a tiny, muted tickle of delight. In some nebulous way, rhyme gives the content an added luster, and the listener an extra degree of satisfaction. Consider the millions of readers, adults and children alike, who have been entertained by the Dr. Seuss books. Prose would never have sufficed.

Because of the universal appeal of verse, it has wonderful potential for the puppet playwright and its use should at least be considered. Prosody, as the art of versification is called, is a fascinating subject that has many facets, but only the elementary aspects are necessary to begin to have fun writing light verse.

Even though some of us are not poetry lovers, we all know a verse when we see one. But unless we have studied poetry, we are, perhaps, unaware that prosody analyzes and catalogs the structure of verses and poems. All the syllables in a line of poetry are divided into small groups called feet. Each foot has a rhythm, or a meter, that consists of one accented syllable and one or more unaccented ones. Each combination has a name. "da-*DA* da-*DA*" is called an iambic meter, while "*DA*-da-da *DA*-da-da" is called a dactylic meter, etc. Each line of poetry has a certain number of feet—monometer, pentameter, and the like.

So a poem can be written in "iambic trimeter" or "dactylic pentameter," and so on. But it's the feel of the rhythm, and not the nomenclature, that's most important.

One book I have found invaluable is *Words to Rhyme With* by Willard R. Espy. It not only includes a rhyming dictionary with one-, two- and three-syllable rhymes, but it also explains the various poetic structures and provides examples. In addition to a rhyming dictionary, a versifier needs a thesaurus handy as a resource for words, ideas, and inspiration. It is not hard to produce rhymes and even the rhythms. The hard part is to make the verse seem natural and easy. Verse that sounds contrived or artificial is not pleasing. A little work can lend a lot of sparkle to a script.

Some scripts, of course, are written entirely in verse, which lends a certain fairy-tale charm. But verse also can be used in selective ways. I sometimes have relied on verse to help differentiate characters—especially to indicate a different level of being. Few of us regularly speak in rhyme, so when a wizard, a fairy godmother, or a leprechaun uses rhyming verse, he is immediately distinctive, set apart from the earthly mortals capable only of prose. The contrast will confer an almost magical quality.

Other similar distinctions also can be made. In *The Saga of Grime and Glory*, I used prose for the more prosaic narrative segments (explanations and transitions), while the characters spoke in rhyming verse. Such dialogue seemed quite normal, puppets being what they are.

NARRATOR: Out of the annals of dastardly deeds and tender passions comes this moving story never before told but destined to touch the hearts of all who hear. Our gripping tale begins in the office of Casius M. Grime, a rich, prominent landlord and financier.

GRIME: My middle name is "Money" and
           They call me "Cash" for short.
           For fun and games I always read
           The daily stock report!

Variations of rhythm and meter also can be used to enhance the particular characteristics of the various puppets. A clock puppet might speak in iambic (two syllables with the accent on second syllable) diameter (two meters to a line).

CLOCK: Tick tock! Tick tock!
           I am a clock.
           I speak in rhyme
           And I keep time,
           And go "Bong! Bong!"
           The whole day long!

A music-box dancer might speak in a way that would augment her movements. A waltz beat (**1**-2-3 **1**-2-3), which is a dactylic meter (one accented syllable followed by two unaccented ones), might be used.

DANCER: Beauty is mine as I twirl on my music box,
           Exquisite elegance, grandeur and grace.
           Lovers and friends I can't have, though I cry, because
           Never can I leave this porcelain place.

There are many combinations of rhyme patterns and meters with which you might want to experiment. The possibilities are restricted only by the playwright's imagination. I find I often use iambic with three and four feet to a line (tetrameter and trimeter), as in *The Princess and the Pea*. The following verses are spoken by one of the potential brides who tries to endear herself to the prince.

WILHELMINA: You now are privileged to meet
           The Princess Wilhelmina.
           My famous lineage long has ruled
           The kingdom of Selena.
           My pointed head just fits a crown.
           I have a queen-sized nose.
           My blood is blue as blue can be
           And I wear jeweled clothes.

Rhyming can inexplicably contribute to the humor of a line or a situation. The use of verse also can lighten a script whose subject matter is dramatically dull, such as "electrical safety" or "saving fossil fuels." In my play about the history of early Seattle, several pioneers were complaining about the lack of women in the new settlement. Satirizing their predicament, I elected to have them explain their situation in limerick stanza pattern:

MAN I: There's one thing that's wrong with this place,
           We don't have enough frills and lace,
           Or ribbons or bows
           Or fancy silk clothes.
           A womanless town's a disgrace!

MAN II: I don't have a woman to wed,

To clean up my house—make
my bed,
To wash and to scrub
And cook up my grub,
Chop wood every day and
bake bread!

Now, if you have your script idea and you have your resource books nearby, you are ready to begin to work—and it will be work. Sometimes the rhymes seems to flow and the verses almost write themselves. Other times you can spend hours on one quatrain. But don't give up. If the word "woman" doesn't fit, substitute "maid," "girl," "dame," or "sweetie-pie." Something will eventually work. If "ill" doesn't have enough syllables, try "ailing," "poorly," "afflicted," or "indisposed." (Or you can have your character recuperate.)

If you were writing *The Frog Prince* in rhyme, you might think along these lines when the princess refuses to kiss the frog as she promised:

PRINCESS: I am a royal princess.
                  I couldn't kiss a frog!
                  I need a rhyme for "frog."
                  There's "hog," but it's not
                  right.
                  No need for "synagogue."
                  And "eggnog's" out of sight.
                  O.K. Then I'll try "toad."
                  "Bestowed" is what a kiss is.
                  There's "road,"
                  "explode," and "load."
                  Oh, what a problem this is.

                  Retreat! Review! Rethink!
                  Redo.

                  Should stick to prose! Oh
                  well, here goes.

PRINCESS: Of course, I didn't mean it,
                  You slimy, bumpy thing.

And you can't make me do it.
My father is the king!

And so another milestone on the road to "The End," even though "thing" is such an easy rhyme it's almost a cop-out.

Anyone with a sense of rhythm and a rhyming dictionary can launch himself into verse. It can be frustrating, but when the rhymes gel, it is tremendously gratifying. It may not be poetry, but it will have a flair, it can give your script a certain charm, and it can be fun.

Chapter 8

Adaptations

For various reasons, we playwrights find ourselves adapting stories for the puppet stage. Sometimes we choose an old favorite for economic reasons. It may prove to be much more marketable than something unknown. Sometimes, because of time limitations, it's easier to start with someone else's general idea than to start from scratch. (Shakespeare did it so why can't we?) And sometimes, there is a favorite story or a book that we simply love and want to make into a play.

Bringing a story to life is an exciting and fun project and sounds easy enough, but effecting such a metamorphosis can be anything but simple. Consider the successful books that have been made into movie flops. The writer and director somehow failed to capture the flavor of the book and/or the essence of the characters as they switched from the literary to the dramatic. We are dealing with two very different mediums and, although the goal of each is to communicate, there can be a tremendous difference between the written word and its dramatized corollary.

Both plays and books or stories incorporate characters, plots and atmosphere, words and pictures. But a play also features movement and sound. In any good adaptation, the essence of the story is retained while, by some mysterious dramatic alchemy, the story moves from the realm of imagination to a here-and-now experience. Descriptive prose, thoughts, feelings, written dialogue, and pictures are transformed into a blend of spoken words, action, sound, scenery, and props.

Things actually happen. Though committed to maintaining the integrity of the book, one can seldom expect to transpose from page to stage directly.

Granted, some simple picture books can be enacted on the stage in their entirety. But as a story becomes more complicated, such a presentation becomes not a drama but a dramatic reading. Of course, the narrative technique is invaluable to playwrights at times, but its use must necessarily be limited. Theatre is a matter of showing, not telling.

Suppose a boy in a story is described as "frightened." "His scalp prickled and his skin crawled as he entered the old barn. All the horror stories he had ever read came flooding back to his mind." If this boy becomes a character in a play, the audience needs to know his condition, but you can't just inject the words of the story and have the boy gasp "I'm scared. My scalp is prickling and my skin is crawling. All the horror stories I've ever read are flooding back into my mind," unless the play is a spoof. Nevertheless, all of his feelings need to be communicated, but in dramatic terms. He might say something to another person about how scared he is. Perhaps his voice quivers as he whispers how this is just like all the horror stories he's read. Or, instead of dialogue, the playwright might want to resort to a shadowy stage, eerie music, and a character who hesitantly enters, shivering and shaking, and perhaps starts violently at the slightest noise. It's up to the playwright how to communicate the boy's fear.

If the book describes a house as a place that immediately invokes a feeling of warmth and comfort, you must figure out some way to get these perceptions across to the audience in the language of the theatre. The set might require homey touches—a fireplace and over-stuffed chairs, pleasant music. A character could exclaim how it's always so wonderful to come home to this cozy house. The owner of the house might bustle about singing, then welcome a newcomer with an offer of coffee. The narrator might set the stage. It's the playwright's decision.

Suppose a man is described as "happy about his lot in life." What does this man do or say to let everyone know how he feels? Does he laugh? Does he dance? Does he sing? Does he cheerily greet those he meets? It's the playwright's job to find a way to project his contentment.

Finding a good story is not usually a problem. However, sometimes a story, even though it makes captivating reading, may have little promise for dramatization. For instance, we all know that anything can happen in a book. It all depends on the imagination of the author, his ability to write with authenticity, and the reader's willingness to be swept along. But on the puppet stage, some marvelous episodes have trouble happening—believably, that is. They may require impossible ingenuity from the director and promise horrendous problems for the technical staff. Stories with such segments should be seriously questioned as potential productions.

Other books may adapt poorly because their success rests on their lyrical qualities, the aesthetics of their illustrations, or their special appeal to the imagination. These stories often lack one of the essential ingredients of drama—action—and therefore will make poor plays.

As a playwright considers his choice and his subsequent adaptation, he can never afford to forget that the audience is out there. And that audience must **understand, care,** and **be satisfied**. To guarantee these responses, you must follow the same principles as when writing an original play. And if the adapted story violates any of these principles, then you should consider changes in the story or another story choice. A bored reader simply lays down his book. But a bored member of an audience can cause a disturbance, can go to sleep, can develop a sudden need to go to the bathroom, or leave for good. Not fun! We want to try to forestall such reactions as we adapt our stories.

Simplify the Story

A general rule for all writing is to eliminate the superfluous. This rule is especially important when dramatizing traditional folktales that tend to be repetitive. Numerous old stories are structured as journeys with a series of encounters. The swineherd meets an old lady, then a boy, then a girl, a baker, a miller, and so on. Now, preschoolers may love repetition and delight in hearing the same question asked and the same answer given over and over again, but too much repetition on the stage becomes very boring for a general audience. They tend to think, "Let's get on with it." If one's audience is always 3- and 4-year-olds, or if one manages to make each encounter unique and exciting, then it may be safe to stick to the story. Otherwise, some changes are in order.

Actually, the fewer scenes and the fewer characters needed to tell the story, the better the pacing. Often, various episodes can be telescoped into one scene. The various encounters can happen in one place, or the protagonist can simulate walking. Such streamlining also means fewer puppets and props, a boon to small companies with few puppeteers. Furthermore, the fewer the scenes, the fewer the needed transitions. And you must minimize transitions because, as mentioned before, they often take time and impede the flow of the action.

Many times, characters whose function in the story is the same can be easily eliminated without detriment. I'm not suggesting that a porcine hatchet job be done to produce "The One Little Pig," but I am saying that Cinderella could do as well with a stepmother and one stepsister instead of two (done successfully by Seattle Puppetory Theatre).

Change the Story if Necessary

The popular children's stories heard and read for generations often are dramatized for young audiences. Unfortunately, charming old tales are not necessarily charming when dramatized. In folktales, characters often *are* for no good reason, *do* or *go* with little or no motivation, and are inconsistent in their behavior. Undefined characters and unmotivated action do not usually result in highly successful drama. Most audiences unconsciously want reasons for what they see on the stage. I have heard playwrights defend their faltering plays by boasting about how they "stuck exactly to the story." What a mistake! Many of these old stories need attention and revision if headed for the stage.

When I adapted the story of *Rumplestiltskin* for a Seattle Puppetory Theatre production, I read various versions. Some of the characterizations in this old tale consistently bothered me, and I made some changes.

In the first place, I looked at the king, a most unpleasant character, who threatened to kill the miller's daughter if she did not manage to spin his straw into gold. He was obvi-

ously a greedy, cruel soul with no heart. And yet, this miller's daughter ends up marrying this horrible person! How could she ever be expected to live happily ever after? Not a happy ending for this poor young queen or a satisfying ending for the audience. So I made the king more compassionate and altruistic. In my version, he ruled over a kingdom that was destitute. Money was needed to repair roads and bridges and to build a new water wheel for the royal mill. Grasping at straws, this monarch hoped the miller's daughter could save the kingdom. Now he doesn't seem like such wretched husband material.

Secondly, in the original stories, Rumplestiltskin gets so angry that he either splits in two or he stamps himself into the floor, never to be heard from again. Now what kind of justice is this? This little man wanted a child. He bargained with the miller's daughter, promising to spin the straw into gold. Rumplestiltskin kept his promise. She did not want to keep hers. So the little fellow generously gave her another chance. He again kept his promise. She could keep the child. Yes, it's only an old folktale, but there was something unsettling about it. Rumplestiltskin did everything right and he comes to a bitter end. What underlying message was this play giving? No future in keeping promises?

I felt I had to make a few changes. In my version, Rumplestiltskin is presented as a poor, lonely little man who wants a baby to love. When he loses his chance, all is not lost. The royal couple asks him to be the godfather of the baby, which lessens his disappointment and rewards his integrity. As an added touch, he goes to stay at the new mill, where the miller hopes his guest will be able to change wheat into diamonds.

If a playwright fiddles around with an old folktale, he is asking for possible complaints from the fans of the old version. He must be

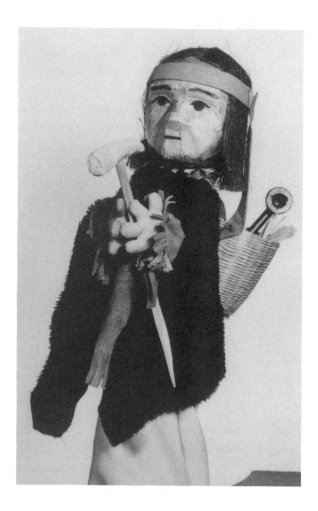

Netak sets off for the mountains in *The Miser of Mount Rainier.* Puppet by Betsy Tobin and Jean Mattson.

sure that he actually has created a better story and be ready to explain and defend the changes.

Some time ago, the Seattle Puppetory Theatre adapted *The Miser of Mount Rainier*, a northwest Indian legend. Because of the nature of the story and the fact that the storyteller was such a traditional part of Indian culture, we elected to forgo dialogue and use narrative for our project. We revised the narrative to fit the dramatic needs of a play, and we employed an actor whose rich and resonant voice made the Rip Van Winkle/Scrooge tale come alive. The only dialogue was the conversation between the Elk God and the

Thunderbird, as they discussed how best to deal with the miser. *The Miser of Mount Rainier* was a very popular show in the schools of the northwest.

The Funny Little Woman as a Puppet Play

To exemplify a possible adaptation, I will use a picture storybook currently on the market, *The Funny Little Woman* by Arlene Mosel. This is the story of a Japanese woman who makes rice cakes and who is always laughing. One of her rice cakes rolls away and down into a hole. She tumbles in also and finds herself in a dark cavern, where she meets jizos and an oni, Japanese folk characters. The oni, a monster of sorts, takes her to his home, gives her a magic rice paddle, which makes rice continually, and forces her to make rice cakes—and more rice cakes. She finally steals the rice paddle and escapes in a boat.

Frantic about losing his rice maker, the oni follows her to the lake and slurps up all the water. Her boat is beached until he spews out the water. She then manages to row away and return home, where she happily sells rice cakes for the rest of her life.

Now, granted, this book is charming to read. The many illustrations are delightful as they depict her cozy little house and her tumbling down, down, down into the underground pathway. The relationship of the underground tunnel to her little house on the surface is graphically presented. Each page is filled with beautiful pictures following the strange adventures of the little woman. Now, what kind of a puppet show will this delightful book make? Unless significant changes were made, the play would be rather weak for several reasons.

Most importantly, the audience would end up not caring too much about what happens to the little woman. We wouldn't worry about her, because there is no real threat other than the darkness of the tunnel. The jizos say they are mean, but they don't show it. The oni doesn't seem to present much danger; he wants his rice cakes, but otherwise he is rather benign. The little woman never acts as if she is afraid—she is laughing all the time. She sneaks out of the oni's house simply because she's tired of making rice cakes and wants to go home.

To make the audience really care about this little woman, she needs to be in much more of a predicament. She needs to be homesick. She needs to fear the oni. To be caught by the oni again should be a frightening prospect. It will be a stronger play if the suspense builds and culminates in the boat scene.

The little woman's merry face gives her a certain appeal in the book, but we know little about her other than she makes rice cakes. Furthermore, she had no right to steal the rice paddle from the oni. Such unjustified behavior is not endearing. Her character seems to need further development so that we identify and/or sympathize with her.

Furthermore, the producers of this puppet play might have real problems in making the scenes believable and effective. It could be done—but not easily. The little woman's tumble down into the tunnel is beautifully illustrated in the book, but to recreate this episode as effectively on the stage would be a tremendous challenge to the scene designer. Likewise, a puppet who can swallow a lake is a tall order—then to expel it, even taller. The puppet maker might have a few difficulties. If these essential scenes are presented ineffectively, the audience will not be satisfied.

Of course, some of these episodes could be replaced by clever use of narration, sound effects, and music, but eliminating any of the exciting scenes will leave the audience feeling a bit cheated.

My conclusion about this little book is

that, although it is engaging because of its beautiful artwork, it would be a questionable choice for an adaptation. For such an endeavor, you would need to consider further character development, a magnification of the problems that beset the little woman, and solutions for the challenging production problems involved.

Remember the Copyrights

One important aspect of adaptations is the matter of copyrights. Dozens of wonderful books in print would make excellent puppet shows. But they belong to their authors (sometimes their publishers). An author has put time and effort into his creation and is trying to make his living by doing so. One should never use someone else's work without his permission. Sometimes the author will grant permission without a fee and sometimes he will negotiate for the payment. Some authors refuse to allow anyone else to use their works.

Most authors will not object to classroom use, but if there is a question (if there is any profit to be made, you must get permission) it's best to check before going ahead. The publishers can usually forward letters to their authors.

Chapter 9

Productions with a Message

Sometimes puppeteers need to develop a play on a particular subject. You might be commissioned by the National Parks Department to produce a show on saving the environment. Or maybe an organization wants to commemorate some aspect of the Civil War or, again, a high school teacher might want to develop a production that augments the social studies curriculum. Any such situation challenges the imagination. Just as a playwright's work can bring a story to life on the stage, so he can make history live or make safety rules seem vitally important. But a play is a play, and the principles are the same.

The Seattle Puppetory Theatre has done a number of shows with messages and particular themes and has found that these shows can be every bit as interesting and fun to write and produce as any other story—and sometimes even more so.

Zap Happy

Some years ago, Seattle Puppetory Theatre received a contract from Seattle City Light to develop a puppet theatre presentation on electrical safety. The company wanted to prevent the accidents that happen because children do not understand the potential danger of electrical wires and substations. The show was to be performed in dozens of elementary schools in Seattle.

We read all the company's safety manuals and watched some of their videos. We knew we did not want to preach. The show had to be fun and entertaining to meet our goals, but it also had to be educational to fulfill Seattle City Light needs.

When a particular subject has little dramatic potential or audience appeal, you may have to step outside the subject and find characters who might somehow be intimately involved with the subject. Our story was structured around Ginger Lee, a student in an elementary school, who has a problem completing an assignment on electrical safety. Our target audience of children could identify with the protagonist and *care* about what happened. We limited our use of electrical terms and explained them simply so that the children would *understand*. The ending was *satisfying* to a young audience in that Ginger managed not only to solve her problem but also to outshine the other kids and an adult. Furthermore, the play satisfied the sponsors by teaching the kids exactly what would happen if they flew kites near electric wires, built a tree house close to electric wires, or trespassed into an electrical substation.

Four or five years after this Seattle City Light tour, we were performing another show in one of the Seattle schools, and one of the sixth-graders ran up to us and said, "I remember you. You did the show where the man got 'zapped.'" He must have been in kindergarten or first grade when he saw *Zap Happy*. Somehow, at that moment, it all seemed worthwhile.

Gold Nugget Champ

When Washington had a centennial a few years ago, grant opportunities multiplied. Actually, we didn't get our act together in time to apply for any of them, but we did end up with several different plays based on the research I did.

While reading about the effects of the gold rush in Seattle, I ran across an account of how unscrupulous men would steal dogs—any breed—and sell them to unsuspecting prospectors as sled dogs, supposedly an absolute necessity in Alaska. So I wrote a play about a boy whose dog, Champ, had been stolen. His problem was solved when he got his dog back. Puppet dogs are usually crowd pleasers and, indeed, our *Gold Nugget Champ* proved to be a successful addition to our repertoire. In addition to presenting a good story, we were able to communicate the general milieu of the times, some of the frenzied optimism that prevailed, and the tragic realities that awaited many of the eager prospectors.

The Big Pig War

A humorous and somewhat bizarre incident in northwest history also piqued our interest. It seems that in 1853, England and the United States were involved in a controversy known as the Pig War. An insignificant boundary dispute between farmers resulted in a dead pig. This innocuous squabble escalated into an ominous confrontation between warships and militias before the matter was finally settled. This story provided the basis for a fast-moving, interesting play. The conflict was between two governments with two conflicting ideas about the location of what is now the boundary between Canada and the United States. The climax, of course, was when they finally agreed on the line of demarcation and

war between England and the United States was fortunately averted.

High Priority

Several years ago, Seattle Puppetory Theatre received a grant from the Washington Commission for the Humanities to develop a puppet project with a group of "lifers" at the Monroe State Reformatory. We began by discussing ideas for a play, knowing that it would be more meaningful to them if we incorporated some of their own thoughts and feelings. I listed several ways to get story ideas—a problem to be solved, a question to be answered or a conflict to be resolved. "Do you have any problems?" I inadvertently asked. Their incarceration had not squashed their senses of humor. They laughed and we were off to a good start.

Rich tries out his puppet, Casper, in "High Priority," produced at Monroe State Reformatory.

Several in the group were involved in the literacy program at the prison. One served as an assistant to the college teacher who came each week for classes. Another was learning how to read through the program. They all agreed that illiteracy and the resulting frustrations are among the major reasons a person turns to crime. This issue became the basis of the play. I wrote the script using all of their ideas. Joan King directed the group in the construction of the puppets, sets, and props. The play was produced and performed for school children, families, and friends.

Sometimes the information or the message that needs to be communicated simply does not inspire the playwright with ideas for a story. Then, perhaps, the story format needs to be looked at from a slightly different perspective. Instead of a protagonist with a problem or a conflict, a historical or thematic question can be asked that will cement various loosely related scenes into a meaningful whole as the question is answered. The focus in this case is on the development of a personality, an institution, a place, or on the scope of a particular field or subject.

For example, suppose a decision has been made to present a play about the life of George Washington Carver. That should be fairly easy research. Much material has been written about this man. But before beginning, a playwright must decide on his perspective. As has been noted, in writing most plays, the perspective involves deciding from whose point of view the story is going to be told. In this case, we know it is George Washington Carver's story. That has been set. The perspective involves how we approach his story. What question are we going to answer?

We could ask the question, "Who were the people who made an impact on Carver's life?" In that case, we would probably include scenes about Aunt Susan and Uncle Moses, who took him in after his mother was kid-

napped; Dr. and Mrs. Milholland, who encouraged him to try again, this time successfully, to enroll in college; and Booker T. Washington, who hired him as a college professor. The climax would probably include Dr. Carver's achievements and the recognition of the influence many had upon this life, while stressing the strength and abilities that enabled him to benefit from these influences.

In another approach, we could ask, "How did the son of a slave become the famous scientist whose face appears on a U.S. postage stamp?" This play would focus on the main events in his life: his struggle to get an education, his trouble with racism, his experiments with the lowly peanut, his persistence and the gradual gaining of respect and credibility. This second approach would be leading up to a slightly different climax—his crowning professional achievements and final recognition of his genius by the academic and commercial world.

Perhaps the important question to be answered might be, "Who was George Washington Carver, the man?" To do this approach justice, you would have to include not only Dr. Carver's dedication to science, but also his love of flowers and plants, his intense desire to help his people, his lifelong interest in art and painting, and his extreme modesty and humility. For the third approach, the ending should somehow be a summation of the qualities, attitudes, and achievements that made George Washington Carver an outstanding human being.

These are only three of the questions that might be asked. Among other possibilities are, "How does the work of George Washington Carver influence my life?" and "What is the importance of the lowly peanut?" In each of the options, the underlying story and the protagonist would be the same, but the play script would be quite different because of the perspective involved. It would be up to the playwright to decide.

The same process in regard to perspective would be operative whether the subject we're talking about is Christmas carols or the art of puppetry. And most of the same writing principles apply. The audience must **understand, care** (the subject must be presented as important, relevant, and interesting), and be **satisfied**.

As with writing any play script, the audience must know what's going on. The subject matter and the playwright's perspective should be communicated to them in some way—by the title of the play, by the program, or by introductory narration or exposition. The development of this perspective (the sequence of events that eventually answer the question) comprises the middle of the play. And the climax obviously comes when the question has been adequately answered. Narration would be especially useful for this form to bind the scenes together as a whole.

I enjoyed researching and writing a number of plays with thematic threads for Seattle Puppetory Theatre. The following listings are among them:

Peter Puget and Captain Vancouver confer in *How Now Seattle*.

How Now Seattle

When I was researching for the centennial celebration, I read all about early Seattle from the time Captain Vancouver sailed into the Strait of Juan De Fuca in 1792 to the Alaskan Gold Rush in 1890. It was an exciting story that answered the question, "What made Seattle the great city it is today?" I tried to choose the main events that contributed to the growth of the area. Because of the colorful characters and the interesting episodes involved, it was not hard to present an entertaining show. The final scene depicted the gold rush, which changed Seattle from a dull little western town into an important commercial center. The show turned out to be a hand puppet and shadow puppet production. A little satire, a bit of rhyme, some music and song were blended into a 45-minute show.

We found that there are streets named for some of the children who were in the first landing party in the area, so we capitalized on this fact and wrote a song that they sang as they were unloading the boat and getting settled.

> We've come in covered wagons 'cross the prairie.
> It was bumpy. It was dusty. It was bad.
> There were deserts. There were rivers. It was scary.
> But the best adventure that we've ever had.
>
> We may be only children on this shore-a
> But we'll go down in history just same.
> 'Cause we're Olive and Virginia and Lenor-a
> And there'll be streets right in Seattle with our name.

Oh, we're Olive and Virginia and Lenor-a.
To be pioneers is really quite a chore-a.
It's a struggle to survive.
It's a trick to stay alive
But we did and didn't ask for any more-a.

The activities of the early explorers and settlers make a fascinating story. The schools loved this show because it fit right in with their required segment on Washington history. And the kids discovered that history can be fun.

Nuclear Follies

A few years ago, when the cold war was still hot, we wanted to write a show that was entertaining, but that brought out the idiocy of the whole nuclear buildup. "Where is this nuclear arms race leading us?" We therefore developed a production that we called *The Nuclear Follies*. In it, a community of puppets finally realizes that if the world goes up in smoke there won't be any puppeteers! No puppeteers! No live puppets! Horrors! Panicking, the puppets get busy and decide to do what they do best—entertain. They will put on a show that will not be just another government-sponsored song and dance.

They line up their acts: a magician who miscalculates when he puts his guns, grenades and bombs into the hat and produces not a dove, as he expects, but a dead duck; dancers who become atomized during the final chorus; and a fast-talking salesman who is selling the elixir that mortals have long been waiting for—the Cure for the Common Cold War! We included singers and dancers and even a stand-up comic.

MAN # 1: Say, do you know what they call a bunch of hand puppets without puppeteers?

MAN # 2: No, what do they call a bunch of hand puppets without puppeteers?

MAN # 1: A hollow cast! (Ha-ha-ha-ha!)

We had fun and we presented our message.

Celebration

We were approached by a community college to do a show for their holiday family night. Because of the variety of ethnic groups in their student population, they wanted a program that would incorporate a number of cultures. I decided to have a holiday theme and present various holidays around the world. We would answer the question, "How do different people of the world celebrate?" noting that they all have holidays, at which time they give thanks for something outstanding in their lives or commemorate someone or some important historical event.

No problem. All I had to do was look up the various holidays and dramatize them. Again, not as easy as it sounds. There was no lack of holidays. Every country has its family holidays, its national celebrations, and special religious days. However, we had to find celebrations that would lend themselves to dramatic scenes, preferably featuring the children of the various countries, or at least visually interesting rituals of some kind. One difficulty was the sameness of many of the celebrations. We needed variety. Furthermore, we wanted holidays that would lend themselves to our format, beginning with January and ending with December. Finally, we needed to include cultures from each continent so we would encompass the whole world in our presentation. It was a matter of blending all our needs into the dozens of holiday observations we found. (We really celebrated when at last we premiered our show, *Celebration*.)

We introduced each one of our twelve holidays with several slides flashed on a large screen above and behind the hand puppet stage. A narrator's voice accompanied the slide projections and bridged the transitions between the scenes. The finale stressed the fact that the whole world celebrates, though perhaps differently, with the same feeling of gratitude and joy of living, reaching out to all with good wishes, understanding, and above all, hope for the future.

If you are developing a show for a committee or an organization that knows nothing about puppetry or playwriting but, nevertheless, knows exactly how everything should hang together, things can be tough. In order to do a good job, it is necessary to understand the principles of playwriting, then be able to articulate not only what you want to do and why you want to do it, but also what you do not want to do and why not.

Chapter 10

Actors and Puppets Together

I have heard some puppeteers who insist that puppets should perform only with other puppets and never be combined with actors in performance. They say such a union diminishes the magical quality of the puppet's performance and mars its impression of reality. This is not so, in my opinion. Some of the most engaging shows I have seen featured a blending of puppet and actor. When effectively coupled with a living entity, the puppet can become even more imbued with life and truth than when interacting with its inanimate colleagues.

Mrs. Button and Jiggles, the clown, work together in *The Return of the Bounce*. Puppets by John Bartelt and Joan King.

One of my favorite shows, produced by a Bulgarian company, presented a prime example. I will never forget that performance. Onto the stage, which was set as the rear of a very elegant theatre, an actor, costumed in brocades and white wig, entered, holding in his arms a little white dog. They take seats in the back row. The overture and the first act of the puppet show are presented without incident. We all enjoy the performance. The dog sits quietly watching until, during the second act, a puppet cat appears in the show. The dog responds in typical canine fashion, zooming after the cat. The results are totally devastating, believable, and hilarious, all heightened by the actor's responses. A lasting impression!

Through the years, Seattle Puppetory Theatre has successfully developed several shows utilizing live persons interacting with the puppets. One story line that worked well involved an unhappy, destitute person (actor) who befriends a turtle that suddenly is able to speak and sing. The puppet turtle ends up performing successfully for the public on the stage and saving the person from penury. Similarly, *The Magic Teakettle*, a Japanese folktale, would lend itself beautifully to this type of production, with a cast of actors and a puppet teapot.

In these various cases, the puppet must be in a position so that his movements seem natural and intrinsic. The turtle can be placed on a table or a rock so that the puppeteer has easy access to the puppet, and any movements seem spontaneous and genuine. The audience must not be aware of the mechanics behind the scene. A screen or a curtain on an otherwise natural set seems contrived and detracts from the realism of the story. Granted, this can severely tax the ingenuity of the technical director, but a successful solution can mean a popular production.

Several years ago there was a rash of shows in which the puppeteers were in plain view of the audience. This convention involved the puppeteer functioning not only as manipulators but also as various characters in the story. Seattle Puppetory Theatre produced *Cinderella* using this format. The two actors in our show were sometimes puppeteers, but also took the parts (as actors) of the servant of the prince, the doctor, and the fairy godmother.

This maneuvering can be tricky business. The subtle changing of roles must be communicated to the audience, whether by action, costume, or mien, to insure their understanding and continued involvement. When the distinctions are clear, this type of play often develops fascinating momentum.

The play *The Puppeteer* can be most easily done with an actor and puppets. The play is about a puppeteer who yearns to be the director of a traditional theatre and to direct actors, not puppets. He dreams that his puppets come alive and are so temperamentally difficult to deal with that he finally is grateful and satisfied to have his little puppet company. The play, as written, includes a segment in which the puppeteer/actor actually performs part of his show. The audience sees the puppets as puppets being manipulated and then, later, as living creatures.

When the Seattle Puppetory Theatre produced the northwest Indian story *The Miser of Mount Rainier,* all the characters were puppets except for the Elk God and the Thunderbird, two spirits of the mountain. The puppeteers themselves were masked and costumed and appeared as larger-than-life, powerful entities.

Likewise, a human actor also can add vitality to any story that features a monster or a giant.

Combining puppets and actors may not suit every company's needs or abilities, but if those involved enjoy performing in front of an audience, instead of being hidden behind a puppet stage or curtain, a puppet/actor production may be an option.

Chapter 11

Developing a Play with a Class

When a teacher or a leader wishes to produce a play with a class or a group, he usually looks in books or catalogs for a play to use. Discovering that the plays available will not fit the particular class situation, he realizes that he must develop a script. Should he go ahead and write the play himself or do it collectively with the class or group? It's easier to write it oneself, certainly, but involving the class can be a rewarding experience (at least for the class). The input of fifteen or twenty stimulated children can result in an interesting, lively script, and the excitement of their participation should compensate for the use of class time and teacher effort. However, some students inevitably become personally involved and get carried away with wild ideas. The teacher must be able to affirm these ideas while explaining audience dynamics. Clarence's idea is good, but may not work because of the way audiences react. The onus is placed on the audience where it belongs.

The same basic principles pertain to a group effort as to a single playwright. Attention must be paid to the structure, characters, action. Consistency, motivations, believability, perspective, and the like need to be explained. The class must be made to understand the importance of thinking about the audience at all times during the playwriting process.

Several years ago a teacher who had received a grant from an arts commission asked Seattle Puppetory Theatre to help her third-grade class develop a hand puppet produc-tion. The kids wanted to write it from scratch, and I was all for it. I had hoped to develop an original script, discussing the various approaches, working with play structure, motivations, and so on. However, they had already decided they wanted to dramatize the story of *Cinderella*. There were twenty three kids in the class and, of course, they all wanted to make a puppet and be in the show. I explained the cast limitations and the other production difficulties with this particular story—the changing of the pumpkin into a coach and the shoe on a hand puppet (most of them do not sport feet), but they were adamant. They had their hearts set on *Cinderella*.

I spent three sessions with the class delving into all aspects of the Cinderella story. After briefly sketching out the familiar plot, we talked about our characters. We mulled over the relationship between Cinderella and her father and their background together. It was to be a loving relationship, and the father was unaware of the way Cinderella was being treated. We discussed Cinderella, who was to be sweet and forgiving. The stepmother remained as she is usually portrayed, selfish and ambitious. We discussed how the stepsisters would exhibit their selfish, unpleasant personalities. We considered various names for them, and eventually chose Ruby and Pearl—their mother's little gems. These names provided interesting opportunities for dialogue.

The fairy godmother had to be defined. We explored a number of possibilities. She could be magical and ethereal. She might be sweet and angelic. She could be grandmother-ly. She ended up being a practical, helpful person who spoke crisply and directly.

Somewhere along the line it was decided that the prince should have two brothers (probably because we needed more puppets to accommodate our surplus of puppeteers). And so we developed obnoxious personalities for Philander, who is obsessed with clothes, and Adelbert, who is a glutton.

After all the main personalities were forged, we talked about the plotting of the story. What would our first scene be, and what would happen? We worked through each scene. We talked about the motivations for any appearances. To further fulfill our need for puppeteers, we added a king and decided that there would be a program during the ball featuring a magician, madrigal singers, and a puppet announcer who would introduce the whole performance.

The addition of the prince's two odious brothers turned out to be brilliant, providing a satisfying twist in the climactic scene. The fairy godmother with a final stroke of her magic wand causes the two step sisters to fall madly in love with Philander and Adelbert. They obviously deserve each other. Cinderella and the prince, of course, live happily ever after.

I included the performers at the ball reluctantly. Adding songs or material that does not further the action is not recommended, as has been mentioned. But sometimes it is a matter of the rock and the hard place. In this case, both acts were brief and they provided Cinderella and the prince more time together before the midnight hour. (An audience can tolerate only so much dancing.) Fortunately, several of the students made their puppets, but preferred to function backstage on sound, lights, and props. (All went well, and the audiences of other students and parents rated the show an unqualified success.)

I find that for the lower grades, it works best if I write the final script, incorporating all the ideas that evolve during the classroom discussions. I can take care of the important details, such as motivations, transitions, blocking, and so on. (Primary children can write simple playlets and should be encouraged to do so, but they cannot be expected to understand the more complicated aspects of playwriting. It is very important that the audience **understands, cares,** and **is satisfied,** so that the applause will be loud and the accolades many.)

In the upper grades, each student can write his own script. These scripts can be discussed and suggestions made. One or more can then be chosen for the performance, and the final script collectively developed. Participation in the writing and production of a play is a never-to-be-forgotten experience. Every child should be so lucky!

Chapter 12

And Now the Mechanics

When a playwright has refined all his ideas for sets, dialogue, and stage direction, he must then be concerned about the actual written format. How can he write his play so that it is easily understood by those who will read it? There is plenty of effort involved in play production without the initial problem of deciphering the script. The reader should have no difficulty distinguishing the speaker from the speech, the blocking directions, or the stage business.

There are general rules for scripting with variations. All suggested script formats require that each scene begin with, if not a description of the set, at least its location. Characters' names are always in capitals when identifying dialogue or action. Margins of at least one inch are recommended. Directions for stage action and information about the characters' behavior are included in parentheses and are sometimes printed in italics.

There are several accepted ways in which dialogue can be written. Most traditional theatre plays place the character's name in the center.

MRS. CLIFFORD:
(Haughtily surveying the store)
Yes, you can help me, young man. I'd like to buy a full set of rain gear—hat, slicker, and boots, in yellow—for my pekinese.
(She picks up her dog)

In the format I usually use, the characters' names stand out on the left, which, I feel,

speeds the assimilation of the script by the readers. I want it to be easy to use.

MRS. CLIFFORD: *(Haughtily surveying the store)* Yes, you can help me, young man. I'd like to buy a full set of rain gear—hat, slicker, and boots, in yellow—for my pekinese. *(She picks up her dog)*

There are usually more blocking directions in scripts for puppet theatre because of the necessity to consider the movement of the puppeteers as well as the puppets. The use of the right or the left hand is often critcal. To facilitate the actions of a puppet, a puppeteer may need to change puppets from one hand to the other or exchange puppets with another puppeteer. Sometimes, a puppeteer may need help in handling his puppet's props. (As a possible aid, I have included manipulation charts for *most of the plays; see the appendix. Of course, more puppeteers can be utilized than are indicated in the charts.)*

Play publishers often provide their own script requirements. For instance, the editors of *Plays, The Drama Magazine for Young People* require the same information, but in a slightly different format. They will provide a manuscript specification sheet upon request.

When submitting a play to a publisher, you should have a title page that includes a brief description, such as "hand puppet play"

and the author's name in the center of the
page. A copyright notification would be on
the bottom left. A second page includes the
cast of characters and a brief description of
the play. If the play is lengthy, the time and
place of the scenes might be listed.

Chapter 13

Now Go Forth

I find it tremendously exciting to sift through the avalanche of ideas for plays and find a promising nugget that may hold the possibility of a rich story. It's a unique thrill to create characters in your mind who actually come to life on the stage. But writing plays also is hard, frustrating work! It is a struggle to contrive a story that does not seem contrived. It takes patience, persistence, and concentration to fashion appropriate dialogue from the plethora of words and phrases spinning around in one's brain. But it is tremendously satisfying to finish a scene that feels right.

But this satisfaction is ephemeral until the play is, at long last, forged through performance. The anxieties of writing are mild when compared to the agonies surrounding the premiere. Although you can be somewhat optimistic if you have focused on the audience's *understanding, caring,* and *satisfaction*, you must await the dramatic culmination for final validation of your judgment.

Whatever the audience reaction to his play, however, the playwright will have profited from his experience. His reflection on his characters, their motivations, their personalities, and the consequences of their actions will have enlarged his horizons. Every completed script will provide growth and direction to his work. Moreover, the playwriting process never fails to impart insights into and understanding of the happenings on the larger stage whereon we all perform.

Curtain going up!

Part II

Play Scripts

Introduction

Following are a group of plays that have been used by the Seattle Puppetory Theatre. Several were originally commissioned by other organizations but most were written solely for the company's use. The majority were intended to be performed by two people. However, they can be performed by more than the prescribed number of puppeteers, but not fewer.

As I have mentioned, to avoid manipulation muddles, a playwright must be aware of possible blocking possibilities as he writes. When I provided scripts for the librarians of the King County Library System, Joan King and I developed blocking charts that we included with the scripts. These charts are especially worthwhile if the number of puppeteers is limited to two. A number of charts are included in the appendix. The playwright may want to consider using this chart idea. Such charts can validate his structural decisions and offer invaluable assistance for the puppeteers during their initial rehearsals.

These plays have been performed for thousands of children and their families in hundreds of places. Their heartwarming responses have made the whole production process a pleasure. (If it weren't fun, we wouldn't do it—it's too much work.) It is hoped that these plays will continue to be enjoyed by the puppeteers who perform them and the countless people who love puppet shows.

All of these plays may be used without royalty payments. Audiotapes are available for some of the plays. Write to Seattle Puppetory Theatre, 13002 10th Ave. N.W., Seattle, WA 98177-4106.

The Ant and the Grasshopper

by Jean M. Mattson

CHARACTERS
Ant
Grasshopper
Narrator's voice

PROPS
Guitar
Bag of wheat
Leaves

SET PIECES
Bushes or tree
House with a window
Piles of snow

This version of Aesop's fable requires one set and includes two scenes. It can be performed by one person. However, as a two-person play, the grasshopper can be made to fiddle with more zest and abandon. Stick puppets can also be used.

SCENE I: BUSH OR TREE STAGE LEFT. ANT'S LITTLE HOUSE STAGE RIGHT.

INTRODUCTORY MUSIC

(ANT enters stage left with a grain of wheat, crosses stage and enters house. He comes out without the grain, crosses and exits stage left. GRASSHOPPER enters stage right with his guitar, crosses stage, sits down by the tree, and strums and sings.)

HOPPER: I live in the grass and I hoppity hop.
I sing and I play and I hate to stop.
I sing and I play and dance in the sun
'Cause summer is made to enjoy—have fun!

(ANT enters stage left with another grain and crosses stage. Hopper sees him.)

Oh, hi there, Anty-panty. What are ya doin' there anyway?

ANT: Oh, Hopper, hi. I'm carrying wheat.

HOPPER: Oh, yeah?

ANT: Yeah. The farmers always spill some grain when they go to the mill. I bring it home. Sometimes it's oats, sometimes it's corn. Today they're grinding wheat—that's my favorite. Time to store up for winter.

HOPPER: Grain by grain? That'll take you forever.

ANT: Well, I've got all summer.

HOPPER: But the summer goes fast, li'l buddy. You oughta stop that running back and forth and enjoy the sun.

ANT: You're right. The summer goes fast. That's why I'm running back and forth. It'll be snowtime before you know it. You'd better do some planning, Hopper.

HOPPER: Relax, li'l buddy. Come on. I'll play you a li'l ant song. *(Starts to sing.)*
There was an ant who liked to eat.
He hauled in oats and corn and wheat
And filled each cranny, crack, and shelf
And left no room for his own self.
Ha-ha-ha. Ho-Ho-Ho. Come on, Anty-panty. Have a little fun.

ANT: No, Hopper. Thanks, but I've still got a lot to do. You know, there's plenty of wheat out there. One farmer had a hole in his sack. You could store some away for the winter yourself.

HOPPER: Maybe later, li'l buddy. I'm happy now just singin' and dancin'.

ANT: Suit yourself. Gotta go now. Time's a-wastin'. *(Exits.)*

HOPPER: *(Shakes his head.)* And you're a-wastin' time. *(Starts to sing again.)* Wheat, huh? Well, maybe I'll hop down to the mill. I could stand a chomp or two for lunch. *(Hops off singing.)*

TRANSITIONAL MUSIC

NARRATOR: Soon the summer was over. The leaves turned brown and swirled off the trees. *(Leaves swirl.)* Winter came and the cold winds blew and the snow covered the fields and forest.

(Piles of snow appear on the ground, the tree, and ANT's roof.)

SCENE II: SAME AS BEFORE. A WARM GLOW SHINES OUT ANT'S WINDOW AND DOOR.

(ANT opens his window and looks around.)

ANT: Well, it looks like the worst is over. But it'll still be a while 'til spring. Brrrr, it is cold out here. *(Closes the window.)*
(HOPPER enters stage right haltingly.)

HOPPER: *(Weakly.)* I live in the grass but I can't seem to hop.
I'm feeble from hunger, I'm about to drop.
Hop—hop ahhhh. Hop—hop ahhh. Oh.
Hey, there's Anty-panty's house. Yeah, and in his house are all those grains of wheat he was stashin' away last summer. Yeah. *(Approaches the house.)* Hey, Anty-panty. It's your old pal, Hopper. *(No response.)* Hey, Ant, it's me.

ANT: *(Sticks head out window.)* Oh, hi, Hopper. How are you doing?

HOPPER: Not so good, ol' buddy. Well, actually, I'm starving, like as in no food for a week. Just grass. Well, I got to thinking about all that wheat you got stashed away in there.

ANT: But, Hopper, I just have enough to last me until spring. The snows came early, you remember, and I had to stop working before I was really finished. I'm sorry.

HOPPER: Yeah, but all I've got to eat is grass. Have you ever tried to eat grass? Think about it, Anty-panty. Stringy and scratchy and some of it's slimy.

ANT: Well, I am sorry, Hopper, but I can't help you now. I wish I could.

HOPPER: But, ol' buddy. *(Gets idea.)* How about if I do a little soft-shoe for ya. A little entertainment. Brighten up the dark days. *(Tries to dance.)*

ANT: No thanks, Hopper. Just sing yourself a few songs. That will tide you over. Spring is just around the corner. *(Closes the window, then opens it again.)* There was still some corn by the mill wheel before it snowed. You maybe could dig for it.

HOPPER: Ohhhhh. Ohhhh.
               I'm a grasshopper having a big tummy ache.
               I know I was stupid and I made a mistake.
               I danced and I sang at my own great expense. *(Starts to exit right.)*
               I gotta quit that and start using some sense.
               Gotta quit being lazy. Can't romp and croon.
               Gotta settle right down. Gotta change my tune. *(Stops and looks back at the house.)*
               Down by the mill wheel, huh? Ohhhh.
               Gotta change my tune. Gotta change my tune. *(Fades as he exits stage right.)*

FINALE MUSIC FADES IN

NARRATOR: And when spring finally came there was a grasshopper who was much skinnier and much wiser.

MUSIC SWELLS

Production Notes

There are no outstanding production problems in this play.

The Frog Prince

by Jean M. Mattson

CHARACTERS
Witch
Prince
Frog
Woman
Princess Granola
King
Narrator's voice

PROP
Golden ball

SET PIECES
Bushes and/or trees
Castle walls and
    banner
Well

This old fairy tale can be performed by one puppeteer but would be easier if performed by two. It has four scenes and two sets. The frog should be a stick puppet. The other characters may be stick or hand puppets.

INTRODUCTORY MUSIC

NARRATOR: Once upon a time in the tiny kingdom of Rosania, there lived a kind, young prince who had not yet found a suitable wife. News of this unmarried prince and his kingdom spread far and wide—even to the land where lived the Witch of Murk.

MUSIC FADES

SCENE I: THE WITCH'S CASTLE.

WITCH: So, I hear the prince of Rosania needs a wife. How fortunate. Have I not been looking for just such a prince. *(Cackles.)* Who would make a better bride than I? I can think of no one. The time has come for Rosania and the Land of Murk to become one. I must go immediately to Rosania and arrange a royal wedding. *(Cackles and disappears—sound effects.)*

TRANSITIONAL MUSIC

SCENE II: PRINCE'S CASTLE. CASTLE WALLS AND BANNERS (Optional).

PRINCE: *(Enters left.)* The royal ledgers must be checked and all my subjects must be notified that—*(Sound effects as WITCH appears.)* Whaaaat! Where—who are you? I heard no visitor come to the gates.

WITCH: *(Beguilingly.)* Oh, I have come from the Land of Murk, my prince, to fulfill your destiny.

PRINCE: To fulfill my destiny? I'm sorry but—what do you mean?

WITCH: I mean—I have come to fill your empty heart, of course. I will sit beside you on the throne. I have come to be your bride.

PRINCE: *(Stunned.)* But—I—well—I am—I thank you for your kindly offer, but, you see, I am not yet ready to choose a bride.

WITCH: The Land of Murk and Rosania shall be one. My power will be yours. Other kingdoms will fear you. Gold and riches will be showered upon you and your domain.

PRINCE: You cannot buy happiness. What you suggest is out of the question.

WITCH: What? You reject me? You refuse my offer? I won't have it! You will pay the consequences—do you hear? No one rejects the Witch of Murk!

PRINCE: I am sorry but—under the circumstances I . . .

WITCH: Sorry, he says. You'll be more than sorry! You've had your chance!
Until a girl that's sweet and pure
Will give a willing kiss,
You from this moment on will be
A slimy frog like this!
(Sound effects as PRINCE disappears and FROG appears. WITCH cackles.) You might as well get used to your green skin because it will be a long time before any girl agrees to give you a smoogie. *(Cackles and disappears with sound effects. PRINCE croaks and hops away stage left.)*

TRANSITIONAL MUSIC

NARRATOR: And so the prince hopped away. Unhappily, he wandered from place to place looking for someone who would break the spell.

SCENE III: ON A ROAD. TREES OR BUSHES.

(FROG enters stage left as WOMAN enters stage right.)

FROG: I beg your pardon. *(She looks around.)* Down here. It's me. *(She gasps.)* Please, I need someone to kiss me. Please give me a kiss.

WOMAN: Good heavens. I must be hearing things. I thought that frog asked me to kiss him. I must be going crazy! Help! Help! *(Runs off stage right.)*

FROG: I might just as well be dead. No girl will want to kiss a frog.
(FROG slowly hops off stage left.)

TRANSITIONAL MUSIC

NARRATOR: At last discouraged and dejected, he wandered into the garden of a castle where there was a nice clean well.

SCENE IV: CASTLE GARDEN OF THE KING. A WELL IS CENTER STAGE.

(FROG hops in stage left, hops upon the rim of the well and looks in.)

FROG: This is as good a place as any, I guess. *(Jumps into the well. GRANOLA enters stage right and plays with her ball. KING enters stage right.)*

KING: Granola, my dear, we must talk. We must think about the future. Some day you will be queen.

GRANOLA: Some day—but not now, dear papa.

KING: No, not now, but your father is growing older, my dear, and I must think of your future and the future of the kingdom.

GRANOLA: You're such a worrywart, papa.

KING: You need to marry. There must be children to carry on the family name.

GRANOLA: Well, I don't want to think about it now. There's no one I want to marry and, besides, I want to play with my ball.

KING: What a worry this is. Oh, what a worry. *(Exits stage left. GRANOLA plays with her ball, laughing and running about until the ball falls into the well.)*

GRANOLA: Oh, my ball. My golden rainbow ball. Uh—uh. *(Looks into well.)* Oh, it went way down so I can't reach it. Oh, I can't possibly climb down into the well. Ohhh, It's my favorite thing in the whole world. *(Cries.)* Oh, how could that have happened? *(Sits down, her back to the well.)*

FROG: *(Jumps to rim of the well.)* What's the matter?

GRANOLA: Oh, I lost my ball in the well—my golden rainbow ball. *(Unhappily.)*

FROG: Maybe I can help.

GRANOLA: *(Turning.)* Oh, if you—oh. Are you talking? Why, you're a frog.

FROG: Yes, I'm afraid that's what I am—a frog. A talking frog.

GRANOLA: Oh, my goodness. And you can get my ball back for me?

FROG: I can do that, but you must promise to do something for me.

GRANOLA: Oh, anything.

FROG: You must promise to give me a kiss.

GRANOLA: I—ahhhh—kiss a frog?

FROG: Yes, kiss a frog.

GRANOLA: Ahhhhh. *(Thinks.)* Yes, yes. I will. I will. Just get my golden ball. *(Frog hops into the well and returns with ball.)* Oh, my ball. My lovely golden ball!

FROG: And now—your promise.

GRANOLA: My promise?

FROG: My kiss.

GRANOLA: You expect me to kiss you—a slimy, icky green frog. That's the last thing I want to do. I think you should just get back into the well where you belong. *(FROG looks at Granola and then sadly hops into the well.)*

KING: *(Enters stage right.)* I thought I heard you crying, Granola.

GRANOLA: And I was, too, because I lost my ball. But you know the strangest thing happened. A frog jumped out of the well and I promised to kiss him if he'd get my ball back. Isn't that silly?

KING: Did he get it for you?

GRANOLA: He surely did. Here it is.

KING: And did you kiss him?

GRANOLA: Of course not. Why would I ever want to kiss a frog, Papa?

KING: Because you made a promise, Granola. My dear, I have tried to train you so when it is time for you to rule the kingdom you will do so with integrity and honor. A queen must always keep her promises.

GRANOLA: Oh, Papa, why do you have to be so high-minded and noble?

KING: Think about it, my dear. *(Exits stage right.)*

GRANOLA: *(Puts down ball.)* He actually wants me to kiss that wretched frog! Imagine, my own father. *(Thinks.)* My own father! Just because I made a promise. I did—make a promise. But why should I . . . Oh, Oh . . . *(Wails.)* All right. All right. I guess I'll have to do it. I'll close my eyes and make it quick. *(Goes to well.)* Frog. Frog. Come up. Come up here. *(Frog appears.)* I've decided I have to keep my promise. Just sit right there. *(Takes a big breath, kisses frog, and turns away. Sound effects as FROG disappears and PRINCE appears.)* All right. I did it. Are you satisfied?

PRINCE: Completely.

GRANOLA: Ahh— *(Turns around.)* Who are you? Where's that frog? *(Looks around.)*

PRINCE: I am that frog.

GRANOLA: What do you mean—you're that frog. I just kept a promise. You see, I kiss—ahh—well, never mind.

PRINCE: Granola, some time ago the wicked witch of Murk put a spell on me and turned me into a frog.

GRANOLA: Really? I don't believe—are you sure? I mean—well, why did she do that?

PRINCE: Because I would not agree to marry her. The spell would be broken only by the willing kiss of a girl. And you saved me. You were honest and honorable enough to keep your promise and kiss a frog.

GRANOLA: Ohhhh. Oh, am I glad I did! Oh. Oh. Oh!

PRINCE: Not half as glad as I am.

GRANOLA: Oh, wait until my father hears this. Come on, he'll be interested in meeting you—in more ways than one. Papa! Papa!

NARRATOR: And, of course, the old king was delighted. Granola found that she didn't mind in the least kissing the prince, and it wasn't long before a royal wedding was announced. The Witch of Murk was never heard from again. The old king's worries were over. Granola became an admirable queen, and they all lived happily ever after.

Production Notes

Golden ball—A styrofoam ball on a stick can be used to good advantage.

Magic spell— Sound effects and a flicker of lights will make the switch from Prince to Frog and Frog to Prince magical.

The Lion and the Mouse

by Jean M. Mattson

CHARACTERS
Lion
Mouse
Bushes and trees
Grass
Narrator's voice

PROPS
A net—a trap for the lion

SET PIECES
Bushes and trees
Grass

This play, an Aesop fable, has one set and two scenes. It is written for one puppeteer.

SCENE I: THE JUNGLE. THERE ARE TREES , BUSHES, AND GRASS.

INTRODUCTORY AFRICAN DRUM MUSIC

> *(LION enters stage right.)*

LION: I am a lion. Bingle—bangle—bungle!
I am the king of this whole big jungle. Do-de-de-do-do. Do-de-de-do.
Yep, I'm the king. Everybody—and I mean everybody—listens to me. I am strong.
I am smart. I do what I want to do—when I want to do it. And right now I want to
take a nap. *(Looks around.)* Here's a nice spot for my after-lunch nap. Yeah. Lots
of soft leaves here. A little sun coming through the trees. And nobody—I mean
nobody—better bother me. *(Yawn.)* Ahhh. *(Lies down.)* Feels good. Nice warm
sun. *(Dreamily.)* Just what I need—a little snooze. *(Pause. Lifts his head.)* Do not
disturb. *(Snores.)*

> *(MOUSE enters stage left.)*

MOUSE: *(Singing.)* Once there was a little mouse, little mouse, little mouse.
Once there was a little mouse, as big as he could be.
How he scurried here and there, here and there, here and there.
How he scurried here and there to see what he could see.
Oh, and I've seen a lot today. It's the first time I've been out by myself and I didn't
know the world was so big. It's been fun. I've seen trees and vines and flowers and
all kinds of funny animals. Oh, I've been busy. And now I need a nap. *(Sees LION.)*
Oh, there's a big pile of fur. It looks so soft and it looks so warm—a good place to
curl up. *(Approaches LION.)* My goodness! That looks like a nose! My goodness!
It is a nose!

LION: Umph. Uh-uh what's this. Who's bothering me? *(Stands up and puts his paw on
the MOUSE.)*

MOUSE: *(Crying.)* Hey, don't do that. Let me up. You're squashing me.

LION: Who are you, anyway? Who dared to wake me up?

MOUSE: I'm a mouse. And I didn't mean to bother you. Let me up. I can't breathe.

LION: Do you know who I am? I'm Lion, the king of the jungle. And nobody—I mean
nobody—wakes me up when I'm taking a nap.

MOUSE: I didn't know. I didn't know.

LION: Too bad. I'll just have you for a little snack.

MOUSE:	Oh, no, no. Please don't eat me. Let me go. Please let me go.

LION:	Why should I let you go, rodent?

MOUSE:	Ahhh—ahhh. Because—someday maybe I'll be able to do something for you.

LION:	Ha-ha-ha. You, a little pip-squeak like you, do something for me? What a joke—and I do mean joke! Ha-ha-ha.

MOUSE:	But it's true. There may be a time when you will need me.

LION:	Ha-ha. Never. But, you know, I'm really not hungry 'cause I just had lunch. And you're such a brave little pip-squeak, I think I will let you go. *(Lets MOUSE up.)* But don't you ever—and I mean never— wake me up again. You hear?

MOUSE:	I promise—cross my heart and hope to—ahhh—cross my heart and cross my fingers, and I'd cross my ears if I could.

LION:	Yeah. Well, O.K. There you go. *(MOUSE exits stage left. LION yawns.)* Now, maybe I can take my nap.

(LION lies back down.)

TRANSITIONAL MUSIC

NARRATOR: The lion forgot all about the little mouse. And several weeks later . . .

**SCENE II:	SAME JUNGLE SCENE.**

(LION enters stage right.)

LION:	I am a lion. Bingle—bangle—bungle!
I am the king of this whole big jungle.
Do-do-dedo-do. Do-do-dedoo.
Do-do-dedo-do. Do-do-dedoo. Eeeeeeowww!
(LION falls as if into a hole and then crawls up inside the net.) Wha—ohhh— this is a trap. I fell into a trap. Ugh—ugh—grr. *(Tries to get out of net.)* I'm caught. I can't seem to out of this. *(Roars and pants.)* Oh, I've got to get out of here. When those hunters come back they'll put me in a cage and take me to some circus—or maybe they'll even kill me. Ohhh. Ohhh. Somebody's got to help me—some hippopotamus or a baboon—or somebody. I'll just wait. Somebody's got to come. *(Sounds exhausted.)*

(MOUSE enters stage left.)

MOUSE: *(Singing.)* Once there was a little mouse, little mouse, little mouse,
              Once there was a little mouse who loved to sing and play.
              And he had the grandest time, grandest time, grandest time.
              And he had the grandest time, all the livelong day.
              Oh-oh. There's that lion sleeping again. I'd just better tiptoe out of here right now.
              (He starts to back away.)

LION: Hey, is that somebody? Who's there? Who's there?

MOUSE: I'm going. I'm going. I didn't know you were sleeping there.

LION: No, I'm not sleeping. I need help. Can't you see? I've been trapped. I'm in this net
              and I can't get out.

MOUSE: *(Approaches and looks at the net.)* My goodness! You sure are caught—like a rat
              in a trap. Maybe I can help.

LION: Oh, I wish you could, but what can a little pip-squeak like you do?

MOUSE: I'll show you. I may be small, but I've got very sharp teeth that can chew through
              just about anything. It'll take a little time. Gnaw—gnaw—gnaw—gnaw. It's
              coming. Gnaw—gnaw—gnaw—gnaw. Just a little more now. Gnaw—gnaw—
              gnaw. *(Net falls away from LION.)* There. I did it. What did I tell you?

LION: I can't believe it. You, the little pip-squeak. How can I ever thank you?

MOUSE: You already have.

LION: You are an amazing little pip-squeak.

MOUSE: *(Singing.)* I am just a little mouse, little mouse, little mouse.

LION: *(Singing.)* You may be a little mouse, little mouse, little mouse.

              You may be a little mouse, but you rescued me.

              (LION and MOUSE walk off together.)

MUSIC FADES IN

NARRATOR: *(Over music.)* And from that day on the lion was much more respectful, not only of
              the little mouse but of all the other animals in the jungle.

FINALE

Production Notes

NET—Part of an onion sack can be used as the net in which the lion is trapped.

The Bad-Tempered Wife

by Jean M. Mattson

Based on a Norwegian folktale.

CHARACTERS
Poova, a middle-aged Laplander
  man
Morgrid, Poova's wife
Mountain troll
Narrator's voice

PROPS
Basket
Pillow
Rope

SOUND EFFECTS
Birds twittering

SET PIECES
Cottage (Optional)
Barn
Trees and bushes
Bush with yellow
  cloudberries

This is a play in two scenes with two sets written for two puppeteers.

SCENE I: A FARM. STAGE RIGHT A COTTAGE. STAGE LEFT A BARN.

Morgrid berates Poova in *The Bad-Tempered Wife.*

INTRODUCTORY NORWEGIAN FOLK MUSIC

NARRATOR: Once, a long time ago, a gentle young reindeer herder named Poova married a happy
young Laplander girl. Everyone expected them to have a long and happy life together on their little farm. Unfortunately, things did not work out quite that way. As the
years went by, their once-pleasant relationship somehow changed.

MUSIC FADES

MORGRID: *(Screaming from offstage.)* Poova! Poova! Where are you, Poova?
(Enters stage right.) Poova, come here. I know you're out there behind the barn.
(Pause.) Come out here this minute. *(Peevishly.)*

POOVA: *(Enters stage left with pillow.)* Yes, Morgrid, my little apple dumpling.

MORGRID: Don't you "apple dumpling" me, you lazy oaf. You should be working and you were
back there gazing at the glacier on the mountaintop.

POOVA: I was feeding the reindeer, Morgrid.

MORGRID: I suppose you were feeding the reindeer pillows? *(Grabs the pillow.)* Why don't
you ever do any work around here?

POOVA: Now, Morgrid, my little spritz cookie, don't say things like that. I mended the roof
now, didn't I?

MORGRID: And you waited until I thought the rain water would sweep us right into the fjord.
You never do anything on time. Not since I married you have you done anything on

time. *(During the next few lines, MORGRID goes into the cottage or upstage and exchanges the pillow for a basket.)*

POOVA: I got up in time to see the sun come up this morning, Morgrid, my little krumkaka.

MORGRID: Oh, yes, you manage to do the foolish things on time—and all the time. My mother told me I should marry a man who spent his time usefully. I should have listened to her. *(Continues to mutter.)*

POOVA: *(Under his breath.)* Wish you had, Morgrid. Wish you had.

MORGRID: Poova, I want you to try to do something useful for a change. Here is a basket.

POOVA: You want me to look at that basket?

MORGRID: No, I do not want you to look at that basket. I want you to take that basket and go up to the mountains and pick cloudberries for supper.

POOVA: But, Morgrid, the cloudberries grow in the high country where the mountain trolls live.

MORGRID: Trolls or not, I want cloudberries for supper. Now, take the basket and remember— the green ones are sour.

POOVA: The green trolls? *(Picks up basket.)*

MORGRID: No, you nincompoop! The green cloudberries. I want you to pick only the nice ripe, plump, sweet yellow ones. *(POOVA picks up a rope and starts to exit stage center.)* Fill up the basket—all yellow berries—*(Screaming after him as he disappears.)*—and be back in time for suuuup-per! Hmm. If it weren't for me, we wouldn't have any sweet berries for supper, lunch, or breakfast. *(Starts to leave stage right.)* If it weren't for me, we wouldn't have a lot of things around here. *(Exits and then re-enters.)* If it weren't for me! *(Exits.)*

TRANSITIONAL MUSIC UP AND FADES

SCENE II: IN THE MOUNTAINS. A TREE STAGE LEFT. CLOUDBERRY BUSH CENTER. ADDITONAL BUSHES STAGE RIGHT.

POOVA: *(POOVA enters stage left, deposits his rope, and puts basket down left of bush.)* I've only found three berries all day. *(Looks into basket.)* Oh-oh, only two now. I must have lost one. Oh, how can I go back and face Morgrid, my little ginger snap, if I have only two berries? *(Sees bush of cloudberries.)* Oh, those look like cloudberry bushes. *(Looks at bushes.)* Yes, they are. And chock full of cloudberries. How lucky! *(Slips.)* Ohhh. I didn't see that hole there with all those bushes growing around it. Why, I almost fell in. *(Looks into hole.)* My, that is a deep hole. That is dangerous. *(Shakes his head.)* Well, I'd better get busy and pick some of these berries. *(Picks a few.)* It's so peaceful and quiet around here. *(Birds twitter. He sighs and sits down under the tree.)* Morgrid and I used to walk in these woods. That was before she got her bad temper. *(Dreamily.)* That was fun. She never laughs anymore, though. Never even smiles. Those old times—were—good—times. *(Drifts off to sleep and snores.)*

MORGRID: *(Offstage.)* Poova! Poova!

POOVA: *(Waking up.)* Oh—oh—I guess I fell asleep. And I just had the awfulest nightmare. I dreamed Morgrid had climbed up here and was chasing all the birds away. *(Lies down.)* That was—a terrible—dream. *(Drifts off.)*

MORGRID: *(Offstage.)* Poova! Poova, you lazy good-for-nothing. Where are you? Wait till I get my hands on you. *(Enters stage left and crosses stage without seeing POOVA.)*
            I knew I should come up here and check on you. *(Sees him.)* Ah-ha, there you are. *(Tiptoes over to him and screams.)* Poova!

POOVA: *(Jumping up.)* Oh—did you ever see a dream walking—and screeching?

MORGRID: So there you are—and snoozing again. This is what you've been doing all day—by the looks of this basket. *(Looks into it.)* You're about as good at picking berries as a fish is at wearing shoes.

POOVA: Morgrid, my little bowl of fruit soup, I've been climbing all day.

MORGRID: "All day! All day!" he says. Then, Poova, you should have a whole basket full of cloudberries.

POOVA: You don't understand, Morgrid. I didn't find any cloudberry bushes at all until just now—when I was ready to come home.

MORGRID: I should have come up here with the basket, and I should have picked cloudberries for supper. I'll have to do it now anyway. *(Furiously raving and picking berries putting them in the basket.)* I don't know why I never learn. You would think I would learn after twenty years. It's always the same. *(Continues to mutter.)*

POOVA: Watch where you're stepping, Morgrid.

MORGRID: What do you mean? *(Continues to pick and rave furiously.)* I always watch my step. The only time I didn't watch my step was when I married you twenty years ago. Then is when you should have warned me. *(Continues to mutter.)*

POOVA: But, Morgrid, be careful. There's a big deep hole over there.

MORGRID: Careful! I'm always careful. Telling me to be careful. What do you mean—"hole"? Ahhhhhhh! *(MORGRID disappears into the hole.)*

POOVA: *(Peering into hole.)* Morgrid. *(Pause.)* I think she fell into this big hole. *(Looks again.)* Yep, she did. *(Cautiously.)* Morgrid, my little glob of raspberry frosting. Hmmm. I don't think she can hear me. *(Louder.)* Morgrid, my little lump of curdled cheese. Hmmm. *(Very loud.)* Morgrid, you old sour lemon. I can say that because she can't hear me. *(Looks around.)* Hey, look how quiet and peaceful it is all of a sudden. The wind rustling the pine branches. *(Birds twitter.)* The birds singing. Hmmm. I think maybe I'll go home now. It must be quiet and peaceful down in the valley too—I mean, with Morgrid up here. *(Starts to leave and stops.)* No, I can't do that. *(Pauses.)* No, I can't. *(Pauses.)* Yes, I can! *(Turns and takes a few steps and stops.)* No, I'll have to pull her up. Now, where did I leave my rope? *(Looks around and then goes upstage and picks up the rope.)* This should do it. *(Looks into hole.)* Morgrid, are you down there? Here, now. I'm going to let down a rope. Morgrid, here it comes. Oh-oh, she must have caught hold of it. *(Pulls the rope tight.)* All right, Morgrid, hang on. Up you come.

TROLL: *(Head appearing out of hole.)* Let me out of here. Let me out.

POOVA: Oh, a mountain troll. Yiiiii! Get back into your hole. Get back in there. *(Tries to push TROLL back into hole.)*

TROLL: Oh, please—please. I can't go back into that hole now. *(Climbs out.)* I couldn't do that. There's a woman down there who's making so much racket, I couldn't stand it. She woke me up and she won't shut up. I've never heard such a commotion in all my life—and I'm over 3,000 years old.

POOVA: Sounds like Morgrid.

TROLL: Yeah, I've captured a lot of humans before and took 'em to my home down there, but I've never had one around like that. "Wash behind your ears," she says. Imagine—a troll washing—anywhere! "Stop spittin' on the floor," she says. Been spittin' on the floor for 3,000 years. No human's going to tell me to quit. *(Spits.)* "Don't pick your nose," she says. Huh, I'll pick my nose when and if I want to. Us trolls like to pick our noses. See. *(Picks his nose.)*

POOVA: Yes, that's her.

TROLL: I tell you, it's awful down there. Even a troll can't stand that. Thanks for pulling me out. Not many humans would help out a mountain troll. *(Looks around.)* My it's nice and peaceful out here! I'll just go over there and finish my nap. Wake me up in about an hour. As long as I'm out here, I might as well go down the mountain and steal a few babies and kidnap a few princesses. *(Lies down under the tree and immediately snores loudly.)*

POOVA: Well, now, I guess I really should get Morgrid out of that hole. But I don't feel much like it. Well, if I do pull her out, there's got to be some changes. Got to be some changes. *(Picks up rope.)* Morgrid, here comes the rope. *(Puts rope into hole.)* Oh-oh. There's someone on the end of the rope. I hope it isn't another troll.

MORGRID: *(Muffled voice.)* Hurry up and get me out of here. It's about time you did something to get me out of this hole. *(Continues to rave.)*

POOVA: *(As MORGRID raves on.)* It's my wife alrighty. *(Pulls her out as she continues to speak in one continual tirade.)*

MORGRID: You are as bad a puller-upper as you are a berry picker, you bumblefingers you. I don't know why I didn't marry a man who could do something right—anything. I'm not particular. Just some little thing—some time. *(Continues to mutter.)*

TROLL: *(Waking up.)* What's that? What's that? Oh, it's her! It's her! Help! I can't stand it. I can't stand it. Help! Help! *(Jumps down into hole.)*

MORGRID: That troll didn't wash behind his ears. I could see. I could tell he didn't. Nobody listens when I tell them exactly what they ought to do. *(Continues to mutter.)*

POOVA: *(Interrupting.)* Morgrid, will you please be quiet for once? *(POOVA puts his hand on her mouth.)* Now, tell me what a troll is, Morgrid.

MORGRID: You dunderhead! What is the matter with you? Everyone knows a troll is a filthy creature who never washes behind his ears, who spits on the floor and picks his nose, and they are ugly and smelly and mean most of the time. Some of them have three or five heads and they scare everybody.

POOVA: It would take something really awful to drive a troll away, wouldn't it, Morgrid?

MORGRID: Of course it would, Poova, of course it would.

POOVA: You did it Morgrid, You scared that troll away.

MORGRID: I did not!

POOVA: You did too! I have a wife who is so bad-tempered she can even scare trolls away. I don't like having a wife who is so bad-tempered she can even scare trolls away. Do you want to be a wife who is so bad-tempered you can even scare trolls away?

MORGRID: No.

POOVA: It wasn't always like this, Morgrid. It used to be very pleasant. We used to walk in the woods and laugh and . . .

MORGRID: That was before you got so hard to get along with. Oh, I remember. Don't think I don't remember . . .

POOVA: *(Interrupting.)* Morgrid, quiet. *(She stops. Sound of birds.)*

MORGRID: What's that?

POOVA: That's the birds' singing. *(They look up.)*

MORGRID: Oh, for goodness sake. I thought they stopped singing twenty years ago.

POOVA: No, Morgrid. They've been singing, but you've been yelling and and screaming so much you couldn't hear them.

MORGRID: Ohhhh. Have I been making that much racket?

POOVA: Yep. 'Fraid you have, Morgrid. 'Fraid you have.

MORGRID: Ohhhhhh. *(Walks away.)*

POOVA: *(Following her.)* Remember how much fun we used to have walking in the woods and talking? We used to tell stories. Wasn't that fun, Morgrid?

MORGRID: Yes, it was.

POOVA: You haven't laughed for a long time, Morgrid. Come on now, think of something funny. Let's have a little laugh.

MORGRID: No—

POOVA: Morgrid, come on. Remember how that troll looked when he jumped back into that hole. He was pretty funny, now, wasn't he?

MORGRID: *(Shakes her head.)* Nooooo.

POOVA: He was pretty surprised. Wasn't he now, my little sticky bun?

MORGRID: Well, yes—*(Starts to relent.)*—and his ears did flap—*(Giggles.)*—and his nose was twitching. Guess he was pretty funny. *(Laughs.)* He was surprised. Funny old troll.

POOVA: You're laughing, Morgrid. You're laughing. Just like old times. Come on, let's go home. Things are going to be different from now on. Things are going to be different. *(Exits stage left.)*

MORGRID: *(As she follows.)* He was pretty funny. Oh, I forgot the basket *(Picks it up and moves upstage. TROLL climbs out of the hole not seeing MORGRID.)*

TROLL: Is she gone? Whew! Us trolls aren't supposed to be able to stand clanging church bells, but church bells are like music compared to that screeching crow.

MORGRID: *(Who has been sneaking up on him.)* Boo!

TROLL: It's her again. It's her. Help! Help! Get me out of here. *(Jumps into hole.)*

MORGRID: *(Peering down into the hole.)* I did scare that troll back into that hole. I really did scare him away. *(Shaking her head.)* Oh, my goodness. *(Exits stage right.)* Poova! Poova!

NORWEGIAN MUSIC SWELLS

NARRATOR: Morgrid's experience with the troll made a big difference. Although life on the farm was not perfect, Poova and Morgrid lived more or less happily ever after.

FINALE

Production Notes

Cloudberry—Yellow chenille balls from ball fringe sewn or glued to a bush make wonderful cloudberries. Painted wooden beads or paper circles also can be used. Berries need not be actually picked. Miming the action is sufficient.

The Rope— Two ropes make the maneuver easy. The one that Poova takes with him and places on the ground is permanently coiled. (Poova, of course, hands it to his puppeteer.) When he needs the rope to throw into the hole, Poova's puppeteer hands him the second rope, which has a loop on one end into which Poova's hand can fit.

The Big Pig War

by Jean M. Mattson

CHARACTERS

Narrator
Griffin, a farmer with
    livestock
Customs Officer*
Cutler, a farmer
Man I & II
Woman I & II*
General Harney*
Admiral Baynes
Official in Washington, D.C.
Official in London
An American coolhead*
4 Sheep
2 Pigs, one with wings

* Can play dual roles

PROPS

Flagpole with British flag
    that can be run up
Flagpole for American flag
    that can be run up
Hoe
Gun
Soldiers
3 Ships: a warship, a 31-gun
    frigate, and 10-gunner

SOUND EFFECTS

Explosion
Gunshot
Scratching pen
Galloping horses

Pig oinks
Marching soldiers
Boat sounds
Telegraph keys

SET PIECES

Trees and bushes
2 Cabins
Fence
A fort
2 Cannons
2 Desks

This hand puppet play is written for three puppeteers. It has four sets and a number of brief scenes. This historical event lends itself well to dramatization—a conflict that escalates almost to war before its final resolution.

NARRATOR: *(Outside stage.)* Many people do not know that the northwest had its very own war 130 years ago. The island of San Juan was the scene of this conflict known as the Pig War. *(Explosion and many oinks.)* Yes, that's right—the Big Pig War! And this is the way it happened.

One hundred and forty years ago when Great Britain and the United States agreed on the dividing line between Canada and the United States, they never quite figured out who owned all the Islands north of Puget Sound. Nobody really cared though because nobody was living on the islands then. But in the year 1853 that began to change.

INTRODUCTORY MUSIC

SCENE I: COUNTRYSIDE WITH TREES AND BUSHES. THE ACTION FLOWS FROM ONE SCENE TO ANOTHER WITH NO DEMARCATIONS.

GRIFFIN: *(Several sheep enter stage right baaing and gamboling. Griffin enters stage right with two more sheep.)* Come on. Get a move on. That's right. Right in there. There ya go! *(Single sheep jumps.)*

CUSTOMS OFFICER: *(Enters stage left.)* What do you think you're doing with those sheep?

GRIFFIN: Well, I'm not playing hide-and-go-seek!

CUSTOMS: You're on United States property.

GRIFFIN: Nothin' of the kind. It's British. The Hudson Bay Company sent me here to raise these sheep and that company has been hunting and trapping in these parts for years. Don't you tell me I don't belong here.

CUSTOMS: Well, I am telling you. And I am also telling you, if you keep these sheep here, you've gotta pay taxes for grazing on United States land.

GRIFFIN: You've got that a little wrong, you have. This land belongs to Britain, and I'll not pay you one penny. *(Exits stage right herding the sheep.)*

CUSTOMS: We'll just see about that. *(Watches GRIFFIN go, then turns around shaking his head. A sheep enters stage right and butts him, baaing. Sheep exits stage left. He shakes his fist and exits in a huff stage left. GRIFFIN enters stage right dragging pole and puts up British flag stage right. Exits stage right. CUSTOMS OFFICER enters stage left, sees flag, reacts, exits stage left and re-enters with flagpole with the American flag, which he places on stage left.)*

NARRATOR VOICE: A year later, no taxes had been paid.

(Several sheep enter stage right. CUSTOM OFFICIAL enters stage left.)

CUSTOMS: Well, if he won't pay his taxes, we'll just take some of those wooley old sheep of his. *(He stomps off stage left and and returns carrying a sheep. The other sheep run into the woods.)* We'll show him. *(Exits left.)*

GRIFFIN: *(Enters.)* Stealing my sheep, are they? And scaring my lambs into the woods. Well, I'll have them arrested. We'll get them off this island. *(Exits stage right and sheep follow.)*

NARRATOR VOICE: So things went along for a few years with people sneering and snarling at each other. *(GRIFFIN and MAN I enter and snarl at each other and exeunt.)* There was plenty of nasty feeling. *(CUSTOMS OFFICER enters and crosses to British flag on right. GRIFFIN enters stage right, not seeing CUSTOMS OFFICER, and crosses to American flag on stage left. They each lower the other's flag, turn, see what has happened, stalk over to their own flags, and raise them again, shaking their fists.)* But nobody wanted to start any real honest-to-goodness trouble. *(They exeunt, turning several times to glare.)* Time passed, and more people came to the island. The Hudson Bay Company built a trading station and increased their livestock herds. *(Cabin with company sign goes up on stage right. Pigs enter.)* American gold miners who hadn't found any gold came to stake out claims and become farmers. *(Cabins go up on stage left.)* One of these farmers was a man by the name of Cutler.

(Cutler enters stage left, hoes, plants, weeds, etc., and puts up a fence. Activity lasts approximately one minute.)

CUTLER: Now that's what I call a humdinger of a 'tater patch. *(He brushes his hands off and exits stage left.)*

(Pigs enter stage right, snort, and root around. They finally end up in CUTLER's yard and knock over his fence.)

CUTLER: *(Enters, yelling at the pig.)* Hey, get outa my 'tater patch, you goldern pig. Get outa there! *(Pigs run. CUTLER exits and returns with his gun. One pig returns. He chases it back and forth . They run off stage left. An explosion, and the pig squeals. CUTLER enters stage left and stalks over to GRIFFIN's.)* Griffin! *(GRIFFIN enters stage right.)* I'm here to tell you I shot your pig!

GRIFFIN: You what?

CUTLER: I shot your old pig 'cause he knocked down my fence. Now, I'm willing to give ya $10 for that pig, but from now on I want you to keep your pigs outa my patch or I'll shoot every one of 'em. *(CUTLER starts to leave.)*

GRIFFIN: This island doesn't belong to you in the first place. *(CUTLER turns.)* Furthermore, if you can't protect your potato patch you should go home to America. *(Exits stage right.)*

CUTLER: This is America! *(He furiously fidgets.)* Well, this has gone far enough. *(Exits stage left.)*

                (Cabins, trees, and bushes disappear.)

NARRATOR: Word about this fight spread.

                (The following segment involves people meeting, talking, and spreading rumors. We hear the buzz of the conversation and then certain remarks leap out at us.)

                (Two people meet center stage, talking unintelligibly.)

MAN I: Did you hear about that pig? *(He mumbles on.)*

MAN II: And he shot him daid! Yes! Daid as a doornail. *(Exeunt, mumbling.)*

                (Two more people enter talking unintelligibly.)

WOMAN I: A pig, you say? A pig? A bloomin' porker? Why I never heard of such . . . *(etc., etc.)*

WOMAN II: I heard he shot them all—down to the last little piggie. Can you imagine? *(etc., etc.)*

NARRATOR: Rumors flew and tempers flared as far away as General Harney's office in Ft. Vancouver in southern Washington.

GENERAL: *(Enters stage right.)* Send Captain Picket to the San Juan Island with his regiment. He is to build a fort to protect the Americans from the Indians—and from the British! *(Exits.)*

NARRATOR: All of a sudden there was a lot of American activity on the island.

                (A pause as a fort appears stage left. Soldiers march back and forth upstage. Two cannons appear stage left.) Before long, a British warship from Victoria appeared in Griffin Bay—the Satellite. And then another—the Tribune, a 31-gun frigate with a crew of 325 men. The next day, the 10-gun Pumper arrived. *(Ships sail from stage left to stage right upstage during the narration.)* It was not a friendly situation. Over 1,000 men were on the alert with orders to fight if the other side made a false move.

(Comes out in front of the audience if not already there.) Now let's stop for just a moment and find out what the British and the United States governments thought about what was going on up in the northern part of the North American continent.

(Set pieces disappear and desks appears on stage right and stage left.) Well, the two governments didn't think anything about the situation—because they didn't know about it. In those days, it took weeks for news to travel from the Atlantic to the Pacific coast. A letter was written in San Juan and sent by boat to San Francisco. *(Boat sounds.)* Then it went by Pony Express to Ft. Leavenworth. *(Sound of horses galloping.)* From there it was telegraphed to Washington, D.C. *(Sound of telegraph clicking)* or sent by ship to London. *(Boat sounds.)* When the messages finally arrived—

(Yankee Doodle music as American flag goes up.)

MAN IN WASHINGTON: *(Enters stage right and sits at his desk.)* What's this? Colonel Picket's men and Company I of the 4th Artillery? Good grief! Because a man shot a pig? Well, this government certainly doesn't have time to deal with trouble in the northwest. We've got the Civil War to tend to! Tell them to settle it! *(Exits stage right. Desk disappears. British military music, perhaps "British Grenadiers." British flag goes up stage right.)*

MAN IN LONDON: *(Enters stage left and sits at desk.)* Trouble in North America? Well, we can't have that now, can we? It's much too far away. And besides, we're too busy with these wars in Europe. Oh, no—no—no—no. There is a bloody limit! Tell them to settle it! *(He exits stage left. Desks disappears.)*

NARRATOR: These messages were sent back to the northwest. *(Sound effects in reverse, but much faster.)* But before they arrived, the pig controversy escalated. The hotheads got even hotter.

Admiral Baynes of the British Navy and General Harney of the American Army glower at each other in *The Big Pig War.* Puppets by Joan King.

GRIFFIN: *(Enters stage left.)* Admiral Baynes, we need to protect the British flag and our citizens from insult, bloodshed, and pig-killers! Let's fight! *(Growls and snarls.)*

ADMIRAL BAYNES: *(Enters.)* Now just a minute. If we fight, we would win the battle, but we'd be surrounded. There are thirty times as many Americans as British in the northwest. Imagine what would happen if we went to war! No. A war is simply out of the question. *(Exeunt stage right.)*

GENERAL: *(Enters stage left with American coolhead)* As a general in the United State Army I feel qualified to assess this situation. We need a war to let Washington know we're important out here. Let's fire the cannons! Brings on the troops. *(Growls and snarls.)*

AMERICAN COOLHEAD: No, General. If we actually fight, we'd lose. They have more guns. We'd be slaughtered by the royal navy. We'd better think twice about this—or 50 times—before we fire that first shot. *(Exeunt stage left.)*

NARRATOR: And they did think about it. Fortunately there were a few smart men in the northwest who knew that killing each other was a terrible way to settle an argument. And not one bullet was fired. Actually, they thought about it for the next twelve years, until the leaders in London and Washington finally had time to get together and figure out who owned what.

   (The leaders enter, man from Washington stage right and man from London stage left.)

WASHINGTON: We want the San Juan Islands, and we want our fisherman to be able to fish off the eastern coast of Canada.

LONDON: Well, you give us 15 and a 1/2 million dollars and you can have them both.

WASHINGON: Agreed! *(They shake and walk to their respective flags. Final music begins—"God Save the Queen" and "My Country 'Tis of Thee.")*

NARRATOR OUTSIDE THE STAGE: The solution wasn't too hard after all. Both sides were satisfied after their little talk. San Juan and the other islands in the group were made part of Washington as they are today.
   And that's the story of the Big Pig War—a reminder that very few things are worth going to war over—and a pig is certainly not one of them.

   (Leaders exeunt and a pig with wings appears on center stage, rises, and floats slowly away.)

FINALE SWELLS

Production Notes

The number of scenes and the pace of this play present difficulties for two puppeteers, for which it was originally written. The addition of more puppeteers and/or backstage help makes production much easier. This play can be done with a narrator outside the curtain at all times.

Flagpoles— The flagpoles are major props and need to work smoothly. They can be made by placing two screw eyes at the bottom and top of a 1/2-inch dowel and threading a cord loop through the eyes. The two flags are appropriately attached to the cord. When clipped or clamped to the playboard, the dowels become respectable flagpoles on which the flags can be raised or lowered by pulling the cord.

The Christmas Constellation

by Jean M. Mattson

CHARACTERS
Two carolers
Mrs. Simms, bakery proprietor
Mr. Hill, toy store proprietor
Mr. Conover, a craftsman
Ellen Conover, five years old
Davey Conover, her brother,
    nine years old
Dr. Alexander
Ollie, a dog
Narrator's voice

PROPS
Rocking chair
Cake boxes
Sign
Broom
Bag of cookies
Pitcher and cups
Christmas tree cake
Rocking horse

SET PIECES
A bakery with window
A toy store with window
A streetlight (Optional)
The Conover home
2 Beds
Table

A Christmas play in two sets and two scenes that embodies the Christmas spirit and provides a chance for a great variety of interesting puppets to be incorporated into the production. It can be produced by two puppeteers.

SCENE I: **A STREET. THERE IS A BAKERY ON CENTER LEFT WITH A LARGE SIGN, "CHRISTMAS TREE CAKES." A TOY STORE ON CENTER RIGHT. A STREETLIGHT IS DOWN STAGE LEFT. LIGHTS ARE ON IN THE SHOPS.**

INTRODUCTORY MUSIC (A CHRISTMAS CAROL)

VOICE-OVER: Christmas is a time of dreams and stars and joy, when children believe in miracles and parents pause to contemplate the wonder of it all.

> *(Caroling is heard offstage, growing louder. CAROLERS enter stage right and cross to lamppost, where they finish the carol. MRS. SIMMS sticks her head out of her shop and wishes them a Merry Christmas. They respond, cross stage, and exeunt stage right as they begin to sing "Deck the Halls." MR. CONOVER comes out of the toy shop carrying a rocking chair. He is followed by MR. HILL.)*

MR. HILL: I'm sorry I can't buy your chair. The craftsmanship is beautiful. It really is. It's a work of art. But this is a toy store, Mr. Conover, and a rocking chair is not a toy.

MR. CONVOVER: You're sure you can't take it? I—I need the money. It's Christmas and—my kids . . .

MR. HILL: If you had come in earlier, I might have found a buyer—it being Christmas and all, but—on Christmas Eve? *(Shakes his head.)*

MR. CONOVER: *(Despondently.)* Yes, I understand. I know I'm late. Ahh—well—thank you. *(Starts off stage right and turns.)* Thank you. *(Exits stage right.)*

> *(MR. HILL watches him go, shaking his head. MRS. SIMMS comes out of the bakery.)*

MRS. SIMMS: How are you doing, Mr. Hill?

MRS. HILL: It's been a busy day.

MRS. SIMMS: Well, at least you didn't have to get up at four o'clock to put yeast into your doll houses.

MR. HILL: Maybe not, but I had to put seventeen wagons together. I think every child in town is getting a wagon from Santa Claus.

> *(MR. HILL exits into shop. MRS. SIMMS takes her sign down and exits into shop. BOY enters stage right and goes into bakery. MR. HILL enters with*

broom and sweeps sidewalk. Boy comes out of bakery carrying a cake box, followed by MRS. SIMMS.)

MRS. SIMMS: Carry it carefully now. Your mother wants a plum pudding, not a plum pancake.

BOY: I will. I will. *(Exits stage right.)*

MR. HILL: *(Stops his sweeping and looks up at the sky and shivers.)* Brrr. It's getting colder—and clouding up too. We may get some snow after all.

MRS. SIMMS: We may get that snow after all.

           (Sounds of children coming.)

DAVEY: *(Offstage.)* Hurry up, Ellen. It's getting dark.

MRS. SIMMS: Oh, the Conover children. I wonder if I have any cookies left. *(Exits into bakery. (MR. HILL puts his broom inside and starts to roll up awning or wipe off window.)*

ELLEN: Star light, star bright. First star I see tonight. I wish I may, I wish I might, get the wish I wish tonight. *(Davey and Ellen enter stage left.)*

DAVEY: You are silly, Ellen Conover. The stars aren't even out tonight.

ELLEN: I know—but . . .

MR. HILL: *(Interrupting.)* Say, there. It's getting ready to snow. You'd better go home and get your winter coats on.

ELLEN: This is my winter coat, sir.

MR. HILL: *(Disconcerted.)* Ohhh—ahhhhh. *(Observes both children.)*

ELLEN: *(Looking in the toy store window.)* Oh, look at that beautiful princess with the star in her hair. Isn't she just the prettiest doll you've ever seen?

DAVEY: The sign says she's the sug—ar plu—m prin—cess. Sugar plum princess.

ELLEN: *(Sighing.)* Ohhhh.

DAVEY: Oh, look at that boat. It has real sails and a little flag. Sir, you have beautiful toys. Does that little rudder really work?

MR. HILL: That it does. She's quite a boat. *(To ELLEN.)* And what were you wishing for so hard, young lady?

ELLEN: A Christmas dinner—if Papa gets some money. And a rocking horse if Papa has time to make it.

MR. HILL: Is that right? Well, Merry Christmas. *(Goes into his shop.)*

               (DAVEY puts his arm around ELLEN as they look into window oo-ing and ah-ing, "Oh, look there" and "See that.")

ELLEN: Where's Ollie, Davey?

DAVEY: I don't know. Here, Ollie. Come on, boy. He was right behind us just a minute ago. Here, Ollie. *(Bark is heard offstage.)* Oh, here he comes. *(DOG enters stage right.)* We thought we'd lost you. *(DOG whines and they pet him. All three look into bakery window.)*

ELLEN: I just love bakeries. They smell so good. Look at all the tarts and breads—and—that wonderful green Christmas tree cake. Look, Davey. The ornaments are red cherries and sugared candies. Doesn't that look good, Ollie? *(DOG whines.)* I'm hungry, Davey.

DAVEY: Shhhh, Ellen.

MRS. SIMMS: *(Coming out of bakery to take a wreath down.)* Well, hello there. You are the Conover children, aren't you?

DAVEY: Yes, ma'am.

ELLEN: Is that Christmas tree a real live cake that you can eat?

MRS. SIMMS: Yes, it is. Pistachio frosting and a chocolate trunk.

ELLEN: Oh, I wish I may—I wish I might—

MRS. SIMMS: *(Thinks a moment as she looks at them.)* Ahh, I'm closing up now and—ahhh—l just happen to have some sugar cookies left. Would you like some?

BOTH CHILDREN: Oh, yes, please.

               (MRS. SIMMS goes into the store and brings out a bag, handing it to Davey.)

MRS. SIMMS: There you are. *(They thank her and the DOG whines.)* Oh, so you want one too, do you? I may have a crust or two. *(DOG pants and whines. She enters bakery and comes out with bite for the dog.)* There you go. *(DOG gulps it down.)* Well, aren't you going to eat yours too?

DAVEY: No, I'm going to save mine for Christmas.

ELLEN: I think I'll eat mine now, Davey.

DAVEY: You know what I think we should do?

ELLEN: What?

DAVEY: Give our cookies to Papa for his Christmas present.

ELLEN: But I'm hungry.

DAVEY: Don't you want a present for Papa?

ELLEN: *(Almost tearful.)* Yes, I do.

DAVEY: Come on then. *(They exeunt stage left.)*

            (DOG exits and then re-enters and whines.)

MRS. SIMMS: No—no. No more cookies for you. *(Whines.)* That was the last cookie in the store. Go on, now. Go on home. *(DOG moves to stage left and sits.)*

DOCTOR: *(Enters stage left.)* Oh, Mrs. Simms, I was afraid I'd be too late.

MRS. SIMMS: You were close, Doctor.

DOCTOR: *(Looking back left.)* Did you notice those children? They weren't dressed for this kind of weather.

MRS. SIMMS: Yes, the Conovers.

DOCTOR: So they are the Conover children.

MRS. SIMMS: Yes. They don't have a mother, poor things.

DOCTOR: I know. The father is a patient of mine. He's been sick all year.

MRS. SIMMS: Hmm. Well, it's freezing out there, Doctor. Come on in. I've got your wife's order ready to go. *(MRS. SIMMS and DOCTOR enter bakery. Dog watches them go. DAVEY calls from offstage, "Ollie." DOG takes one last look at bakery and then exits stage left. Light goes off in store. MR. HILL comes out and locks door. He approaches the bakery.)*

MR. HILL: *(Calling.)* Mrs. Simms. It's time to close up.

MRS. SIMMS: *(Offstage.)* Yes, I know. This is my last order.

DOCTOR: *(Exits from bakery.)* Oh, Mr. Hill, hello.

MR. HILL: Merry Christmas, Doctor.

DOCTOR: Merry Christmas. *(DOCTOR starts off stage left, then turns.)* Do you by any chance have anything suitable in your store for an extra little gift for my wife?

MR. HILL: Let's see. Does she like to play with dolls that cry or a Chinese top?

DOCTOR: *(Laughs.)* Well, just thought I'd ask. I've had so many patients lately, I just haven't had time to think about Christmas.

MR. HILL: Well, it's time to think about it now, Doctor. And have a merry one. *(DOCTOR exits and MR. HILL walks over to bakery. Lights go off in bakery and MRS. SIMMS comes out.)* You did say those were the Conover children?

MRS. SIMMS: Yes, I did. Nice children. I hope Christmas doesn't pass them by altogether. *(Mr. Hill and Mrs. Simms exeunt.)*

TRANSITIONAL MUSIC

SCENE II: **THE CONOVER HOME. THERE IS A BED STAGE RIGHT, A BED STAGE LEFT, AND A TABLE CENTER STAGE. VARIOUS OTHER FURNISH-INGS. THE STAGE IS DARK.**

(ELLEN, DAVEY, and the DOG enter.)

ELLEN: It's dark. Papa's not home yet.

DAVEY: Come on. I can light the lamp. *(Pause.)* Be careful. *(Lamp lights.)* There. Let's put the cookies over here so Papa won't see them until tomorrow. *(They do so.)*

ELLEN: I'm wishing Papa gets some money. He said he wasn't coming home until he did. What if he never comes home!

DAVEY: Don't say that, Ellen! He'll be home. It's Christmas Eve! Come on, let's have a glass of milk . *(Davey pours milk for them and they drink.)*

ELLEN: I'm wishing we have roast turkey tomorrow, Davey. I'm hungry.

DAVEY: That's a good wish, Ellen.

(DOG whines.)

ELLEN: Ollie's hungry too.

DAVEY: I know, Ollie. But you just wait. We'll have a big dinner tomorrow. I know we will.

(DOG sits and DAVEY pets him.)

ELLEN: I'm cold, Davey.

DAVEY: Come on, Ellen. I'll tuck you into bed. *(ELLEN climbs into bed stage left, and DAVEY covers her.)*

ELLEN: Weren't those toys wonderful?

DAVEY: Yes, they were. And they worked. They really worked. *(DAVEY turns down the lamp and climbs into his bed stage right. The DOG lies down close to DAVEY's bed.)*

ELLEN: *(Dreamily.)* Are there really sugar plum princesses, Davey?

DAVEY: Oh, I think so, Ellen.

ELLEN: Did you see—*(Yawns.)*—how her star—sparkled, Davey?

DAVEY: Uhhuh. *(Yawns.)*

ELLEN: I— wish—I may—I wish—I miiiiiight—

MUSIC FADES IN AS ELLEN GOES TO SLEEP. LIGHTS DIM

DREAM SEQUENCE

(After a brief pause, the lights come up and the sugarplum fairy floats in and slowly moves to each bed. As she disappears, the boat floats over to Davey's bed, the music fades and other characters appear as the appropriate music fades in. The characters move appropriately (the soldiers do a marching maneuver, etc.), but briefly. Suggestions for puppets to be used in this are listed in the Production Notes.)

DREAM SEQUENCE MUSIC FADES TO SAD OR MINOR MUSIC

(Conover enters stage right with rocking chair. He puts it center stage. He looks fondly and kisses each child. He pets the DOG, then goes offstage right and brings in rocking horse, which he places by DAVEY's bed. He returns to the table, sits, and puts his head on the table in despair.)

MUSIC FADES

(After a pause, a knock is heard. CONOVER gets up to open it stage right.)

CONOVER: Oh, Dr. Alexander.

DOCTOR: You didn't pick up your medicine today, Conover. I was afraid you might be needing it over Christmas.

CONOVER: Well, you see—I didn't have money to pay you.

DOCTOR: I know you'll pay when you can. You always have.

CONOVER: How kind of you, Doctor. I do appreciate it—*(Knock on the door.)* Now who could that be? *(Goes to open it.)*

MRS. SIMMS: *(Enters with cake.)* Merry Christmas! *(Sees DOCTOR.)* Well, hello again, Doctor. *(Doctor answers.)* Mr. Conover, your children were admiring my green Christmas tree cake today. Unfortunately, it did not sell. Now I ask you, what good is a Christmas tree cake after Christmas? Huh? So I thought I'd bring it over to them. *(Puts cake on the table.)*

CONOVER: *(Puzzled.)* Why, the children will be—I hope they were not a bother.

(The DOG jumps up and comes over to the table and whines.)

MRS. SIMMS: No, of course not. *(To the dog.)* Oh, I remember you. And you can't have any of this cake, but you might get to lick the box if you're a good dog.

CONOVER: Go, lie down, Ollie. Go on. *(Dog lies down. Knock on the door.)* Now what? *(With wonder. He goes to answer the door.)* Mr. Hill, what can I do for *you*, sir?

MR. HILL: *(Entering.)* Well, Conover, I understand that you make rocking horses.

CONOVER: I just made one for my children for Christmas, that's all. *(Points to it.)*

MR. HILL: *(Sees doctor and Mrs. Simms.)* Oh, hello, Doctor, Mrs. Simms. *(They respond. Mr. Hill goes over to the horse. They all look at the horse as Mr. Hill mutters and "Hmms.")* Excellent! Excellent! Now, I could use these, Mr. Conover. You make me six of these and you've got a deal. I've brought you a toy boat and a sugarplum fairy as an advance—if that's satisfactory.

CONOVER: *(Incredulous.)* Well—yes—I . . .

MR. HILL: Oh, Doctor, you were looking for a gift for your wife. Would she like a new rocking chair? Mr. Conover has one of the most beautiful rockers I've seen anywhere. *(Takes him over to the rocker.)* And it's for sale!

DOCTOR: *(Looking at the rocker.)* Ahhh—yes. *(To himself.)* A fine piece. Why, this is extraordinary, Conover. I had no idea you were such an artist. My wife would love this. Actually, so would I. May I buy it?

CONOVER: You want to buy it? *(Unbelieving and ecstatic.)* Why—why—I don't know what to say. *(Looks at all of them.)*

DOCTOR: How about "Merry Christmas"?

(All wish each other "Merry Christmas," CONOVER saying many "Thank you's." Everyone exits stage right, with the DOCTOR taking the chair.)

MUSIC FADES IN, POSSIBLY "I HEARD THE BELLS ON CHRISTMAS DAY"

(CONOVER looks at the cake. He goes to each bed and kisses each child. He pats the DOG, who whines. He turns down the lamp and moves stage left, stopping to look back and shake his head before he exits.)

VOICE OFFSTAGE: *(As CONOVER crosses to stage left, shakes his head and exits.)* Christmas is a time of dreams and stars and joy, when children believe in miracles and parents pause to contemplate the wonder of it all.

FINALE

Production Notes

Craft stores often carry small rocking chairs and rocking horses. Night lights make good puppet lamps.

The Christmas Dream—The various parts of this sequence should be accompanied by a medley of musical pieces segued to match the various puppets that float in and out of the dream. The "beautiful sugarplum fairy doll " floats over to Ellen's bed. A toy boat sails over to and hovers above Davey's bed. Chinese puppets do a brief dance. Soldiers march in a short drill. Santa Claus puts down his pack, surveys contents, and nods. Christmas elves frolic. Sparkling stars float in the firmament. Cakes, tarts, and breads drift tantalizingly about. Candy canes cavort and create a word, a Christmas tree, or a star. Raggedy Ann and Raggedy Andy keep time to "Turkey in the Straw." The possibilities are endless, limited only by the availability of the puppets and the director's imagination. The use of black light for this scene would make it even more magical and dreamlike.

Cinderella

by Jean M. Mattson

The familar old fairy tale with an interesting, new perspective.

CHARACTERS
Cinderella in rags
Cinderella in ball gown
Cinderella's father
Cinderella's stepmother
Ruby—Cinderella's stepsister
Pearl—Cinderella's stepsister
The King
Prince Frederick
Prince Adelbert
Prince Philander
Messenger
Fairy godmother
Performers at the ball

PROPS
Bucket
Firewood
Suitcase
Broom
Tiara
Scroll
Pumpkin
Cage
Coach
Menu
Glass slipper
Godmother's wand

SET PIECES
Fireplace
Mirror
Trees and bushes
Colonnade
Giant urns

SOUND EFFECTS
Godmother's wand
Trumpet

This play was written with the help of a third grade class at Perkins Elementay School in Seattle,Wash. through a grant from the Seattle Arts Commission. It includes five scenes and three sets: Cinderella's home with fireplace, outside the house and the palace. The production can accomodate a classroom of performers. However, it also can be produced with three or four puppeteers.

INTRODUCTORY MUSIC

SCENE I: **CINDERELLA'S HOUSE. THERE IS A FIREPLACE ON STAGE LEFT AND GENERAL LIVING ROOM ACCOUTERMENTS, PERHAPS A CHAIR AND TABLE. THERE IS A WINDOW ON STAGE RIGHT AND A MIRROR STAGE LEFT.**

RUBY: *(Offstage.)* Cinderella, bring me my wash water. *(Cinderella enters stage right with a bucket and exits stage left.)*

STEPMOTHER: *(Offstage.)* Ella, have you brought the wood in for the fire?

                   (CINDERELLA enters stage left and places some logs on the fire. Her father enters stage left with his suitcase.)

CINDERELLA: *(Turns to him.)* Father, do you have to go?

FATHER: *(Putting down suitcase.)* I'm sorry, Ella, but you know I must. You'll be all right. Your stepmother will take care of you. And I'll be back soon.

STEPMOTHER: *(Entering with Pearl and Ruby.)* Have a good trip, Antoine. *(Kisses him.)*

FATHER: Good-bye, my Dear.

STEPMOTHER: Say good bye to your stepfather, Girls—Pearl—Ruby.

RUBY: *(With a quick kiss.)* Bye. Don't forget to bring me a present.

PEARL: *(With a quick kiss.)* Me too. Tah-tah.

CINDERELLA: Good-bye, Father. *(Throwing her arms around him and crying.)*

                   (Father pats CINDERELLA, embraces his wife, and exits stage right.)

RUBY: What a sniveler you are, Cinderella! *(She goes to the mirror and preens.)*

PEARL: You baby! *(Throws herself into a chair.)*

STEPMOTHER: Cinderella, your father has enough to worry about without your whining and pouting.

CINDERELLA: I'm sorry.

STEPMOTHER: Now go and feed the chickens and gather the eggs for breakfast. *(CINDER-ELLA exits stage right.)*

RUBY: Have her fix breakfast now, mama. I'm hungry.

PEARL: Stop thinking about your stomach, Ruby. I need her to iron a blouse for me to wear.

STEPMOTHER: First she makes breakfast and then she changes the beds. *(Exits stage left.)*

RUBY: Not until I've had my nap! *(Voice rising to be sure her mother hears.)*

PEARL: When is she going to iron my blouse?

RUBY: You're not the only one that needs things done around here, Pearl. I've got a petticoat that needs—*(Trumpet sounds.)* Oh, what's that? *(She runs to the window.)* Oh! Oh! Pearl, it's a messenger from the palace!

PEARL: *(Runs to the window.)* Oh, it is. It is. Mother! Mother! A messenger from the palace! Oh, what do you suppose he wants. How exciting. Oh, I can't wait. *(Keeps bubbling.)*

(STEPMOTHER enters stage left and hurries across stage to admit the messenger.)

MESSENGER: *(Enters.)* Hear ye! Hear ye! A message from the King to the loyal subjects of the land. You are cordially invited to the royal ball on Saturday next to celebrate the birthday of Prince Frederick, the heir to the throne.

(A trumpet sounds and the MESSENGER exits stage right.)

PEARL: Oh, Mother. A royal ball! I could dissolve with excitement! *(Giggles, twirls around, and exits stage left.)*

STEPMOTHER: The king has three sons—all unmarried, I might add. What an opportunity!

RUBY: One prince is exciting, but threeeeee! *(Laughs.)* What'll I wear? What'll I wear?

STEPMOTHER: You'll wear a ball gown, of course, Ruby. We'll have to see about this at once.

PEARL: *(Enters with a tiara on her head and goes to the mirror.)* I can wear my tiara. Doesn't it make me look fetching?

RUBY: I'll carry my silk fan. *(Giggles.)* Ohhh. I can hardly wait.

CINDERELLA: *(Enters.)* Oh, how wonderful to go to a royal ball.

STEPMOTHER: Oh, Ella. I'm afraid you won't be able to go. Your father left only so much money for us to use until he returns, not enough for four ball gowns. You understand what I'm saying, I'm sure.

CINDERELLA: Yes. I understand—but I don't think that it . . .

STEPMOTHER: Please, Ella. You don't want me to have to tell your father I've had a problem with you, now, do you?

(CINDERELLA shakes her head and turns away.)

PEARL: You would feel out of place at the palace anyway. Mother, I want lace and ruffles and I'd like to have pleats in the back. *(Exits with STEPMOTHER stage left.)*

RUBY: *(Tearing herself away from the mirror.)* Can I have pure silk? I want pure silk with gold stitching on the collar. Motherrrrrr! *(She exits stage left.)*

CINDERELLA: Oh, dear—I wish Father were here. *(Exits stage left.)*

TRANSITIONAL MUSIC

SCENE II: **CINDERELLA'S HOME.**

(CINDERELLA enters stage left with a pot, which she places in the fireplace. PEARL enters stage left dressed for the ball.)

PEARL: Cinderella, fix the comb in my hair. *(She sits in the chair and CINDERELLA fusses with her hair.)*

RUBY: *(Enters stage left dressed for the ball.)* Tie my sash, Cinderella. *(CINDERELLA does so.)* Oh, don't pull it so tight, stupid.

PEARL: *(Preening at the mirror.)* Oh, I'm fit for a king. I don't know why Mother didn't name me "Diamond" instead of Pearl.

RUBY: *(Nastily.)* "Oyster" would be more appropriate.

PEARL: Oh, you nasty thing!

STEPMOTHER: *(Enters stage left.)* Oh, let me look at my two lovely little gems. *(Indulgently.)* Ruby and Pearl. Precious!

RUBY: *(Tittering.)* I can hardly wait to dance with a prince—a real live prince.

PEARL: Three of them, Ruby. Three of them. *(Laughs ridiculously.)*

STEPMOTHER: Now, Ella, be a good girl and tidy up a bit while we're gone. Come now, girls.

                (She exits with PEARL and RUBY. CINDERELLA watches them go, then sits down and cries.)

GODMOTHER: *(Appearing suddenly.)* Now, now, what be those tears about, my little lady?

CINDERELLA: Oh, who are you? I didn't see you come in.

GODMOTHER: Never you mind. You just tell me why you are crying your little eyes out.

CINDERELLA: Oh, I'm being selfish and silly to cry, but I do so want to go to the royal ball. It's in the palace and there will be music and I could dance with a prince and—*(She sobs.)*

GODMOTHER: You really want to go, don't you?

CINDERELLA: Oh, yes.

GODMOTHER: Then you shall go.

CINDERELLA: But I can't. I don't have a dress and I have no way of getting there. *(Sobs.)*

GODMOTHER.   Well, we'll be seeing about that. Now listen carefully. Close your eyes and turn yourself around.

CINDERELLA: But I—

GODMOTHER: Just do—do—do, my child. *(CINDERELLA turns around.)*
                Tiddledy-dee and tiddledy-down.
                I want to see a beautiful gown. *(CINDERELLA appears in gown.)*

CINDERELLA: Ohhhh, I can't believe it. It's beautiful. *(She goes to the mirror and parades about.)*

GODMOTHER: Well, of course. You couldn't be going to a ball in rags, now could you?

CINDERELLA: Who are you?

GODMOTHER: I be your godmother, child, a special kind of godmother. And now, if you'll be meeting me outside with a pumpkin and some mice, we'll be taking care of another little matter.

CINDERELLA: Mice and a pumpkin?

GODMOTHER: You be hearing right. Now skadaddle.

CINDERELLA: *(As she exits stage right.)* I'll see if we have any mice in our trap. I know we have a pumpkin.

GODMOTHER: Hurry. Hurry, or you'll be late for the ball. *(Disappears.)*

TRANSITIONAL MUSIC

SCENE III: **OUTSIDE THE HOUSE.**

(GODMOTHER appears and CINDERELLA enters stage left with a pumpkin and a cage, which she deposits on the ground.)

GODMOTHER: Fine, child, fine.
Tiddledy-dee and tiddledy-doach *(Touching pumpkin and cage with her wand.).*
I want to see a royal coach. *(Pumpkin and cage disappear and a coach appears.)*

CINDERELLA: *(Awestruck.)* A coach! A coach—finer than I've ever seen!

GODMOTHER: Get in. Get in! *(CINDERELLA enters coach and looks out of the window.)* Have a wonderful time, but remember one thing. You must leave the ball by midnight.

CINDERELLA: I do?

GODMOTHER: Yes, you do. Twelve o'clock. Not a minute later. That's just the way it is.

CINDERELLA: All right. Twelve o'clock. And thank you. You *are* a very special godmother.

GODMOTHER: *(As the coach moves off stage.)* Remember—when the clock strikes twelve!

(She disappears.)

TRANSITIONAL MUSIC

SCENE IV: THE PALACE.

(PRINCE FREDERICK and the KING enter stage left.)

FREDERICK: What a splendid celebration, Father. Thank you so much.

KING: It is going well, isn't it. Perhaps with all these people around, you will find a girl who will interest you. You will be King Frederick some day, you know, and every king needs a queen.

FREDERICK: *(With little interest.)* Oh, yes, Father.

KING: But you'd better go and greet your guests. *(He waves him away. FREDERICK exits stage right. KING shakes his head. ADELBERT enters stage left with menu.)*

ADELBERT: Oh, Father, I've been looking all over for you. This is supposed to be the celebration of the year, and I don't see wild boar meat crumpets on the menu. I can't really celebrate without wild boar meat crumpets.

KING: Well, that's too bad, Adelbert, but try to enjoy the party anyway. I'm sure there are plenty of other delicious tidbits.

ADELBERT: Well, mock turtle pie isn't the same. It just is not the same.

PHILANDER: *(Enters stage left.)* Father, you should sack your tailor. He's a royal pain. He did not have my blue velvet frock coat ready for this ball. I had to put on this wretched rag. It doesn't match my eyes, and it has too little lace around the collar. I feel like a sight. Just look. *(Turns around to show himself.)*

KING: You look elegant, Philander. Really, you do. Now, both of you forget about your problems and celebrate with the rest of us. *(Exits stage right.)*

PHILANDER: Adelbert, you have been in the kitchen snitching again. You've got cherries jubilee on your sleeve.

ADELBERT: Oh. *(Slurps it off.)* Oh, yum, not bad . . .

(RUBY and PEARL enter stage left.)

PEARL: Oh, this palace is wonderful!

RUBY: Yes, but it's so big. Where do we go? *(Looks around. Sees the princes.)* Excuse me, but we ladies are looking for Prince Frederick.

ADELBERT: He's our brother. May I introduce my picky, clotheshorse brother, Prince Philander.

PHILANDER: And this is my yum-yum brother, Prince Adelbert.

RUBY: *(Tittering.)* Well, we're really looking for the birthday prince.

ADELBERT: I'll show you where to find him—and the chocolate eclairs. Come on.

RUBY: Oh, good. Ladies do have to eat, after all. *(Laughs.)* Come on, Pearl.

                 (ADELBERT leads the girls off stage left, followed by PHILANDER. FREDERICK enters stage left. CINDERELLA enters stage right.)

FREDERICK: Oh, hello. *(Evidently impressed.)*

CINDERELLA: Hello. *(With wonder.)*

PRINCE: I don't think we've met.

CINDERELLA: No, I don't think we have. How do you do. *(She curtsies.)*

FREDERICK: I'm Frederick. I have a job at the castle so I hang around here most of the time.

CINDERELLA: And I'm just a girl who came in a pumpkin.

FREDERICK: What a charming way of putting it. I'm delighted to meet you. *(Music starts.)* Ahhh, would you care to dance?

CINDERELLA: Oh, yes. Yes, I would love to. *(They dance off stage left.)*

MESSENGER: *(Enters stage left.)* To celebrate the birthday of Prince Frederick, we now present the entertainment of the evening. *(Introduces the singers who perform.)* And now, to entertain us with his mysteries and magic we present *(The magician, who performs briefly.)* And coming from the Far East to entertain for Prince Frederick's birthday is *(The dancer or dancers.) (There is applause after each act.)* And now, please enjoy the music and the dancing. *(Messenger exits stage left and STEPMOTHER enters stage right and meets RUBY and PEARL entering stage left.)*

STEPMOTHER: Where have you been? I've been looking all over for you. Have you met Prince Frederick?

RUBY: Well, we have tried, but he's been dancing with some floozy in a blue *(or whatever)* dress.

PEARL: She's a cow, that's what she is, and she's taking up all of his time.

RUBY: And the evening is almost over. I haven't had one dance with him. Oh—there is that awful Adelbert—and Philander too. They have been following us all night. Let's get out of here.

(STEPMOTHER, PEARL, and RUBY exeunt stage right. ADELBERT and PHILANDER enter stage left.)

ADELBERT: There they are. *(The two princes race across the stage after RUBY and PEARL. CINDERELLA and FREDERICK enter stage left.)*

CINDERELLA: It's a perfectly lovely ball.

FREDERICK: I could dance all night with you. *(Clock strikes 1-2.)*

CINDERELLA: The music is so beautiful. *(Clock strikes 3-4.)*

FREDERICK: When can I see you again? *(Clock strikes 5-6.)*

CINDERELLA: *(Hears the clock.)* Oh—what time is it? *(Clock strikes 7-8.)*

FREDERICK: It's almost midnight. *(Clock strikes 9-10.)*

CINDERELLA: Oh—oh. *(Starts to run.)* I must go. *(Clock strikes 11-12. She exits stage right.)*

PRINCE: What—where are you going?

CINDERELLA: *(From offstage.)* Good-bye. Good-bye.

(FREDERICK stands bewildered and then hurries after CINDERELLA. KING enters stage left. PRINCE re-enters stage right.)

KING: Oh, there you are, Frederick. Some of the guests want to congratulate you.

FREDERICK: *(Despairingly.)* She's gone.

KING: Who's gone?

FREDERICK: The girl I danced with all evening. And that is the girl I think I would like to marry, Father.

FATHER: Really? Well, who is she?

FREDERICK: I don't know. She didn't really say.

KING: *(Puzzled.)* Didn't say?

FREDERICK: No. She rushed off at midnight before I could find out. I ran after her, but she's disappeared. All that I found was this slipper—this tiny glass slipper.

KING: *(Looking at it.)* Not many feet could fit that little thing.

FREDERICK: Father, I have to find that girl.

                  (KING and FREDERICK exeunt stage left.)

TRANSITIONAL MUSIC

SCENE V: CINDERELLA'S HOUSE.

                  (CINDERELLA enters stage right with an armload of wood, which she deposits by the fireplace. STEPMOTHER enters stage left.)

STEPMOTHER: Ella, I want you to do the sweeping, the dusting, and the washing this morning. Your father will be home any day, and we want the house to be nice for him, now, don't we?

CINDERELLA: Yes, Mother. *(Exits stage left.)*

                  (RUBY and PEARL enter stage right.)

RUBY: Oh, oh, oh. I am so peeved about not dancing with Prince Frederick.

STEPMOTHER: But you did dance with that other prince, dear.

PEARL: *(Sarcastically.)* You and Adelbert make such a nice couple, Ruby.

RUBY: In a pig's eye, Pearl. The lout was hanging on my arm all evening—when he wasn't stuffing his mouth. You and Philander were getting along famously, though. *(Spitefully.)*

PEARL: "Famous"? Phooey! He wanted me to stand with him all the time when we weren't dancing. He didn't want to sit down because it would make his britches shiny. *(Petulantly.)* And I wanted to dance with Prince Frederick. I could just pinch that floozy in the blue dress.

                  (Trumpet sounds.)

STEPMOTHER: Oh, is that another messenger from the palace?

(The three run to the window to look.)

RUBY: Oh, it is! It is! *(STEPMOTHER goes to stage right to admit messenger.)*

MESSENGER: *(Enters with a pillow on which sits the glass slipper.)* Hear ye. Hear ye. A glass slipper was lost at the royal ball. The King has decreed that the lady whose foot fits the slipper will be Prince Frederick's bride. *(Appropriate uproar from the sisters and STEPMOTHER.)* Do you have unmarried ladies in the house? *(RUBY and PEARL scream.)*

STEPMOTHER: Ruby, you first.

PEARL: Motherrrrrr!

RUBY: I'm the oldest and the more mature. *(PEARL flounces. RUBY sits down and tries on slipper.)* Oh, I know it will fit. I know it. *(She tries, grunts, and groans.)* It will! It will!

STEPMOTHER: All right, Pearl. Ruby's foot is just a trifle too large.

PEARL: A trifle! Like putting a cow in a birdhouse. *(Ruby is still trying.)* Ruby, it's my turn. *(PEARL yanks RUBY up.)* Bigfoot! *(Ruby flounces away and PEARL sits down and pushes and snorts.)* Just a little more. A little more should do it.

MESSENGER: I'm sorry, Mademoiselle. *(He retrieves the shoe against Pearl's protests as CINDERELLA enters stage left.)* Oh, another lady.

RUBY: Cinderella, a lady. *(Laughs derisively.)*

PEARL: She never even went to the ball.

MESSENGER: And now you, miss.

PEARL: Why are you trying it on her?

MESSENGER: My orders, miss. *(CINDERELLA sits down as the sisters loudly protest.)* It fits. The slipper fits. I must summon Prince Frederick. *(Exits stage right. The sisters and STEPMOTHER look at each other and then at CINDERELLA in shock. GODMOTHER appears.)*

GODMOTHER: Ella, we have some unfinished business.

RUBY: Who is she? *(Looking around.)* Where did she come from?

GODMOTHER: Tiddledy-dee and tiddledy-reen.
                 We need to dress the future queen.

                 (CINDERELLA is changed into her ball gown. Ruby and Pearl gag and faint.)

STEPMOTHER: Ella! *(Looks aghast at Cinderella and her daughters.)*

FREDERICK: *(Enters and looks at CINDERELLA, amazed.)* It is you!

CINDERELLA: Yes, and you—you are here with Prince Frederick?

FREDERICK: I am Prince Frederick.

CINDERELLA: But I—but I thought—

FREDERICK: Oh, I thought I might never find you again. Joy of my life, come, my coach is waiting.

                 (FREDERICK bows and CINDERELLA curtsies. He then escorts CINDERELLA as if in a dream. STEPMOTHER watches in a daze. ADELBERT and PHILANDER enter stage right.)

ADELBERT: We understand that Ruby and Pearl live here.

PHILANDER: We want to marry them.

STEPMOTHER: Ahhh—yes—but—I'm not sure that the girls will want to—I mean—this is so unexpected—and—I don't know if—*(Looks at girls on the floor.)*

GODMOTHER: Oh, I'll take care of everything. You really deserve each other. *(She touches RUBY with her wand.)*
                 Tiddledy-dee and tiddledy-dirt.
                 Awake with love for Adelbert. *(RUBY stirs and GODMOTHER touches PEARL.)*
                 Tiddledy-dee and tiddledy-dart.
                 Philander is your one sweetheart. *(GODMOTHER disappears and girls revive.)*

RUBY: *(Sees ADELBERT.)* Oh, Adelbert, my dream Prince. I've waited for you all my life. *(She throws her arms around Adelbert.)*

ADELBERT: Oh my little cream puff, would you like to join me for lunch?

PEARL: Philander, my heart's desire. My own true love. *(She tries to hug him.)*

PHILANDER: Oh, careful, my dear, you'll wrinkle my ruffle. Come, we'll go to the palace. *(The princes escort sisters out stage right.)*

STEPMOTHER: *(Dazed.)* Well, I'm a royal mother-in-law. Won't my husband be surprised! *(She shakes her head, dazedly.)*

MUSICAL FINALE

Production Notes

Slipper— If this play is produced with hand puppets or rod puppets, the glass slipper is somewhat of a problem. The sisters and Cinderella can sit with their backs to the audience as the messenger fits the slipper. Or, to be more convincing, the puppet can sit on a chair or stool so that her side is visible. A foot, ankle and pantaloon can be fitted on a stick and maneuvered under the skirt so that it appears to be part of the puppet.

Magical changes—Cinderella in rags can simply be quickly exchanged for Cinderella in her ball gown, and likewise for the cage and the pumpkin. A flashing of lights and sound effects will increase the sense of magic.

Ruby's and Pearl's ball gowns—Two puppets may be used for each character, of course, or each puppet can be made with a ball gown underneath a plain everyday dress that can be easily removed for Scene II.

In order to give each member of the original class a part, the play included several entertainers in the ball scene. If included (they need not be), these acts must be brief and exciting enough to counteract the interruption of the flow of action.

The Fisherman and His Wife

by Jean M. Mattson

The familiar old tale of ambition and greed.

CHARACTERS
Fisherman
His wife
Wife as prosperous
  housewife
Wife as lady of the manor
Wife as King
Wife as Pope
Fish

PROPS
Fishing pole
Fishing sack

SET PIECES
Fisherman's hut
Cottage
Mansion
Castle
Cathedral
Seashore with trees
  and rocks

A play in thirteen short scenes and two sets, but a number of set pieces. It is written for two puppeteers.

INTRODUCTORY MUSIC

**SCENE I: OUTSIDE THE
            FISHERMAN'S HUT.**

(Fisherman looks out the window of the hut.)

FISHERMAN: Another day. The sun is out.
            *(Enters from the hut with fishing
            creel on shoulder.)*
            And look—the sky is blue.
            It's such a lovely morning.
            I feel so good, don't you?

The Fisherman and His Wife.

WIFE: *(In rags, enters from hut.)*
        I'm miserable! I'm miserable!
        I feel like such a frump.
        Though I deserve the finer things,
        I live in this old dump!
        Why did I wed a fisherman,
        Who fishes in the sea?
        Whose luck is always awful
        So he can't buy things for me.

FISHERMAN: Why can't you see the
            brighter side?
            Forget your misery.
            Our situation could be worse.
            And you look just fine to me.

WIFE: Why do you blabber gibberish?
        You should be out there catching
        fish!
        Now, go! And don't you dare come
        back
        Until you've filled your fishing sack!

TRANSITIONAL MUSIC

*(WIFE enters hut. FISHERMAN picks up
his pole and exits stage left.)*

MUSIC FADES TO SURF SOUND

SCENE II: SEASHORE.

*(FISHERMAN enters stage right and
makes a few casts into the water.)*

FISHERMAN: I'll catch something big
            today.
            I'll show her good and proper.
            She'll have to—oh—oh—oh—
            what's that?
            I think I've hooked a whopper!
            *(FISHERMAN struggles with
            FISH, which splashes on the end
            of his line.)* A golden fish! Oh, what
            a prize!
            But wait, can I believe my eyes?

FISH: Now, fisherman, you look again.
        I am no common flounder.

FISHERMAN: You're right. I'll take you to
            my wife.
            My good luck will confound her.

FISH: I am not good to eat. I am
  The King of all the sea.
  So spare my life. You must remove
  The hook and set me free.

FISHERMAN: Oh, very well, King of the
  sea,
  I'll let you swim away.
  I know it's right for me to do.
  But what's she going to say?

(FISHERMAN *releases fish and exits.*)

SURF TO TRANSITIONAL MUSIC

SCENE III: OUTSIDE HUT.

(*Fisherman enters stage left.*)

WIFE: You're back. So where's my bag of
  fish?

FISHERMAN. Now, Wife, try not to scold.
  I caught the King of all the sea,
  A fish of shining gold.

WIFE: Indeed? A golden fish, you say?
  Now that should help the
  pocketbook.

FISHERMAN: He said he wasn't good to
  eat,
  So I let him off the hook.

WIFE: (*Furiously.*)
  How stupid can you be? But wait—
  The King—you say—the King?
  I've heard that if you save his life
  Then he will grant you anything.
  You go right back and call that fish.
  We'll see if this is so.

FISHERMAN: But I don't want to call him
  back
  'Cause I don't want to know.

WIFE: Here I sit in poverty.
  My clothes are rags and tatters.
  This house is but a hovel—yet
  You act like nothing matters.
  Now, you go back and tell that fish
  You want a bungalow,
  A cottage for your lovely wife.

FISHERMAN: But—

WIFE: Do you hear me? Go!

TRANSITIONAL MUSIC—SURF
SOUND

SCENE IV: SEASHORE.

FISHERMAN: (*Enters stage right*)
  Oh, fish of Gold, King of the sea,
  Oh, high and mightiest.
  Remember that I saved your life
  And grant this one request.

FISH: (*Splashing up out of the water.*)
  Oh, Fisherman, I come to you.
  What is it you would have me do?

FISHERMAN: My wife insists you'll grant
  my wish
  Because I spared your life.
  I want a pretty cottage—not
  For me, but for my wife.

FISH: Oh, Fisherman, my tail will swish,
  And as it does you'll have your wish.
  (*FISH swishes tail and disappears.
  FISHERMAN exits stage right.*)

SURF TO TRANSITIONAL MUSIC

SCENE V: OUTSIDE COTTAGE.

(FISHERMAN enters stage left and surveys cottage.)

FISHERMAN: Oh, Wife, you got your wish,
  I see.
  (WIFE, in nice dress, enters from cottage.)
  And now we can live happily!

WIFE: Look at what that fish can do!
  It's almost too good to be true.
  (They enter cottage.)

TRANSITIONAL MUSIC

(They enter from cottage.)

WIFE: A week in here has made me sure
  This cottage is too small.
  We need a mansion now, my dear.
  Go give that fish a call.

FISHERMAN: Our cottage here is good
  enough.

WIFE: It's much too small, I say.

FISHERMAN: That flounder will be angry.

WIFE: No more talk. Be on your way.
  *(WIFE enters cottage.
  FISHERMAN exits stage left.)*

TRANSITIONAL MUSIC TO SURF SOUND.

SCENE VI: SEASHORE.

(FISHERMAN enters stage right.)

FISHERMAN: Oh, golden fish, King of the
  sea,
  Oh, high and mightiest,
  Remember that I saved your life.
  I have one more request.

FISH: *(Appearing.)*
  Oh, Fisherman, I come to you.
  What is it you would have me do?

FISHERMAN: My wife is discontented
  now.
  She feels we need expansion.
  The cottage seems too small, so now
  I ask you for a mansion.

FISH: Oh, Fisherman, my tail will swish,
  And when it does, you'll have your
  wish. *(FISH swishes and disappears.
  FISHERMAN exits stage right.)*

SURF TO TRANSITIONAL MUSIC

SCENE VII: OUTSIDE MANSION.

(WIFE, in fancy dress, runs out of mansion.)

WIFE: Oh, husband, come and see this
  place.
  We now are "the elite."
  What comfort and what style.
  Husband, wipe your feet!
  *(WIFE exits into mansion.
  FISHERMAN shrugs and follows.)*

TRANSITIONAL MUSIC

WIFE: *(Offstage.)*
  Oh, husband, mine, get out of bed.
  (She appears. He follows rubbing his eyes.)

This mansion may be grand.
But I feel it's not enough. You should
Be king of all this land.

FISHERMAN: Be king. No never. I don't
want
To head up anything.

WIFE: All right. That's fine. Then tell that
fish
Your wife wants to be king!

FISHERMAN: Oh, no!

WIFE: You go!

*(FISHERMAN exits stage left. She exits
into mansion.)*

TRANSITIONAL MUSIC TO SURF

SCENE VIII: SEASHORE.

(FISHERMAN enters stage right.)

FISHERMAN: Oh, golden fish, King of the
sea.
Oh, high and mightiest.
As you can see, I'm back again.
I have one more request.

FISH: *(Appearing.)*
Oh, Fisherman, I come to you.
What is it you would have me do?

FISHERMAN: My wife has now decided
that
She wants to have a throne.
She wants to be a king and have
A castle all her own.

FISH: Oh, Fisherman, my tail will swish,
And when it does, you'll have your
wish.

*(FISH swishes and FISHERMAN
exits stage right.)*

SURF TO TRANSITIONAL MUSIC

SCENE IX: OUTSIDE CASTLE.

WIFE: *(In royal dress, enters from
castle.)*
Prithee thou does now return.
Thy fish hath paid his debt.
We have a royal castle now
From moat to parapet.

FISHERMAN: *(Incredulous.)*
I can't believe you are a king.

WIFE: It's true. You see my crown.
I now decree. You must obey.
Bow, underling. Bow down.
*(She sweeps off. He follows
bowing and bowing.)*

TRANSITIONAL MUSIC

*(WIFE and FISHERMAN enter from
castle.)*

WIFE: Harken how, the king doth speak.
I must enlarge my scope.
Though being king is very fine—
I want to be the pope!

FISHERMAN: Alas, my wife, you can't be
pope.
There's only one of those.
The golden fish, King of the sea,
Can't do what you propose.

WIFE: He made me king! He'll make me
pope!
Now, hie thee to the shore.
And call that fish again and say
"My wife, the king, wants more."

(WIFE exits into castle. He watches her go and then dejectedly exits stage left.)

TRANSITIONAL MUSIC—SURF SOUND

SCENE X: SEASHORE.

(FISHERMAN enters stage right slowly.)

FISHERMAN: Oh, golden fish, King of the
    sea,
    Oh, high and mightiest.
    I come, but I don't want to come.
    I'm feeling quite distressed.

FISH: Oh, Fisherman, I come to you.
    What is it you would have me do?

FISHERMAN: Oh, Flounder, how I hate to
    say—
    My wife wants to be pope.
    I know it's way too much to ask
    I told her not to hope.

FISH: Oh, Fisherman, my tail will swish,
    And when it does, you'll have your
    wish.
    (Fish swishes and disappears.)

TRANSITIONAL ORGAN MUSIC

SCENE XI: OUTSIDE CATHEDRAL.

(FISHERMAN enters stage left. WIFE enters from cathedral in clerical robe and with miter.)

FISHERMAN: Ah, tempus fugit! You are
    pope.

WIFE: Pax vobiscum. See the spire?

FISHERMAN: You now must be contented
    for
    You can't go any higher.

WIFE: I like cathedrals, pews, and chimes
    More than I ever knew.
    Great men bow down to me.
    Husband, kiss my shoe!
    (She sweeps into cathedral.)

FISHERMAN: I do not have a wife or home.
    My life has gone amuck.
    My pulling in that golden fish
    Was anything but luck! *(Exits.)*

TRANSITIONAL MUSIC

(WIFE enters.)

WIFE: The miter fits my head so well.
    But as I wear the stole—

FISHERMAN: Oh, Wife, don't wish for any
    more.
    Please use some self control.

WIFE: The lord of all the universe
    Makes sun and moon to rise.
    I want to do these things, I will
    Not have it otherwise.
    Go fetch your fish and tell him that.

FISHERMAN: But, Wife, this is not right.

WIFE: Hear and obey. I am the pope.
    I will be God tonight!
    (WIFE exits into cathedral. FISHERMAN shakes his head and exits stage left.)

TRANSITIONAL MUSIC TO SURF

SCENE XII: SEASHORE.

(FISHERMAN enters. He turns back, hesitates, and then continues.)

FISHERMAN: *(Hesitantly.)*
> Oh, golden fish, King of the sea
> Oh, high and mightiest,
> I did once save your life, you know.
> I have one last request.

FISH: *(Appearing.)*
> Oh, Fisherman, I come to you.
> And one last thing, I still will do.

FISHERMAN: Oh, King of all the seven seas,
> I shake—my knees are weak.

FISH: Come, come, what does your wife want now?

FISHERMAN: Oh, I can hardly speak.
> She would control the sun and moon.
> Whatever could be worse?
> She now insists she must be Lord
> Of all the universe.
> *(Thunder rolls.)*

FISH: The Lord of all the universe?
> This time she's gone too far.
> Go to your home, oh, Fisherman.
> Where you began—you are!
> *(Thunder rolls. FISH swishes angrily several times and disappears. FISHERMAN backs away cowering and exits stage right.)*

SURF AND THUNDER TO TRANSITIONAL MUSIC

SCENE XIII: OUTSIDE HUT.

(WIFE, in rags, enters from hut, crying. FISHERMAN enters stage left.)

FISHERMAN: Oh, Wife. Oh, Wife. What can I do?
> I asked the fish. I tried.

WIFE: Just tell me, Husband, why at last,
> Was I not satisfied?

FISHERMAN:
> Sometimes we learn too late, my dear.
> Now wipe those tears away.
> I still have you—and you have me
> *(Looks up at sky.)*
> And it's a lovely day.

(They exeunt into hut.)

FINALE

Production Notes

Fisherman's wife—This play can be done using a basic puppet body and adding apron, collars, stoles, and headpieces (kerchief, bonnet, crown, miter, etc.). However, in a more elaborate production, separate puppets, with complete costumes, can be made for each of the wife's new positions.

Staging—A small stage would necessitate scene changes each time the fisherman moves between his home and the sea. If a large stage is used, the home can be on one side and the sea on the other, with the fisherman simulating traversing some distance as he crosses back and forth.

The Golden Axe

by Jean M. Mattson

A well-known Japanese folktale.

CHARACTERS
Tatsuki, an elderly woodcutter
Oshun, his wife
Gonta, a neighbor
Yoshiko, his wife
Goddess of the pool
Narrator's voice

PROPS
Tea kettle
Cracked rice jar
New rice jar
Backpack of wood
2 Iron axes
Folded kimono
2 Golden axes
Bag of rice

SOUND EFFECTS
Splash
Water sounds

SET PIECES
Tatsuki's house
Wood burner
Table
Tatsuki's new roof
Gonta's house
Forest

A play in five scenes that involves two sets, a road with two houses and a forest. It is written for two puppeteers.

INTRODUCTORY MUSIC

NARRATOR: Once upon a time in Japan, there was an honest, old woodcutter called Tatsuki, who lived with his wife, Oshun, in a small house at the edge of a village.

MUSIC FADES

SCENE I: **A JAPANESE STREET. ON STAGE LEFT IS A DILAPIDATED HOUSE WITH A HOLE IN THE ROOF. IN FRONT IS A LOW TABLE WITH CUPS, A BURNER WITH A POT ON IT AND A CRACKED RICE JAR. ON STAGE RIGHT IS A RATHER PRETENTIOUS HOUSE.**

(OSHUN enters from house, stage left, with a teapot, which she puts on the burner. She stirs the pot, then goes upstage to look for her husband and returns to the stirring. TATSUKI enters from behind houses with a load of wood on his back carrying an axe.)

Oshun and Tatsuki ponder their good fortune in *The Golden Axe.*

TATSUKI: I do believe this wood gets heavier every year. *(Puts axe down.)*

OSHUN: Oh, Tatsuki, you look so tired. I think you are working too hard. *(Takes wood off his back.)*

TATSUKI: You worry too much, Oshun. *(He sits down at the table. She pours him tea.)*

OSHUN: Perhaps so, but I see your back bent under your heavy load of wood—and I worry. I see the rice jar cracked and almost empty *(She looks at it.)*—and I worry. I see the sky through the holes in our roof *(Looks at it.)*—and I worry.

TATSUKI: Tomorrow I will get up earlier and climb higher—beyond the blue ridge, and I will find good wood which will bring more money. We will have a new roof before winter comes.

OSHUN: *(Stirs her pot again.)* Even now, you leave before it is light—and come home after the sun sinks into the sea—and we barely survive. And we need so many things. Your coat is in rags.

TATSUKI: The goddess of the woods has always helped us, has she not? *(OSHUN nods.)* Have we ever been hungry? *(OSHUN shakes her head.)* Well, then, do not worry. Things will be better. You will see. Things will be better.

(Oshun picks up pot and they exeunt into the house.)

TRANSITIONAL MUSIC

NARRATOR: Nearby lived Gonta, a greedy woodcutter, who often made money by cheating others. *(YOSHIKO enters from house on stage right. She motions to GONTA to come.)*

YOSHIKO: Look, Gonta! Look at their roof. Like I said, it's falling in.

GONTA: Yes, I see what you mean.

YOSKIKO: We've got to move. This is getting to be a bad neighborhood. We live next door to an old man who can't chop enough wood to make a decent living.

GONTA: He's lazy and irresponsible all right!

YOSHIKO: And his wife is a mess. She never has a lacquered comb for her hair or new sandals.

GONTA: Yes, they do look like beggars.

YOSHIKO: They are a disgrace. The sooner we move, the better!

(Exeunt into their house.)

TRANSITIONAL MUSIC WHICH LASTS DURING VOICE-OVER

NARRATOR: The next morning, Tatsuki did get up especially early and left for the woods, determined to do his best.

(TATSUKI comes out of his house, picks up his axe, and exits.)

SCENE II: FOREST. THE POOL IS CENTER STAGE.

NARRATOR: The climb was long, and he was tired when he reached the top of the ridge *(TATSUKI enters stage right.)* and he found a spot beside a small pool to rest.

MUSIC FADES.

TATSUKI: Oh, that was a climb. *(Puts down his axe and sits by the pool.)* What a beautiful, peaceful place. I could sit here all day and watch the clouds drift by and listen to the wind music. Ahh—but I must get to work. *(He gets up and his axe splashes into the pool.)* Oh, my axe! My axe! It slipped right into the pool. Ohhh. *(Reaches for it.)* It's going down, down, down. What am I going to do? I can't even see it now. I don't dare dive in to look for it. *(Raises his arms.)* Oh, please, Goddess of the Woods, help me find my axe. I have no money to buy a new one. If I do not have an axe, I cannot chop wood, and Oshun and I will starve. Help me!

MUSIC AND WATER SOUNDS

(GODDESS rises from the pool.)

GODDESS: *(As TATSUKI draws back.)* Do not be afraid, Woodcutter. I heard you call me. You see, this pool is my home.

Tatsuki meets the Goddess of the Woods in *The Golden Axe.*

TATSUKI: Ohhhhhhhh.

GODDESS: (*Reaches down and brings up a golden axe.*) Is this what you are looking for?

TATSUKI: Oh, I wish it were. That one looks as though it is made of gold. Mine was only

an old iron one. Could you look just once more—please?

GODDESS: Wait a moment. (*She disappears with water sounds and returns with old axe.*)

Is this yours?

TATSUKI: Yes. Yes, that one is mine. Oh, how can I thank you enough. (*Takes axe.*) Now I can cut my wood and we won't go hungry. How can I ever thank you?

GODDESS: You are a good and honest man. Such honesty deserves recognition. (*She reaches down and brings up the golden axe.*) This golden axe is my gift to you. Take it and have good fortune. (*Water sounds as GODDESS sinks into the pool.*)

TATSUKI: (*Gazing into the pool.*) That surely was a dream. But here is the golden axe. (*Unbelievingly.*) It really did happen. (*Pause.*) Oh, I'll have to try out my new axe. Oshun will be so surprised when she hears about this.

TRANSITIONAL MUSIC

SCENE III: STREET WITH THE HOUSES.

(*TATSUKI enters. OSHUN comes out of the house and they pantomime talking.*)

NARRATOR: And the woodcutter came home and told the whole story to his wife.

MUSIC FADES

TATSUKI: And the goddess was so beautiful and so kind. And she came right up out of that pool and spoke to me. Oh, it has been a remarkable day.

OSHUN: It has indeed. How did you ever manage to bring home so much wood?

TATSUKI: Well, the axe seems to cut the wood like butter. And my pack seemed to weigh almost nothing. It almost floated home.

OSHUN: Oh, we have been blessed. Perhaps I won't have to worry anymore.

TRANSITIONAL MUSIC

NARRATOR: And Oshun did not have to worry. Tatsuki managed to fix his roof that very week. (*New roof goes up.*)

(*GONTA and YOSHIKO come out of their house and look at TATSUKI's.*)

GONTA: I wonder what's going on over there at Tatsuki's. I heard that he was blessed by the Goddess of the Woods up on the mountain.

YOSHIKO: Probably some more of his lies.

GONTA: Well, ever since last week he's been bringing home huge loads of wood. And he's wearing a new coat too.

YOSHIKO: And Oshun has a new comb for her hair—and she was buying fruit and almond cakes at the market yesterday. A real show-off. They can't afford that. I don't like this at all.

GONTA: I don't either.

YOSHIKO: Well, what are you going to do about it? (*She goes into her house.*)

(*GONTA thinks for a moment, surveying TATSUKI's house, then approaches it.*)

GONTA: Tatsuki! Tatsuki!

TATSUKI: (*Comes out of his house.*) Oh, neighbor. Greetings. (*Bows.*)

GONTA: (*Bows.*) Fortune is smiling upon you, Tatsuki. You have been bringing home much good wood this week, I see.

TATSUKI: Yes, ever since last week when I went far into the mountains—beyond the blue ridge.

GONTA: Beyond the blue ridge, eh?

TATSUKI: Yes, that's where I met the Goddess of the Woods. I lost my axe in a deep pool and I called on her to help. She came up out of the pool—that's where she lives—and gave me a wonderful golden axe as a gift.

GONTA: (*Excitedly.*) A golden axe—as a gift?

TATSUKI: You know, ever since then, things seem to have gone much better. I am fortunate.

GONTA: How interesting. A golden axe. Hmmm. Beyond the blue ridge, you say?

TATSUKI: Yes, just past the red cliffs.

GONTA: Well, congratulations on your good fortune, neighbor. May it continue. *(They bow and TATSUKI re-enters his house. GONTA returns to his house. He talks to himself.)* If that woodcutter can get a golden axe out of some goddess up there in the mountains, so can I. Wife! Wife! Yoshiko! Bring me my axe.

YOSHIKO: *(She enters with axe.)* What is it? What's going on?

GONTA: The Goddess of the Woods gave Tatsuki a golden axe. I'm going to get one too. Now, you go and invite everyone to our house tonight. Buy rice cakes and sesame cookies.

YOSHIKO: But Gonta, I . . .

GONTA: Tatsuki thinks he's so smart. I'll show him. I'm going to the mountains beyond the blue ridge and when I get back we'll celebrate _my_ golden axe. *(GONTA takes his axe and exits. YOSHIKO watches him go, then goes into her house.)*

TRANSITIONAL MUSIC

SCENE IV: FOREST.

(GONTA enters stage right with axe.)

GONTA: This must be the place. Yes—there's the pool. Now, I'll just throw my axe into the water and see what happens. *(Throws axe into the water. Splash. GONTA yells.)* My axe! My axe! I've lost my axe. Goddess of the Woods, help me!

MUSIC AND WATER SOUNDS

GODDESS: You called.

GONTA: Oh, please help me. I lost my axe in the pool. I am a woodcutter and I need my axe.

GODDESS: *(Sinks into pool with water sounds and brings up a golden axe.)* Is this the axe you lost, Woodcutter?

GONTA: Yes—yes. That's it. That's the one. Oh, thank you. *(Reaches for axe.)*

GODDESS: You lie, Woodcutter! You lie! This is not your axe. You are a greedy, dishonest man and for that you shall suffer.

WATER SOUNDS AS SHE SINKS INTO THE POOL

GONTA: Come back! Come back! Give me my golden axe. *(Pause.)* Come back again—Goddess. *(Pause.)* Hey, aren't you going to give me my own axe back? *(Pause.)* Goddess! Goddess! She's gone. And I've really lost my axe. This isn't fair. I've been tricked! I've been tricked! *(GONTA exits screaming.)*

TRANSITIONAL MUSIC

SCENE IV: STREETS WITH HOUSES.

(GONTA enters slowly. YOSHIKO sees him and comes out of the house.)

YOSHIKO: You didn't get the golden axe. *(He doesn't answer.)* You didn't get the golden axe? Well, what are we going to do now? I've spent a lot of money on food and sweets. And I've invited the whole village to come to celebrate. How can we pay for all that food? How can I face all those people? *(She exits wailing.)* Stupid! Stupid! Stupid!

GONTA: What bad fortune is mine. Unpleasant neighbors. A wicked goddess. A lost axe—and now—debts and a screaming wife! Suffer! Suffer! Suffer! *(Exits.)*

TRANSITIONAL MUSIC

NARRATOR: And Tatsuki and Oshun continued to prosper. They had money for new mats and new curtains for the doors. They were able to buy plenty of rice and even a kimono that Tatsuki had promised her long ago. *(TATSUKI enters and presents her with a silk kimono.)* And even though Gonta and his wife remained in the neighborhood, Tatsuki and Oshun managed to live happily ever after. *(Exeunt into their house.)*

FINALE

Production Notes

Tatsuki's load of wood—The bundle of wood can be attached to Tatsuki's back by velcro or by hooks that fit into slots sewn into the puppet's costume.

Tatsuki's axe—can be made to fit into a slit cut into a block of wood. This enables him to put it down and pick it up easily.

The pot should be attached to the burner and the spoon to the bottom of the pot.

If the goddess's voice is taped, a nice touch is using reverberation to make the voice sound as though it is coming through water.

Gold Nugget Champ

by Jean M. Mattson

An original story about the Gold Rush of 1897.

CHARACTERS
Jeremy—nine years old
Sam—his older brother
Mrs. Crawford—their
    mother
Mr. Crawford—their father
Mr. Berry—a grocer
A customer
A sled driver
Passenger
Dog owner
Champ—Jeremy's dog

PROPS
Bundles
Wagon
Rope or harness
Bucket
Stick
Suitcase
Basket
Watering can
Slippers
Sled and dog
Bag of flour
Sack of candy
Broom

SET PIECES
Yard with porch & flowers
Pump
Fence
Crawford living room
Chair
Table
Street with storefronts
Boat deck with portholes
Railing with life preservers

SOUND EFFECTS
Galloping horses
Boat engines
Foghorn

A play with four sets and five scenes. It can be performed by two puppeteers.

INTRODUCTORY MUSIC

SCENE I: **YARD OF THE CRAWFORD HOME. TREE ON STAGE LEFT. PORCH INTO HOUSE ON STAGE RIGHT. PUMP ON STAGE RIGHT AND TOY WAGON ON STAGE LEFT.**

(SAM enters stage left with packages. CHAMP bounds from behind the house and jumps up on SAM.)

SAM: Down, Champ. Down, boy.

JEREMY: *(Enters from behind the house.)* Champ, here, Champ. Oh, there you are.

SAM: Yeah, here he is. I almost fell over him.

JEREMY: He's glad to see you, Sam.

SAM: Yeah. *(Goes over to porch.)*

JEREMY: Did you get all your stuff?

SAM: I got the clothes—the parka, the boots, and that kind of thing. Mr. Berry at the Mercantile is going to pack up the supplies. I'm going to pick them up on my way to the boat. *(Turns to enter house.)*

JEREMY: Hey, Sam—*(SAM turns around again.)* What makes you so sure you're going to get rich up there in the Klondike?

SAM: People are hauling out gold by the barrelful, Jeremy. I just heard that one man on the last boat had so many nuggets in his satchel, it broke the handle off!

JEREMY: Wowie! That's exciting.

SAM: Yeah, just think of it. Well, I've got to get going here. The boat leaves in two hours and I've got to get down there early to get a good spot. It'll be jammed. *(Exits into house.)*

JEREMY: Come on, Champ. Let's see if you remember your tricks. *(Does tricks. Dead dog, speaks, sits, and so on.)* Good dog. Say, I wonder if you could be a sled dog. We can pretend my wagon is a sled. *(Gets the wagon. Takes rope out of wagon and harnesses CHAMP to the wagon during following directions.)* Stand still, now. That's a good dog. Now, we'll put this rope around here like this. Just a minute. Now. That looks like it'll work. Now, Champ, they say "Mush" in Alaska when they want you to go. Ya got that? "Mush." Now, let's try it. *(JEREMY gets into wag-*

on.) O.K . . . Mush! *(CHAMP doesn't move.)* Mush, Champ, mush. *(CHAMP sits. JEREMY gets out of wagon and pulls CHAMP up to a standing position.)* Champ, come on. *(Gets back into wagon.)* Now, mush! *(CHAMP lies down. JEREMY sighs and gets out of wagon and unties CHAMP.)* I guess you're just not cut out to be a sled dog. *(CHAMP jumps and barks.)* I'll bet you are thirsty. *(Pumps water into bucket and CHAMP drinks. He barks.)* Oh, you want to fetch, do you? O.K. Here. *(JEREMY throws a stick and CHAMP brings it back twice. Then JEREMY throws it out of the yard and the dog disappears. SAM and MR. CRAWFORD enter from house one with a suitcase, one with a bundle which they put down when they start talking.)*

MR. C.: Have you got your money?

SAM: $500. That's what they say you need.

MR. C.: Are you sure you have everything, Sam? You can't expect to buy anything up there, you know.

SAM: I think so, Papa. Mr. Berry was packing everything on the list and Mama's taking care of my food on the boat.

MR. C.: Sam, I wish—

SAM: *(Interrupting.)* Papa, let's not go through it again. If I decide to go to school at the university, I can go any time. If I want to find gold—I've got to go now before it's all gone.

MR. C.: More people are going to get rich staying in Seattle than up there in the Klondike, son. Why we've sold more at the mill this month than all last year. If you'd—

SAM: Papa, I'm going and that's that.

MRS. C.: *(Enters from house with basket.)* Here's the basket, Sam. Oh, I hope you've got enough along to eat and enough warm clothes. I wish you'd wait until later when it wouldn't be so cold.

SAM: Can't do that, Mama. The sooner I get there, the better. *(Takes basket.)*

MRS. C.: Oh, I will worry about you.

SAM: Mama, I'm nineteen years old. I can take care of myself. *(SAM hugs his mother.)* I'll buy you a new hat Mama. *(Hugs JEREMY.)* I'll bring you back a nugget as big as your fist. Papa, are you ready to go? *(They pick up the suitcase and bundle and basket.)*

JEREMY: Can't I ride along?

SAM: Not enough room—with all my gear. *(They exeunt with "Good byes" and "Good luck" and "Be careful" etc.   JEREMY and MRS. CRAWFORD stand waving as the sound of horse galloping fades into the distance. JEREMY calls CHAMP and exits stage left still calling. MRS. CRAWFORD fills watering can at pump and waters flowers. After a moment JEREMY returns.)*

JEREMY: Mama, Champ's gone.

MRS. C.:   Don't worry, Jeremy. He'll be back. He always comes back. *(Exits into house.)* You'd better get busy, Jeremy. You haven't filled the wood box yet. *(JEREMY exits behind house, continuing to call for CHAMP.)*

TRANSITIONAL MUSIC

SCENE II: CRAWFORD LIVING ROOM. A CHAIR WITH BACK AND SIDE TO THE AUDIENCE ON STAGE RIGHT. TABLE ON STAGE LEFT.

             (MRS. CRAWFORD is dusting furniture.)

JEREMY: *(Enters stage right.)* Mama, he never stayed away this long. You know that.

MRS. C.:   He'll be back when it gets dark. He's a smart dog, Jeremy.

JEREMY: Yeah, he is. He's smart enough to know I'd be worried if he didn't come home.

MRS. C.:   *(Thinks.)* Jeremy, I need a bag of flour. Will you please go down to the Mercantile and get it for me? You can look for Champ on the way.

JEREMY: Yes, Mama. *(Starts to exit stage right.)*

MRS. C.:   Have Mr. Berry put it on the bill. And you can have him add a penny for a candy stick.

JEREMY: And one for Champ?

MRS. C.:   And one for Champ.

             (JEREMY exits and we hear him calling CHAMP in the distance. MRS. CRAWFORD shakes her head and gets a basket of clothes from stage right, which she puts on table.)

MR. C.:   *(Enters stage right with a newspaper.)* Where was Jeremy headed?

MRS. C.:   To the Mercantile to get some flour I don't need. But he's been moping around here all afternoon. I wish that dog would come back.

MR. C.:   *(Sits down in chair and looks at his paper.)* Harriet, I'm not sure that dog will come back.

MRS. C.:   What do you mean, John?

MR. C.:   Ever since that last boat came in from Alaska two weeks ago people have been going crazy.

MRS. C.:   Crazy?

MR. C.:   Gold crazy. The prospectors are buying everything in sight and the stores are selling anything they can get their hands on—for prices you wouldn't believe.

MRS. C.:   *(She brings him his slippers, which he proceeds to put on.)* What does that have to do with Champ?

MR. C.:   Well, some of those rascals are selling sled dogs.

MRS. C.:   So?

MR. C.:   Well, they're selling dogs for sled dogs that aren't huskies or malamutes. They're just ordinary dogs.

MRS. C.:   Who'd buy them?

MR. C.:   Some poor soul from St. Louis who doesn't know a sled from a buck wagon.

MRS. C.:   Oh, John, do you think somebody is trying to sell Champ?

MR. C.:   *(Looking at paper.)* Lots of lost dogs advertised in the paper. Knowing Champ, I'd say he'd be home here now—unless he couldn't get home.

MRS. C.:   Oh, this gold rush is nothing but trouble. Champ is gone. And I'm worried sick about Sam. Did he get on the boat all right?

Mrs. C.:   Along with a million other people and horses and mules and dogs. He'll be all right, Harriet.

MRS. C.:   He's not a rugged pioneer, John.

MR. C.: No, but he's a grown man, Harriet, and we have to let him live his own life. *(She shakes her head. He puts his arm around her and they exeunt.)*

TRANSITIONAL MUSIC

SCENE III: A STREET. THERE ARE SEVERAL STORE FRONTS WITH SIGNS SUCH AS "PORTABLE CABINS," "KLONDIKE OUTFITTERS," "YUKON SUP-PLIES," AND "EAR MUFFS." CENTER STORE IS LABELED "MERCAN-TILE."

(MR. BERRY comes out of store with a customer.)

CUSTOMER: Well, I missed the last boat, but I'm first on the list for the next one. You sure I won't need any more than one gold pan?

MR. BERRY: You only got two hands, haven't you? *(CUSTOMER nods.)* Well, then one oughta do you. *(CUSTOMER thanks him and shakes hands and exits stage right.)* Good luck.

JEREMY: *(Enters stage left.)* Hi, Mr. Berry.

MR. BERRY: Well, hello there, Jeremy. How are you today?

JEREMY: Not so good, Mr. Berry. Champ's lost.

MR. BERRY: Champ?

JEREMY: My dog.

MR. BERRY: Oh, that's too bad, Jeremy. *(JEREMY nods.)* Well, what can I do for you?

JEREMY: My mother needs a bag of flour.

MR. BERRY: She does? She sure must be baking a lot of bread. *(Shakes his head.)* I think I can fix you up. *(He exits into the store. JEREMY starts to follow, but stops when he sees the dog enter stage left pulling a big sled. The DRIVER is whipping him and yelling.)*

SLED DRIVER: Mush, you dumb mutt! Mush! Pull that sled. *(He whips the dog.)* Come on, you stupid mongrel!

JEREMY: *(Running over to man.)* Hey, that's too heavy for your dog. He can't pull that.

SLED DRIVER: Get outa here. This is none of your business, kid.

JEREMY: But you're hurting that dog! Don't you know how that feels? (*Takes hold of DRIV-ER'S arm.*)

SLED DRIVER: Leggo my arm—or I'll show you how it feels, you little crumb! (*Pushes JERE-MY and exits right yelling at the dog.*)

            (*MR. BERRY enters from store.*)

JEREMY: Mr. Berry, did you see that mean man whipping that poor dog? What was he trying to do?

MR. BERRY: He's trying to train him to pull a sled over the snow so he can sell him to a Yukon gold miner.

JEREMY: But there isn't any snow and he didn't look like a sled dog.

MR. BERRY: No, he probably picked him up someplace for twenty-five cents and will sell him for $25. Some scalawags will do anything to make a dollar. Here's your flour. (*Hands it to JEREMY who exits stage left looking back toward where the dog disappeared.*) Hope you find your dog. (*Shakes his head and exits into store.*)

TRANSITIONAL MUSIC

SCENE IV: THE DECK OF A SHIP. THE DECK IS CROWDED WITH BOXES, BALES, HAY, ETC. PORTHOLES IN BACKGROUND. RAIL WITH LIFE PRESERV-ERS ALONG FRONT OF STAGE ON WHICH SAM WILL LEARN. FOG-HORN SOUNDS AND THE ROAR OF THE SHIP'S ENGINE IS IN THE BACKGROUND.

            (*PASSENGER enters stage left and leans on rail. SAM enters stage right with his suitcase and pauses next to the PASSENGER.*)

SAM: You headed for the Klondike too, I suppose.

PASSENGER: (*Without interest.*) Nope, not the Klondike.

SAM: I thought everybody on this boat was headed to the Klondike.

PASSENGER: I'm only going as far as Skagway.

SAM: But the gold fields are over the mountains from Skagway.

PASSENGER: That's right. Two or three months of crawling up mountains, struggling across glaciers, and shooting down rivers. Then you finally get to Dawson City—if you're lucky.

SAM: You don't sound very excited about the gold in the Klondike.

PASSENGER: No, but my brother was excited about it—real excited—until he froze to death going over the mountains.

SAM: Froze to death?

PASSENGER: On Heartbreak Pass. You maybe heard of that. I'm going to Skagway to bring him home.

SAM: Oh, I'm sorry.

PASSENGER: Yeah, well, most of them on that trail don't get rich. They're lucky if they get out alive.

SAM: But your brother had a great dream.

PASSENGER: Oh, sure. A lotta good those nuggets will do him now. Well, I'm going to try to get into the big cabin to get warm before I bed down. You'd better turn in early, or you won't find enough room for your bed roll. *(Exits stage left.)*

SAM: Thanks.

            (DOG OWNER enters stage right with CHAMP on a leash. As he nears stage left, CHAMP turns around and whines. SAM does a double take.)

SAM: Champ, is that you? *(CHAMP pulls on leash and SAM hugs him.)* It is you. *(To DOG OWNER.)* What are you doing with Champ?

OWNER: Champ? This here's "Tiger."

SAM: He's my brother's dog.

OWNER: You're nuts. I paid good money for this sled dog.

SAM: Sled dog? What do you mean "sled dog"?

OWNER: There happens to be snow up there in the Klondike, Mister. Don't you know that? You need sleds to get your gold out and dogs to pull the sleds. Come on, Tiger.

SAM: Well, you can't take Champ. Come on, Champ. See, he knows me. It's him. Where'd you get him, anyway?

OWNER: Listen, fella, I paid $50 for this dog and he's mine.

SAM: Well, you got gypped. He's no more a sled dog than I am. I'll buy him back.

OWNER: If you've got $200 you can have him.

SAM: $200! But you only paid $50.

OWNER: Prices have gone up. Dogs are hard to come by in Skagway.

SAM: I can't afford $200.

OWNER: Take it or leave it, fella. *(When SAM doesn't answer, he shrugs.)* Come on, Tiger. *(CHAMP whines as OWNER pulls him off stage left. SAM looks after them and puts his head in his hands, leaning over the rail. He exits stage right.)*

TRANSITIONAL MUSIC

SCENE V: CRAWFORD LIVING ROOM

(MRS. CRAWFORD enters stage right with broom and sweeps during next conversation. JEREMY enters with his school books, which he throws on floor, and flops into the chair.)

MRS. C.: How was school today, Jeremy?

JEREMY: *(Disinterestedly.)* All right.

MRS. C.: I hope you aren't thinking about Champ so much you're not paying attention in school.

JEREMY: No, Mama.

MRS. C.: *(Looks at JEREMY and thinks.)* Jeremy, Champ's been gone for ten days. I think you'll have to face the fact that he may not be coming back.

JEREMY: I know.

MRS. C.: The Meriweathers have a collie that is going to have puppies soon. Maybe we can get one of them for you.

JEREMY: I don't want a puppy. I want Champ back.

MRS. C.:   Well, I can't say I really want a puppy now either, but I do think that collies are nice dogs.

               (Sound of a dog barking.)

JEREMY: What's that? It sounds like Champ. *(Sits up excitedly.)*

MRS. C.:   Now don't get excited, dear. It's probably some dog on the street.

JEREMY: No. No. It's Champ. *(Jumps up. Sound of a door opening. CHAMP enters followed by SAM.)* Champ! *(Hugs CHAMP)* Oh, where did you find him, Sam?

SAM: I bought him from a miner on the boat, Jeremy.

JEREMY: You bought him?

SAM: Yes, and believe me, Jeremy, Champ's the gold nugget I promised you. After I paid to get him back, I didn't have enough money to go any place but back home. I got off in Ketchican and hopped the next boat back to Seattle.

JEREMY: Then he *was* stolen. Oh, Champ. *(Hugs the dog again.)* Oh, thank you, Sam.

MRS. C.:   Your father will be as glad to hear the news as we are. You'd better go down to the mill right now and tell him.

SAM: Yeah, I have to pick up my gear too. I'll see you soon. *(Hugs his mother.)* And Mama, I am glad to be back. *(Exits stage right.)*

MRS. C.:   Welcome back, Champ. *(CHAMP yelps happily.)* I think the first thing we should do is give Champ a nice bath. *(CHAMP jerks to attention, howls, and runs around the room before exiting stage right with JEREMY chasing right behind him. MRS. CRAWFORD watches them go, shakes her head, and follows them.)*

Production Notes

A two-dimensional cut-out of sturdy material, wood or heavy cardboard, may be used for the sled and sled driver in Scene III. The dog may be a stick puppet.

High Priority

by Jean M. Mattson

CHARACTERS

Melvin Casper—a prison resident
Cook
Guard
McClellen—custody unit supervisor
Supplies supervisor
Parker—a counsellor
Sgt. Lee
Painter—a prison resident
P.A. system voice
Narrator's voice

PROPS

Recipe book
Cannisters
Boxes
Jars
Box
Steam cleaner
Paint bucket and brush
Papers
Book and paper

SOUND EFFECTS

Steam cleaner

SET PIECES

Table with pot and spoon
Basket and 2 buckets
Cupboard
Desk
Counter
Conference room
Table
Waiting room
Bench

This play was written with the cooperation of residents of Monroe State Reformatory under a grant from the Washington Commission for the Humanities. It has six scenes and five simple sets—a kitchen, an office, a janitorial department, a conference room/waiting room and a library.

INTRODUCTORY MUSIC

NARRATOR: Among the rolling hills of Washington rise the walls of the Monroe State Reformatory. Inside these walls, Melvin Casper, a new resident, is finishing the second day of his first job assignment in the main kitchen. We find him here now, sorting out a basket of tomatoes.

SCENE I: **THE PRISON KITCHEN. THERE IS A TABLE DOWNSTAGE RIGHT WITH A LARGE POT AND SPOON. UPSTAGE RIGHT IS A CUPBOARD. ON STAGE LEFT ARE TWO BUCKETS AND A LARGE BASKET.**

(CASPER is busy sorting tomatoes from the basket into the two buckets. COOK enters stage right with a book.)

COOK: Ain't you finished with those tomatoes yet?

CASPER: Almost.

COOK: Well, knock it off for now. I want you to put this spaghetti sauce together. *(CASPER approaches table.)* Here's the recipe. *(Puts book down and opens it.)* All the stuff is there in the cupboard. *(CASPER looks.)* Now get a move on. *(COOK exits stage right.)*

CASPER: *(Looks at the recipe book and then at the cupboard. Takes a close look at the recipe book.)* Oh, who needs a recipe for spaghetti sauce! *(He closes the book with a snap, goes to the cupboard and proceeds to throw this and that into the pot, checking the contents of the containers and nodding as he goes. He stirs the mixture.)*

COOK: *(Entering stage right.)* Everything in?

CASPER: Yeah.

COOK: *(Tastes it. Looks at CASPER.)* Hey, this stuff doesn't taste right. *(Tastes it again.)* This tastes awful!

CASPER: Doesn't it always?

COOK: This mess could start a riot.

CASPER: I just put the stuff in like you told me.

COOK: Look, fella, you fouled up the minestrone soup yesterday. I can't afford to have any-one around who's a dumpaholic. I'll have to talk to McClellan about reassigning you.

CASPER: But I did what you told me.

COOK: Check out, Bud. Now!

CASPER: See ya around.

(CASPER slowly exits stage left, looking back as COOK looks into the pot, shaking his head. Cook exits stage right.)

TRANSITIONAL MUSIC

NARRATOR: It was not long before Casper had an appointment in the office of Mr. McClellan, the custody unit supervisor.

SCENE II: McCLELLAN'S OFFICE. THERE IS A DESK STAGE RIGHT CENTER.

(McCLELLAN and CASPER enter stage left. McCLELLAN sits at desk.)

McCLELLAN: The kitchen staff tells me that you were having some problems there?

CASPER: That's what they say.

McCLELLAN: According to the latest report, the cook gave you a list of the ingredients you were to use and the amounts you were to add to the spaghetti sauce. Right?

CASPER: Right. And I did just that.

McCLELLAN: The report says you ruined the whole batch. What was the problem?

CASPER: That cook always blamed me for everything that went wrong around there. He's a state employee. They're always picking on us, you know that. And he was picking on me.

McCLELLAN: So you think it might be a personality conflict, then?

CASPER: Yeah—yeah. That's it! That's it! And I can tell you something else—as a cook he was a good cement mixer. He didn't know basil from belly buttons!

McCLELLAN: Hmm. Well, we try to find job assignments that are compatible with each resident, Casper. *(Looks at his reports.)* They can use another helper in the Supplies & Janitorial Department. Does that sound like something you could handle?

CASPER: Sure, I can handle that. Piece a cake.

McCLELLAN: There's also a supervisor over there that's easy to work for. You can report there at 8:00 A.M. tomorrow.

          (CASPER exits stage left. McCLELLAN watches him go and then exits stage right.)

TRANSITIONAL MUSIC

SCENE III: SUPPLIES & JANITORIAL DEPARTMENT. COUNTER ON STAGE LEFT.

          (SUPERVISOR enters stage right with papers and goes behind the counter. CASPER enters stage right with box.)

CASPER: Can you check what was on that list of things for the laundry?

SUPERVISOR: *(Looking at the list.)* They need two boxes of soap, a case of bleach, and one can of oil.

CASPER: Coming right up. *(Starts to exit stage left.)*

SUPERVISOR: Oh, yes. The carpets in the main offices need to be cleaned. And you might as well do this one too.

CASPER: Oh. O.K.

SUPERVISOR: The steam cleaner is in the storeroom. You helped the other day. Do you think you can run it by yourself?

CASPER: Piece a cake. *(Exits stage left.)*

GUARD: *(Enters stage right.)* I'm from the cell blocks. And yesterday we ordered a long list of stuff—and we didn't get what we ordered.

SUPERVISOR: What do you mean "You didn't get what you ordered"? We sent over a big load, I remember.

GUARD: Yeah, it was a big load. But we ordered the brown paper towels and we got white.

SUPERVISOR: Well, that can happen.

GUARD: Yeah, but we ordered two cases of bar soap and ten cases of toilet paper. We got two cases of toilet paper and ten of soap.

SUPERVISOR: Well, that is rather . . .

GUARD: And then the brushes . . .

SUPERVISOR: What about the brushes?

GUARD: I mean, we hate to complain but some of the men had a darn hard time brushing their teeth with those scrub brushes.

SUPERVISOR: Well, I'm sorry. We'll get it straightened out. I'll take care of it this right away.

GUARD: Thanks. We'd appreciate that. *(Exits stage right.)*

                (SUPERVISOR looks at his papers. There is a loud noise of rattling, gushing, and pounding. CASPER enters stage left with the steam cleaner, which is violently thrashing and spouting water.)

SUPERVISOR: *(Excitedly.)* What is it? What's wrong? *(He runs around the counter and turns it off.)* What happened?

CASPER: It went crazy, that's what happened. What kind of equipment have you got around here, anyway? I can't run a thing like that.

SUPERVISOR: Never mind. I'll have Nick take care of it. It's never done that before. Always something! *(Goes behind counter.)* Now, Casper, I believe you were the one who made up the order yesterday for the cell block.

CASPER: Yes, I did.

SUPERVISOR: Well, we just had a complaint. Seems the order was screwed up.

CASPER: Well, what do you know!

SUPERVISOR: And that isn't the first time lately that we've had mix-ups. You don't seem to be keeping your mind on the job, Casper.

CASPER: Well, there are a lot of distractions around here.

SUPERVISOR: That may be, but we need someone working here who cares enough about doing a good job to work through those distractions. I don't think you are cut out for this department, Casper.

CASPER: Wait a minute. That's not fair. I work hard pushing these crates around all day.

SUPERVISOR: I am responsible for all the orders that go out of this place, and I need people who pay attention to detail. You're a good worker, but "detail" doesn't seem to be one of your strong points.

CASPER: But I like it here.

SUPERVISOR: We like you too, Casper, but I have to be realistic.

CASPER: This is discrimination!

SUPERVISOR: McClellan will find a place that needs what you have to offer. I'll give him a call.

> *(CASPER exits stage right mumbling and complaining, "They don't know a good worker when they see one," etc.)*

SUPERVISOR: *(Goes over and looks at steam cleaner.)* Never had trouble with that steam cleaner before. I wonder what went wrong? *(Exits stage left.)*

TRANSITIONAL MUSIC

SCENE IV: McCELLAN'S OFFICE.

> *(McCLELLAN and CASPER enter stage left. McCLELLAN sits at his desk.)*

McCLELLAN: The supervisor over there reports that you didn't seem to keep your mind on your work. Orders were always getting mixed up.

CASPER: Yeah, I guess my mind was on other things. It's traumatic to come into a place like this—'n I miss my wife and kids—you know.

McCLELLAN: *(Reading the report.)* You managed to clog up the steam cleaner.

CASPER: Those old machines are always breaking down. How can anybody do a good job with pieces of junk?

McCLELLAN: And you refused to learn how to operate the buffer machine.

CASPER: Well, I'm allergic to wax. Always been sensitive.

McCLELLAN: Seems you are sensitive to a lot of things.

CASPER: Besides, that job is boring. Toting toilet paper and bleach around isn't exactly the most interesting way to spend the day.

McCLELLAN: Uh-huh. Well, my job is not to keep you entertained.

CASPER: Yeah.

McCLELLAN: How about taking some classes?

CASPER: Go to school? No—no. Teachers can't teach me nothing.

McCLELLAN: Casper, it's my job to arrange some kind of productive activities for you while you are here.

CASPER: Listen, they're lucky to have me around.

McCLELLAN: I feel you have potential, but you have to do your part.

CASPER: Hey, I can sing. Maybe I can sing for my supper.

McCLELLAN: We'll see what we can do. I'll talk to you at the 6-month review. In the meantime, I'm assigning you to the print shop.

CASPER: Hey, that sounds like the place for me. *(They exeunt.)*

TRANSITIONAL MUSIC

SCENE V: CONFERENCE ROOM. DOOR STAGE CENTER DIVIDING THE CONFERENCE ROOM WITH TABLE ON STAGE RIGHT AND THE WAITING ROOM WITH a GREEN BENCH ON STAGE LEFT. A "CONFERENCE ROOM 6" SIGN CAN BE SEEN.

P.A. SYSTEM VOICE: Attention Mr. Parker, Sgt. Lee, and Mr. McClellan, your Review Committee meeting will be in Conference Room 6.

(PAINTER enters waiting room stage left with paint bucket and paints the bench. He hangs a sign "Wet Paint" on wall behind the bench.)

PAINTER: They oughta paint these benches red. Liven things up around here. *(Exits stage left.)*

(PARKER, SGT. LEE and McCLELLAN enter stage left with papers. They proceed to Conference Room and sit at table.)

PARKER: Since we have a lot to cover, let's get started. This first man, Melvin Casper, I have not met, but there's a lot of paperwork on him. *(Looks at papers.)* Fired from every job assignment. Doesn't participate in activities.

McCLELLAN: But he hasn't had any actual infractions. In each case, he just didn't work out.

PARKER: Are you telling me! How do you explain the snafu on the state Public Safety manual? That was one of the print shops income-producing jobs. A rush job and it ended up two weeks late.

McCLELLAN: Well, I don't—

PARKER: Plates confused so columns didn't match up. Pages were out of order and upside down. They had new mothers going to the Energy Commission and plumbers applying to the Animal Control Board. Never had trouble until Casper came on board.

SGT. LEE: Sounds to me like blatant irresponsibility.

McCLELLAN: No. I've been working with him. He's willing to work and seems to have real possibilities, but I just haven't been able to figure out what they are.

SGT. LEE: That's for sure. Maybe he needs to be in solitary for a while.

McCLELLAN: He's intelligent, but he's on the defensive for some reason. I can't seem to get to him.

SGT. LEE: I know these guys. It's a waste of time worrying about them.

McCLELLAN: I'm convinced he's worth the effort.

PARKER: Well, let's talk to him.

McCLELLAN: *(Goes to the phone and announces.)* Will Melvin Casper report to Conference Room 6. *(Returns to table. CASPER enters waiting room, knocks, and goes into the Conference Room, where he stands before the committee.)* This is Melvin Casper. Casper, this is Sgt. Lee and Mr. Parker. *(They respond.)*

PARKER: How are you doing, Casper?

CASPER: Well, I'm still here.

PARKER: How's your work going?

CASPER: Haven't found a place that's comfortable yet. But I'm sure I will.

SGT. LEE: Why don't you tell us about the jobs you've had. *(Wants to get rid of this problem.)*

CASPER: Oh, I'm sure it's all in the reports. I don't know why those things happened. It wasn't my fault. I tried to do a good job.

PARKER: All just coincidence, huh?

CASPER: What can I say?

McCLELLAN: If you don't have anything else to say, why don't you step out into the waiting area. We have to discuss several possibilities here. We'll call you.

(CASPER exits into waiting room and sits down on the newly painted bench as the painter re-enters with his bucket.)

PAINTER: Eeowww! What are you doing? You knucklehead, get up off that bench. Ya work your tail off around here and some stupid jerk comes along and . . .

CASPER: Hey, what's with you anyway?

(The Review Committee has risen and is looking into the waiting room to see what the commotion is all about.)

PAINTER: "What's with me," he says. I worked hard on this bench—and then this jerk comes along and sits on it. *(Looks at Casper, who gets up, turns around, and looks at the bench. His back is covered with paint.)* What'sa matter with you? Can't ya read?

(Silence as everyone realizes the truth. Committee members look at each other.)

PARKER: You can touch this up later, George. You did a nice job. Thanks. Come on, Casper.

(PAINTER exits, and CASPER enters meeting area. The Committee sits at the table again.)

McCLELLAN: Now, Casper, I guess we've found the cause of the problem. You had trouble in the kitchen because you couldn't read the recipes. Right? *(CASPER hangs his head.)* You couldn't read the lists in the supply department or read the directions for the steam cleaner? *(CASPER nods.)* And you couldn't tell the difference in the plates at the print shop. *(CASPER shakes his head.)* Casper, I think we need to talk about something we call the Reading Program. *(McCLELLAN looks at PARKER and SGT. LEE, who nod.)* Come on, I'll tell you all about it and sign you up. *(All four exeunt.)*

TRANSITIONAL MUSIC

NARRATOR: A year and a half later, Mr. McClellan found Casper in the prison library.

SCENE VI: PRISON LIBRARY. THERE IS A TABLE CENTER STAGE.

(Casper enters stage left with paper and book, which he lays on table. Mc-CLELLAN enters stage right.)

McCLELLAN: You received a notice today, I believe. *(CASPER nods.)* Could you read it?

CASPER: *(Nods happily and looks down at the paper and reads rather haltingly.)* Melvin Casper is hereby granted a parole.

McCLELLAN: And that's only the beginning of the great things you'll be reading from now on. Congratulations and good luck, Casper. *(They shake hands and exeunt.)*

FINALE

NARRATOR'S VOICE: So as the gates of the prison open to physical freedom in a familiar world, Casper's newly acquired reading skills provide an entrance into a brand-new world full of knowledge, endless possibilities, and promise.

Production Notes

The pot should be attached to the table and the spoon to the inside of the pot.

For Scene V, if the stage is large enough, it can be divided into two sections. Instead of a wall dividing the two, sound effects of a door opening and closing and knocking can create the illusion of two rooms.

Velcro can be used on strips of green, which will attach themselves to Casper's uniform when he sits down on the bench.

King Pinch of Oregano

by Jean M. Mattson

From an old Italian folktale, "The Value of Salt."

CHARACTERS
King Pinch of Oregano
Princess Carrotina
Princess Spinachina
Princess Stringa Beana
Mozzarelli—castle cook
Castle guard

PROPS
Table, with dishes
Salt shaker
Separate dish

SET PIECES
Castle interior
Castle courtyard (which
  includes a tower with
  a window)

A play in three scenes with two sets, castle interior and castle courtyard, written for two puppeteers.

SCENE I: CASTLE INTERIOR.

(KING PINCH enters and moves to center stage.)

K. PINCH: King Pinch of Oregano, that's me.
  A kingly king—as you can see.
  I have a throne. I rule a land.
  I wear a crown and I command.
  I am a king with daughters three,
  Three princesses of rare beauty.
  Carrotina, *(CARROTINA enters left.)*
  Spinachina. *(Enters right.)*
  And Stringa Beana. *(Enters right.)*
  Affairs of state don't bother me,
  Important as they may be.
  What really worries me is what
  My daughters think of me.
  Listen, daughters, hear me well.
  Do you love me? Tell me, tell.

DAUGHTERS: *(All together.)*
  Oh, yes, Father. Yes, Father. Yes,
  Father. Yes.
  Our love for you is bottomless.

K. PINCH: Would you, if I were not king
  Still love me more than anything?

DAUGHTERS: *(All together.)*
  Oh, yes, Father. Yes, Father. Yes,
  Father, Yes.
  We would love you, nevertheless.

K. PINCH: Are you positive?

CARROTINA: Positive. *(Exits left.)*

K. PINCH: Honest?

SPINACHINA: Honest. *(Exits right.)*

K. PINCH: Really?

STRINGA B: Really! *(Exits right.)*

K. PINCH: *(Pacing.)* I'm still not satisfied.
  Do you think they speak true?
  I'll call each one in by herself
  And see what she will do.

K. PINCH: Stringa Beana, Stringa Beana!
  (STRINGA B. enters right.)
  I find that I am sad.
  I must know once and for all time
  How much you love your dear old
  dad.

STRINGA B: Father, must you ask again?
  You must know what I've said.
  But, listen, and I'll try once more.
  I love you—ahh—as much as bread.
  (Exits stage right.)

K. PINCH: Ah-ha. She says as much as
  bread.
  Now that's a wise reply.
  We must have bread to live.
  She means without me she would die.
  Now, Spinachina, dear,
  Come here, come here, come here.
  (She enters right.)
  I have a question I must ask.
  I've simply got to know.
  I must know how much you love me.
  Speak, then you may go.

SPINACHINA: Oh, Father dear, oh, Father,
  mine.
  Why, I love you as much as wine.
  (SPINACHINA exits right.)

K. PINCH: Ah, she loves me just as much as
  wine.
  Now that's a nice new touch.
  For wine gives life a sparkle.
  That shows she loves me much.
  Now, let's see what the third one
  says.

Carrotina, please come in.
(*She enters left.*)
Now, tell me something that will show
Your love for me is genuine.

CARROTINA: Hm. I love you—like—
ahh—I love the sun. (*King nods.
She rubs her chin and paces.*)
No—perhaps a chocolate malt.
No. Diamonds? Rubies? Golden
coins? (*KING leans forward
expectantly.*)
Oh, (*Firmly.*) I love you as much
as—salt.

K. PINCH: Did I hear you say "salt"?
That cheap and common stuff!
It's almost worthless!

CARROTINA: Father—I—

K. PINCH: Enough! I've had enough!
To the tower with this wretch!
To the tower! Hide the key!
She's my daughter so be kind,
But keep her hence away from me!

CARROTINA: But—Father! Please!

K. PINCH: Hear what I say.
Remove her now. Take her away!
(*GUARD holds CARROTINA as
her puppeteer slides hand out of
puppet. He exits with her stage
right.*)

K. PINCH: What have I done to so deserve
Such an ungrateful daughter?
Just how did she forget so soon
The things that I have taught her?
(*KING exits left.*)

TRANSITIONAL MUSIC

SCENE II: CASTLE COURTYARD. TOWER ON STAGE RIGHT.

(*CARROTINA appears in tower window.*)

CARROTINA: Ah, me. I'm so unhappy.
Ah, me. I'm so alone.
I used to always smile
And now I moan and groan.
My tiny window overlooks
The courtyard here below.
I sometimes see the palace cook
Walking to and fro.
(*MOZZARELLI enters stage left.*)

MOZZARELLI: Whenever they want royal
food
They send for Mozzarelli.
They deem my dishes fit for kings.
How they taste and how they smelli.
(*Singing*) Spaaaaa—ghetti! Lasagne.
Raviola! Cacciatore!
Everything-a that I cook-a
Is-a simply—hunky dory!
(*La-la-la's the song.*)

CARROTINA: Mozzarelli! Mozzarelli!
Can you hear me down there?

MOZZARELLI: I can hear you. I can hear
you
But, Princess, please beware.
(*MOZZARELLI looks around
fearfully.*)
If the king knew we had talked,
Oh, my—we'd be in trouble.
He'd probably lop off my head,
And he'd do it on the double.

CARROTINA: You know I'm miserable up
here.
I can't do anything.

MOZZARELLI: But I can't help you now
unless I disobey the king.

CARROTINA: Oh, Mozzarelli, please—for
    me—
    Do just one tiny favor,
    And when you cook the meal tonight,
    Put in no salt as flavor.
    (*MOZZARELLI thinks.*)

MOZZARELLI: Ah, Signorina, very well,
    That favor I will do.
    I'll not put salt in anything.
    I hope that it helps you.
    (Singing.) Spaaaaa—ghetti! Lasa-
    gne! Raviola! Cacciatore!
    Everything-a that I cook-a
    Is-a simply—*(Exits left and
    reappears.)*—hunky dory! *(Exits
    left instantly.)*

TRANSITIONAL MUSIC

SCENE III: CASTLE INTERIOR. A TABLE IS CENTER STAGE.

*(MOZZARELLI enters stage, with tray,
which he places on table and exits.
KING enters stage left.)*

K. PINCH: Mozzarelli! I am hungry.
    Mozzarelli! Where is he?
    Set the table! Bring the food!
    Mozzarelli. Answer me!
    *(MOZZARELLI enters stage right
    with additional dish.)*

MOZZARELLI: (*Singing.*) Spaaaaa—
    ghetti! Lasagne!
    Raviola! Cacciatore!
    Everything-a that I cook-a
    Is-a simply hunky dory!
    (*K. PINCH begins to eat, tasting
    and tasting, then spits the food
    out.*)

K. PINCH: What is the matter? What is
    wrong?
    I cannot stand this food!
    Why, everything is awful—
    The worst I've ever chewed!
    The soup tastes just like water.
    The fish is dull and flat.
    The vegetables are tasteless.
    I can't eat food like that!

MOZZARELLI: King Pinch, I must confess.
    It really is my fault.
    I cooked it all as usual
    Except I left out salt.

K. PINCH: You left out salt? You left out
    salt? (*MOZZARELLI leaps back-
    wards.*)

MOZZARELLI: It's cheap and common
    stuff.
    You said it is quite worthless.
    So I thought you'd had enough.

K. PINCH: Why, salt gives joy to eating,
    Puts zest in every dish,
    Excitement in the sauces,
    And "zingy" in the fish! (*Suddenly
    realizes what he is saying.*)
    Ahhh—ahhh—ahhh. Ahhh—
    Go fetch my daughter.
    (*MOZZARELLI exits stage right.*)
    I know now how she feels.
    I'm as important to that girl
    As is salt to all our meals.
    She loves me. I was wrong.
    That girl is kind and good.

CARROTINA: Father, dear—

K. PINCH: My Daughter!
    How I misunderstood!

CARROTINA: Don't worry, Father. I'm just
      glad
      You know the truth at last.
      Let's have a fine reunion
      And forget about the past.

K. PINCH: Ah, yes, my darling daughter,
      come.
      There's no time for remorse.
      Let's have a banquet now.
      But—pass the salt, of course!
      (*MOZZARELLI enters right and
      shakes salt onto the food on the
      table. KING and CARROTINA
      laugh. MOZZARELLI exits. KING
      PINCH AND CARROTINA rise,
      turn to audience and bow before
      they exeunt.*)

MUSIC SWELLS FOR FINALE

Production Notes

There are no outstanding production problems in this play.

The Princess and the Pea

by Jean M. Mattson

CHARACTERS
King
Prince Harry
Princess Wilhelmina, an
   obnoxious hopeful
Princess Gwen

PROPS
Basket with clothes
Gwen's cloak
Gwen's robe and
   nightcap

SOUND EFFECTS
Bugle fanfare
Gate opening

SET PIECES
Castle interior with
   banners
List of Princesses
   on a stand
Table
Bed with many
   mattresses

A very popular Hans Christian Anderson story with three scenes but only one set, designed for two puppeteers.

INTRODUCTORY MUSIC

SCENE I: CASTLE INTERIOR. THERE IS A TABLE TO THE RIGHT OF CENTER STAGE AND A STAND WITH PRINCESSES' NAMES ON STAGE LEFT.

(PRINCE HARRY enters stage left, head bowed, looks at list of princesses, and paces back and forth.)

KING: I am the king of Wilkenshire.
    And here's my son, Prince Harry.
    We're looking for a maiden fair
    Whom he can safely marry.

PRINCE: Great beauty and perfection
    I do not have in mind.
    I'd like a bride who's pleasant, is
    Considerate and kind.
    Why does it have to be so hard
    To find a wife for me?

KING: Tut-tut, my boy, you know full well
    A princess she must be.

PRINCE: I've looked at princesses all day.
    It's been a real parade.
    I'm sick of golden slippers
    And satins and brocade.
KING: There's yet one more for you to see.
    (Looks at list.)
    She's princess to the core.
    She may well be the charming girl
    That you've been waiting for.

BUGLE FANFARE

(KING and PRINCE HARRY look toward stage left.)

WILHELMINA: *(Enters stage left.)*
    You now are privileged to meet

The Princess Wilhelmina.
    My famous lineage long has ruled
    The kingdom of Selena.
    My pointed head just fits a crown,
    And I have a queen-sized nose.
    My blood is blue as blue can be,
    And I wear jewelled clothes.

PRINCE: Well, thank you, but you just
    won't do.

WILHELMINA: But I came in all this
    weather.
    My coach was almost stuck in mud!

PRINCE: We would never fit together.

WILHELMINA: Well, you'll be awfully
    sorry
    When you realize at last
    That I've slipped through your
    fingers.

PRINCE: My dear, the die is cast.

(WILHELMINA exits left with vociferous exclamations.)

KING: Ah, she's a princess, there's no
    doubt.

PRINCE: But Father, how absurd—
    To think I'd ever marry her,
    That puffed-up jabber-bird!
    And everyone's been just as bad.
    (Looks at scroll.)
    One princess was plain rude.
    And one kept spitting all the time,
    And one spoke just of food.
    I'll tell you, I have had enough!
    This makes me furious.
    Why can't I marry whom I choose
    Without this royal fuss?

Prince Harry reads the list of potential brides in *The Princess and the Pea*. Puppet by Joan king.

KING: It is the law of Wilkenshire—
An ancient king's decree—
A prince can only choose a bride
Who comes from royalty.

PRINCE: I hate that stupid, silly law!
I hate this single life!
The way that things are going
I'll never find a wife. *(Turns away.)*

KING: We've never had a bachelor yet
Upon our family tree.
We'll find a princess. That I know.
Now you just wait and see. *(Pats PRINCE's arm.)*

(NOISE OF GATE OPENING)

What is that rattling at the gate?
Oh, they're letting someone through.
What man would travel in this storm?

PRINCE: I'll go and find out who.
(PRINCE exits stage left.)

KING: *(Looks to see who is coming.)*

My, my, it is an awful night.
The roads would not be safe
Who is it ? *(PRINCE and GWEN enter left.)* Oh, what have we here?
A wet, bedraggled waif?

GWEN: I'm sorry to intrude. I lost
My bearings in the storm.

PRINCE: It's clear she needs some food
And a fire to keep her warm.

KING: *(Looks at her)* You need someone to
wring you out.

PRINCE: She needs dry clothes to wear.

KING: Take her to the kitchen.
We help the beggars there.

GWEN: Oh, no. I am a princess, Sire.

KING: Why, that's ridiculous.
You neither look nor sound like one.

PRINCE: Father, let her speak to us.
(Pause while KING and GWEN sit at the table.)

GWEN: I'm Gwen from Orangeadia.
My father was the king.

KING: What do you have to prove it?

GWEN: I don't have anything.
Our kingdom fell. My parents died.
I've wandered ever since.
I heard your story, and I've come
To meet your son, the prince.

KING: A princess? Ha! You have no crown.
Attendents you have none.

PRINCE: She has a royal flair.

KING: But she needs more than that, my
    son.

GWEN: I cannot blame you if you doubt
    That I am who I say.
    Just give me lodging for the night
    Then I'll be on my way.

KING: Oh, very well. You'll have your bed.

GWEN: Oh, thank you. You are kind.

KING: *(To PRINCE)* Go see that she's
    attended to. *(PRINCE and
    PRINCESS exeunt stage center.)*
    Methinks that love is blind.
    I saw the way he looked at her.
    My son is captivated.
    This girl might lead to problems
    I had not contemplated.
    (PRINCE re-enters excitedly.)

PRINCE: It's very strange. Somehow I know
    That what she says is true.
    She's sweet, compassionate and kind,
    A girl that I could woo.

KING: Now, don't get all excited, son.
    I think that girl's a fake.

PRINCE: I do not want to miss my chance.

KING: Or make a big mistake!

PRINCE: At last I've found the girl for
    whom
    I've waited all my life.
    And I believe her story's true.
    I want her for my wife.

KING: But wait, I think there is a way
    To prove her story true.
    An age-old test that never fails.
    Now, here's what we must do.

    Find featherbeds and mattresses.
    They must be nice and thick.
    We'll settle this once and for all.

PRINCE: Yes, yes, let's make it quick.
    (Exeunt.)

TRANSITIONAL MUSIC

SCENE II: CASTLE BEDROOM. BED WITH MATTRESSES ON STAGE CENTER.

(KING and PRINCE enter.)

MUSIC FADES

KING: See, under all her mattresses
    I slip this tiny pea.

PRINCE: I see. Whatever will that prove?

KING: Now, son, have faith in me.
    A princess has such delicate,
    Such sensitive, soft skin
    That Gwen will surely feel this pea
    If she is genuine.
    Come now, your future rests.

PRINCE: My future? *(Looks at pea.)* On a
    pea?
    *(Exeunt stage left. GWEN enters
    stage right.)*

GWEN: My goodness sake. Could this
    whole bed
    Be waiting just for me? *(Looks at it
    from all angles.)*
    However do I manage this?
    Do I climb or scale or leap? *(Climbs
    up and in with much groaning.)*
    Say this is quite a bed-y-bye.
    Oh, I really have to sleep.

(Much grunting and groaning and moving about. She throws herself all over the bed for some time.)

TRANSITIONAL MUSIC

(Bed disappears.)

SCENE III: CASTLE THRONE ROOM.

(KING enters stage right and sits at table. PRINCE enters stage right.)

PRINCE: Is she awake this morning, sir?

KING: No sign of her as yet.

PRINCE: This waiting makes me anxious.

KING: Come, come, my son, don't fret.
    She'll soon be down. But listen—
    She's coming now, I think.
    (GWEN enters.)
    Good morning, dear. Did you sleep well?

GWEN: I did not sleep a wink.
    I tossed and turned and rolled about.
    I was discomforted.
    I'm every bit as tired now
    As when I went to bed.
    (KING and PRINCE looks at each other.)
    I seemed to feel an awful lump
    No matter how I shifted.

PRINCE: Father, do you now believe?

KING: My doubts have all been lifted.

PRINCE: Thank heaven, that's been settled.
    You are my bride-to-be.

GWEN: *(Puzzling.)* But how—?

PRINCE: You owe it all, my dear,
    To a tiny round, green pea.

KING: And so my son can married be.
    Let there be joy and laughter.
    We'll celebrate a wedding
    And be happy ever after.

FINALE

(As they take their bows.)

Production Notes

List of Princesses—The scroll or book of princesses' names can be on a podium-shaped box, a small table, or a small easel.

Table—A gold lamé cloth can transform a box into a very royal table.

Bed with Mattresses—The bed can be made from a box covered on three sides with quilted striped materal or with a number of fabric strips sewn together and padded. The top of the box should be cut to accommodate the puppeteer's arm. A blanket and a pillow should be fastened onto the top. When the princess is in the bed, the puppeteer's other hand can be used under the blanket to create her restlessness. The hand of the second puppeteer may be needed to help with this movement and also to handle the clamp that must be used to secure the bed to the playboard. The flopping about in the bed should be greatly exaggerated.

The Puppeteer

by Jean M. Mattson

A play based on a Hans Christian Anderson story.

CHARACTERS
Puppeteer (an actor)
Audience member (an actor)
Princess
Frog
Prince
King
Queen

PROPS
Golden ball

SETS
Back of a puppet stage set for the last scene of "The Frog Prince" with a castle, well, and trees and bushes
The playboard as a work table for the puppeteer with piles of cloth, a puppet stand and puppet props

When Hans Christian Anderson was a boy, he made puppets and presented puppet shows. His story "The Puppeteer" reflects this interest. The play combines puppets and actors (three puppeteers, two doubling as actors). It has two scenes and two sets.

INTRODUCTORY MUSIC

NARRATOR: *(Possibly a live announcement.)* When Hans Christian Anderson was a boy he made puppets and presented puppet shows. His story "The Puppeteer" reflects this interest. Our play is based on this story and begins as a puppeteer is concluding his performance of "The Frog Prince."

SCENE I: **ON CENTER STAGE IN FRONT OF THE MAIN PUPPET STAGE IS A SMALL PUPPET STAGE SET SO THAT THE AUDIENCE IS VIEWING BACKSTAGE AND CAN WATCH THE PUPPETEER AS HE MANIPULATES THE PUPPETS. THE PUPPETEER HAS BEEN GETTING READY AS THE NARRATOR IS ANNOUNCING THE PLAY. A CASTLE IS ON STAGE LEFT, A WELL CENTER STAGE, AND FLOWERS STAGE RIGHT. THE PUPPETEER NOW HAS THE PRINCESS ON HIS RIGHT HAND AND THE KING ON HIS LEFT.**

KING: My daughter, I have tried to teach you to behave with integrity and honor because some day you will be queen. You made a promise. Your ball was returned to you, so you must now honor that promise.

PRINCESS: But I don't want to kiss a frog.

KING: Perhaps not. But a promise is a promise *(Exits stage left.)*

PRINCESS: *(Mimics.)* A promise is a promise. Da-de-da-de-da. I'd like to see him kiss an old frog. *(Looks after KING.)* Imagine, my own father wants me to kiss a frog. Ohhh! *(Thinking about it.)* Ohh. All right. I'll close my eyes so I can't see the slimy thing. And I'll hold my breath. *(Leans over well.)* Frog! Frog! Come up. Come up. *(FROG appears on rim of well.)* I will kiss you. *(Leans over, kisses FROG and quickly turns away.)* There! Is that what you wanted? *(Pause.)* Well, is it? *(She turns to well.)* Oh—ahh—where is that frog? *(Looks at PRINCE.)* Who are you?

PRINCE: Clarinda. I am that frog.

PRINCESS: *(Screeches.)* What?

PRINCE: You see, years ago the Witch of Murky placed a spell upon me because I wouldn't marry her. I was destined to be a frog until a girl who did not know about the spell would kiss me. And you, my dear Clarinda, were noble enough to keep your promise. You did kiss me.

PRINCESS: And am I glad I did. Oh, oh, oh.

PRINCE: You are the girl I've been waiting for—in more ways than one. Come, we must talk to your father. (*CLARINDA and PRINCE exeunt stage left. PUPPETEER turns on tape recorder and music swells.*)

PUPPETEER: And so the prince and the princess were married. Clarinda fulfilled her father's expectations and, of course, they all lived happily ever after.

(*Applause. PUPPETEER takes his bow. Applause dies down, and he starts to put away his equipment. *)

PUPPETEER: (*Looking at the PRINCE.*) Oh, your coat needs to be mended. (*Looks at CLARINDA.*) And your hairdo needs a bit of attention. Always something. I suppose I should check them all over.

SPECTATOR: (*Approaching PUPPETEER from stage left.*) Oh, that was a such a nice show. You did a good job. (*PUPPETEER acknowledges the compliment.*) Do you make your own puppets? (*Watches him pack up.*)

PUPPETEER: Yes, I do.

SPECTATOR: What a lot of work!

PUPPETEER: It's a labor of love. (*Continuing to pack equipment.*)

SPECTATOR: Oh, it must be wonderful to be a puppeteer—to perform your shows—to tell stories that entertain people.

PUPPETEER: It has its advantages, of course.

SPECTATOR: But to be welcomed in every town, adored by children, praised, and applauded.

PUPPETEER: Madam, I enjoy what I do or I wouldn't be doing it. But it's not as idyllic as you make it out to be.

SPECTATOR: What more could you want?

PUPPETEER: Well—actually I've always dreamed of directing a real theatre where the actors were real people, not puppets. Individuals who have personalities and lives of their own, not puppets who have no reality except the one that I give them.

SPECTATOR: If your puppets came to life, you'd really be happy, huh?

PUPPETEER: Yes, I really think it would be wonderful to direct live theatre and interact with real actors.

SPECTATOR: You know what they say—"Be careful what you wish for. It might come true." Look, I'm sorry you're not happy, but I really did enjoy your show.

PUPPETEER: Thank you. Thank you.

> *(SPECTATOR exits stage left, PUPPETEER finishes packing and exits stage right.)*

TRANSITIONAL MUSIC

SCENE II: PUPPETEER'S WORKSHOP. SEVERAL PILES OF CLOTH, A PUPPET STAND, AND SEVERAL PROPS ARE ON THE SIDES OF THE TABLE.

> *(PUPPETEER appears inside the main puppet stage with an armload of puppets. He is seen as if he is walking in and putting puppets on a table. He sits down at the table (playboard)*

PUPPETEER: *(Taking off his coat.)* Oh, I am tired, but it was a good audience. *(Checks puppets over.)* Oh, these do need some attention, all right. I didn't notice how the paint was chipped on his face. And the frog's leg is loose. Huh, well, they work hard, they do. *(Pats them.)* And so do I. *(Yawns.)* I am tired. Three shows in one day is getting to be too much. Even if the audiences are—wonderful—and they give me—three curtain calls—Just too—much—I have to—take—it . . . *(Snoozes with head and arms on the playboard. Lights dim.)*

SOFT MUSIC FADES IN AND OUT

> *(Lights brighten and the KING slowly lifts himself up from the play board and stands upright.)*

KING: Come on. Look alive. We've got work to do. Rehearsal schedules, costume fittings. Publicity sessions. Get a move on, everybody!

PRINCESS: *(Rises from the playboard.)* Yes, but I have to talk to our director before I do another thing. *(Approaches PUPPETEER.)* Look at him. Dead to the world. Wake up. Wake up. *(PUPPETEER slowly wakes up.)* I want to make sure my costume is mended before the next show. It should have been done a long time ago. It's ripped on the shoulder and most of the sparkles are gone. Most of the audience comes just to see me. I need to look my best.

PUPPETEER: *(Sleepily.)* Yes, Clarinda. I know.

PRINCESS: And another thing. In my role as princess, I am treated with honor and respect and given attention *onstage*. I think it would be better if I were treated like a princess *offstage* as well, otherwise I might get out of practice.

PUPPETEER: *(Half asleep.)* Well, I don't know about . . .

PRINCE: *(Who has risen during the PRINCESS's line.)* I have an important complaint to make too. My last speech in Act II is inappropriate. I think the wording should be changed to sound more gentile and it should be lengthened.

PUPPETEER: I'll think about it, but, you know . . .

QUEEN: *(Who is now also standing.)* And when am I going to get another part? I'm the puppet with the most experience and there I sit, backstage—or at home in the box. You could have written in a part for a queen mother in "The Frog Prince." And it's not too late. Do you hear?

FROG: *(Who has come alive and has been listening.)* Oh, calm down. At least you get some different roles to play. *(To PUPPETEER.)* Listen, I'm sick and tired of only playing a frog—croaking and jumping in and out of wells. I want to play Hamlet or Hansel—or even the lead in "The Ugly Duckling." Do I make myself clear?

PUPPETEER: Oh, yes, I understand what you are saying, but it is very hard to—

KING: *(Interrupting.)* And another thing I may as well bring up now—before the next script is written. I want you to give me more exit lines. They're the ones that get the most applause. I expect some respect and results here.

PRINCESS: And who put those awful blue jells in the lights? I've suspected it before, but after I saw those publicity shots, I knew that blue was bad for me. I need *red* lights. After all, I deserve to look as lovely as possible. *(Pause.)* Are you listening to me?

(They all begin to speak the following lines at once.)

QUEEN: Do I have your word on my getting a good part in the next show?

FROG: To be in a good part or not to be in a good part, that is the question.

KING: Are you paying attention to what I've been saying?

PRINCESS: I get those lights changed or I refuse to go on.

PRINCE: You'd better listen to what we're saying. Where would you be without us?

(All puppets speak following lines at once.)

QUEEN: What is a director for anyway?

FROG: I want to be a star. Do you hear—a star.

KING: It's time we had something to say about what's going on around here.

PRINCESS: I'm saying this once and for all.

PRINCE: Where would you be without us?

(PUPPETS start hitting PUPPETEER as they become more angry.)

PUPPETEER: *(As they continue to harangue.)* Quiet! Quiet! Stop! You're giving me a headache. I can't breathe. Stop. You're only a bunch of puppets! Get back in your box! Ahhh. Ugghhhhh! *(Flails around. Music swells as lights dim. PUPPETS collapse on playboard as before. Light increases, and PUPPETEER gradually awakes and looks around, trying to understand. He picks up a puppet.)* And to think I wanted you to become alive. *(Thinks.)* That woman! It must have been because of her—but—how strange. I know now how foolish I was. *(Shakes his head.)* Why, my little puppets, you never complain. *(He caresses the PUPPETS as he puts them away.)* I make up the plays as I like them to be and you always do what I want you to. No argument. No prima donnas in the bunch. And this makes me happy. It really does. *(Yawns and sighs.)* And now, I shall go to bed and dream about standing ovations. *(Pats several PUPPETS as he says "Good night.")* Good night. Good night, my friends. Good night, all.

FINAL MUSIC SWELLS

Production Notes

The first scene should have the backstage paraphernalia for the performance of "The Frog Prince" as viewed from the audience. When the show is over, the puppeteer puts away as many of his props and sets as possible into a box or suitcase, then folds up the stage, taking it offstage or leaving it in an inconspicuous place.

Rumplestiltskin II

by Jean M. Mattson

*The traditional spinning-straw-into-gold fairy tale with
more sympathetic characters and a new twist.*

CHARACTERS	**PROPS**	**SET PIECES**
King Reginald	Single sack	Table or stand for records
Queen Mother	Baby	Table
Royal Miller	Straw	Mill
Rosalind, the Miller's	Gold	Pile of flour sacks
daughter		Spinning wheel
Rumplestiltskin		Cradle
Narrator's voice		Trees and bushes
		Fire
		Banners

This is a play in six scenes and four sets, the throne room of the castle, outside the royal mill, the tower room of the castle, and the forest. It can be performed by two puppeteers. References to the writing of this play are included in the chapter entitled "ADAPTATIONS."

SCENE I: A CASTLE. BANNERS ON STAGE LEFT AND RIGHT. TABLE ON STAGE RIGHT. ROYAL RECORDS ON STAGE LEFT.

INTRODUCTORY MUSIC

NARRATOR: Long ago, in a castle far away, lived King Reginald, who was very worried indeed about his kingdom.

(KING enters stage right and paces back and forth, then sits at the table with head in hand. The QUEEN MOTHER enters stage left and watches him for a moment before speaking.)

QUEEN MOTHER: What is troubling you, son?

KING: We have only a few coins left in the counting house.

QUEEN MOTHER: Oh, how terrible!

KING: What does a king do when his gold is gone and his coffers are empty?

QUEEN MOTHER: He simply must acquire more gold and fill the coffers—immediately.

KING: Of course, Mother, of course. But how? That's the problem.

(They both think for a moment. She looks over at the records.)

QUEEN MOTHER: Well, I'll just look in the royal records and see what other kings have done. *(Crosses to records and looks at them.)* Hmmm. Boris, your great, great grandfather waged war on all the other kingdoms. My, he was a nasty one—but he brought back chests and chests of gold. *(Looks up from records.)*

KING: I can't do that. We don't even have an army. Besides, peace is more precious than gold.

(QUEEN MOTHER nods and returns to records.)

QUEEN MOTHER: Well, let's see here. Your great, great grand uncle, King John, raised taxes. Yes—three gold ducats from every subject in the kingdom. *(Looks at them again.)*

KING: You know I can't do that. People are already having a hard time.

QUEEN MOTHER: Yes, and you don't want to ruin your reputation as a kindly king. Oh, no. *(Looks back at records.)* Let's see. Hmmmm. Here's something very interesting.

KING: What is it?

QUEEN MOTHER: Well, centuries ago, it seems, there was a Queen Lulu—who ever heard of a Queen Lulu? It says here that when the treasury was low, she would go to the tower and sit and spin piles of straw into shining gold. Now, what do you think of that?

KING: That would solve the problem, all right. *(QUEEN MOTHER nods. KING crosses to look at the records.)*

QUEEN MOTHER: But these are old records, Reggie. I wouldn't put too much faith in them.

KING: But what else is there? *(Looks at QUEEN MOTHER, who shakes her head.)* Well, then, it's settled. I must find the best spinner in the kingdom. It's our only hope.

(KING and QUEEN MOTHER exeunt stage right and left respectively.)

TRANSITIONAL MUSIC

SCENE II: THE MILL. THE MILL IS ON STAGE RIGHT. TREES ON STAGE LEFT AND FLOUR BAGS CENTER STAGE.

NARRATOR: Nearby the castle in the royal mill lived the miller and his young daughter, Rosalind.

(Sound of mill wheel creaking and grinding to a stop. MILLER enters stage right with bag of flour. Rosalind enters stage left.)

ROSALIND: How is it going, Father?

MILLER: *(Deposits flour on pile of bags.)* This mill is wearing out. The gears are loose and broken and the grinding wheel needs to be replaced. I work twice as hard as I used to to grind a bag of flour.

ROSALIND: Have you reported it to the castle?

KING: *(Shaking his head.)* Many times. But for some reason nothing has been done. I don't know what we'd do if it weren't for your spinning and weaving. *(He sees someone approaching.)* Oh, who's this? *(KING enters stage left.)* Oh, your Majesty! *(MILLER bows.)*

ROSALIND: *(Curtsies.)* Oh, it is an honor, your Majesty. How can we be of service?

KING: Are you Rosalind, the miller's daughter? *(She bows.)* I understand you are known for your exceptional ability at the spinning wheel and the loom? *(ROSALIND modestly acknowledges this with a nod of her head.)*

MILLER: Oh, she is indeed. People journey miles to buy Rosalind's work. Recently, she made a cloth of gold for the wedding of a rich merchant's daughter on the other side of the mountain.

KING: A cloth of gold?

ROSALIND: Oh, it wasn't really gold. They just called it that because it was so soft and shiny and yellow.

KING: How encouraging.

ROSALIND: Encouraging?

KING: Yes. You see, I happen to be looking for someone who can spin straw into gold.

ROSALIND: Begging your pardon, Sire, but that's impossible.

KING: Perhaps, but according to the royal records, it seems to have been done years ago in the tower room of this very castle.

ROSALIND: An old fairy-tale.

KING: You may be right, but we found a spinning wheel in the old tower room and we have supplied it with bundles of straw. It is waiting for a spinster to try to spin it into gold.

MILLER: *(Turning to ROSALIND.)* Rosalind. *(No answer.)* Rosalind, you're the best in the kingdom.

ROSALIND: Father, I can't spin straw into gold. That's ridiculous!

KING: Our country is poor. We have no money to repair the castle or the roads. We can't build bridges. The royal mill needs new gears and another grinding wheel.

MILLER: It does. It does. Rosalind, you know it does!

KING: Something has to be done.

MILLER: What will happen if nothing is done?

KING: The royal kingdom will go down the royal tube. *(Puppet is lowered and raised quickly to simulate "going down the tube.")* Rosalind, will you try? *(MILLER and KING look at her.)* How can you refuse?

MILLER: *(When she doesn't answer.)* Rosalind!

ROSALIND: All right, all right! I'll try.

KING: Good. We'll expect you at the castle in two hours. (*KING exits stage left as they bow.*)

ROSALIND: What am I supposed to do now? Only a magician could do what he wants done.

MILLER: "Only a magician," she says. "Only a magician!" Now, you go into that tower and work harder than you've ever worked before. (*Turns to exit stage right, but stops to look at mill wheel.*) Hmmm. New gears. A new grinding wheel. (*Exits stage right.*)

ROSALIND: Oh, Father! (*Exits stage right.*)

TRANSITIONAL MUSIC

SCENE III: **TOWER ROOM OF CASTLE. PILES OF STRAW AND SPINNING WHEEL CENTER STAGE.**

(*KING and ROSALIND enter stage left.*)

KING: Here is the straw and the spinning wheel—just like the queen had it hundreds of years ago. If she spun gold—so can you. It's our only hope.

ROSALIND: I'm afraid I will only disappoint you, Sire.

KING: Spin, Rosalind, spin. For the love of your country and the love of your king. (*Starts to exit stage right, then turns back, saying insinuatingly.*) For the love of your king. (*Exits stage right. ROSALIND does a double take on his last remark, thinks about it, looks at the straw, then plunges enthusiastically into her work.*)

SPINNING MUSIC AS WHEEL TURNS

ROSALIND: (*Music and spinning wheel stop. She looks at straw.*) Oh, straw! (*More music. She spins. Music stops and she looks at straw.*) It's still straw like I knew it would be. (*More music. She spins. Music stops and she looks at straw.*) Only straw. But how could it ever be anything else? (*Cries unhappily.*)

(*Sound effects, including "Boing," accompany miraculous pop-up appearance of RUMPLESTILTSKIN stage left.*)

RUMPLE: And what, dear lady, is all the crying about?

ROSALIND: *(Turning toward him.)* Oh, you frightened me. Where did you come from?

RUMPLE: Never mind. What is making you cry?

ROSALIND: Oh, the king expects me to spin all this straw into gold. *(RUMPLESTILTSKIN looks at the straw.)*

RUMPLE: A tall order for anyone, I'd say.

ROSALIND: Yes, and if I don't do it, the royal kingdom will go down the royal tube. *(ROSALIND is quickly lowered and raised to simulate "going down the tube.")*

RUMPLE: So it's all on your shoulders, is it?

ROSALIND: It seems to be.

RUMPLE: Hmm. Well, what is it worth to you to have me spin that straw into gold?

ROSALIND: You can spin straw into gold?

RUMPLE: For a price.

ROSALIND: Ohhhhh—. *(Thinks.)* I will give you this gold ring. *(Shows it.)* It was my mother's.

RUMPLE: *(Looks at it.)* It won't do.

ROSALIND: Ahh—I'll give you my gold necklace—the payment I received for my cloth of gold.

RUMPLE: Not quite enough.

ROSALIND: But—but I have nothing else to give you.

RUMPLE: Hmmm—well—ahhh.

ROSALIND: Oh, please.

RUMPLE: Suppose you promise me your firstborn child.

ROSALIND: My firstborn child? But I'm not even married yet.

RUMPLE: Then it won't be hard to promise, will it? *(She hesitates.)* The gold, perhaps, is not all that important, after all.

ROSALIND: Oh, it is—it is. To me, to my father, to the kingdom—*(Meaningfully.)* and to the king.

RUMPLE: Well, then?

ROSALIND: Ohhh—very well, I promise.

RUMPLE: Ha-ha-ha-ha-ha. Then, spin I will. *(Crosses to spinning wheel.)*

SPINNING MUSIC

> *(RUMPLESTILTSKIN spins and ROSALIND becomes tired and lies down, face away from the audience. Straw begins to turn to gold.)*

NARRATOR: The little man continued to spin throughout the night until, in the morning, all the straw was gone and in its place lay piles of sparkling gold. He shook his head in satisfaction, then disappeared as suddenly as he had come.

MUSIC FADES

> *(RUMPLESTILTSKIN disappears into the floor with accompanying sound effects. ROSALIND awakens and sees the gold.)*

ROSALIND: Oh—oh—he did spin it into gold. Oh—your Majesty, he did. He did it. He really did it! *(She runs around the stage excitedly. KING and QUEEN MOTHER enter stage right. MILLER enters stage left.)*

ALL: Gold—it is gold. I can't believe it! She did it! *(They continue to voice excitement.)*

KING: Rosalind, you have rendered a priceless service to your king and your kingdom.

ROSALIND: I really didn't do anything—

MILLER: "Nothing," she says. "Nothing. Nothing." Oh, what a daughter, I have. *(Hugs her.)* What a daughter! New gears—a new grinding wheel. *(Ecstatically dances around.)*

KING: You shall receive a measure of gold—a small token of appreciation.

MILLER: A measure of gold? "A small token," he says. "A small token!" Oh, what a daughter! Come, Rosalind. We must celebrate. *(He laughs and pulls ROSALIND off stage left. She takes a few steps back toward the KING and is yanked off by her father.)*

KING: How can I ever repay that amazing girl?

QUEEN MOTHER: Ahhh, Reggie. I neglected to tell you that—ahh—Queen Lulu, the one who spun the straw into gold, was a miller's daughter.

KING: Really? *(Looks away and then back at her.)* Are you suggesting that I make this whole thing a family tradition?

QUEEN MOTHER: *(Looks at gold.)* Well, that girl would certainly be an asset to the family.

                   (KING looks in the direction where ROSALIND disappeared, looks back at QUEEN MOTHER. They exeunt stage left.)

TRANSITIONAL MUSIC

NARRATOR: And so, King Reginald married Rosalind. The kingdom celebrated and prospered. New roads and bridges were built. The castle was repaired and the mill received new gears and a new grinding wheel. A year passed.

MUSIC FADES

SCENE IV: THE CASTLE. A ROYAL CRIB IS CENTER STAGE. BANNERS RIGHT AND LEFT.

                   (ROSALIND is heard humming a lullaby. She enters stage right holding her baby, whom she places in the crib. Sound effects accompany RUMPLES-TILTSKIN's appearance from the floor stage left.)

ROSALIND: *(Turns and sees him.)* Oh—you!

RUMPLE: Yes, yes, me. I have come for the payment you promised me.

ROSALIND: The payment? *(She slowly realizes what he means.)* No. No. Not—*(She looks into the crib.)*

RUMPLE: Yes, the baby. Your little son—the one you promised me. *(He looks into the crib.)* Such a nice one too. Gootchie—gootchie—goo.

ROSALIND: But—you can't take my baby. *(She pushes him away from the crib.)*

RUMPLE: Dear lady, a promise is a promise.

ROSALIND: But you can't—you can't take a baby away from its mother. I love my baby. *(Leans over baby.)* You can't take him away. Oh, please, give me another chance to make it up to you. Please! *(Kneels and sobs.)*

RUMPLE: *(Listens for a moment.)* Ohhhhhh, why do they always have to cry? *(Listens again.)* Oh, all right, all right. Tell you what. You guess my name, and I'll—I'll forget about my promise.

ROSALIND: I'll try anything—yes, anything.

RUMPLE: You don't know how hard it will be to guess my name. Your chances are slim. But I will return in three days, and if you haven't guessed my name in three tries, the baby is mine. Agreed?

ROSALIND: Agreed.

(RUMPLESTILTSKIN laughs and disappears into the floor with sound effects.)

ROSALIND: *(Picking up the baby.)* Oh, my baby, I cannot bear to lose you.

MILLER: *(Enters stage left.)* Well, Rosalind, how is my favorite grandchild today?

ROSALIND: Oh, Father, you must help me. I never told you about what really happened. *(They begin to exit stage right.)* When I went up to the tower room and the prince left . . . *(Exeunt.)*

TRANSITIONAL MUSIC

NARRATOR: And Rosalind poured out the whole story to her father and begged him to help her. The miller set right out to search the kingdom for any clue to the name of the little man. He visited the villages and hamlets, the highways and the byways, the pastures and the marshes. At last, in the early morning of the third day, after fruitless searching, he came to a small clearing in the forest.

MUSIC FADES

SCENE V: A FOREST. TREES OR BUSHES ON STAGE RIGHT AND LEFT. A FIRE CENTER STAGE.

(Miller enters, hears someone coming and hides behind bushes.)

RUMPLE: *(Entering stage right singing and dancing. Sits by the fire.)*
Oh, I am old and lonely,
I have no friends or kin
Rumple—rumple—stilt
And skinny—skinny—skin.
No one knows where I am going
Or cares where I have been.
Rumple—rumple—stilt
And skinny-skinny-skin.

I need someone to love me
To care, to take me in.
Rumple—rumple—stilt
And skinny—skinny—skin.
But after tonight things will be different—happier. I made a good bargain. I will soon have a child to love and take care of—because nobody knows that my name is "Rumplestiltskin"! *(Laughs.)* Rumple—rumple—stilt and skinny—skinny —skin. *(Exits stage left.)*

(MILLER emerges from the bushes, jumps up and down with joy, and quickly exits stage right.)

TRANSITIONAL MUSIC

SCENE VI: THE CASTLE. BANNERS ON STAGE LEFT AND RIGHT.

(ROSALIND, carrying baby, and KING enter stage right.)

KING: You say he was a tiny little man with a high voice and—

ROSALIND: *(Interrupting.)* Oh, yes, and he could have any one of thousands of names. I'll never find the right one. I know it.

KING: Your father will be back soon. Perhaps he will have discovered something.

ROSALIND: And if he hasn't?

KING: Well, then, he won't take the baby. I won't allow it.

ROSALIND: Remember, that little man can spin straw into gold. *(They look at each other and embrace.)*

(MILLER enters stage left.)

ROSALIND: Father, what did you find out?

KING: Did you learn anything?

MILLER: Yes, I did. I found out the name of the little man is "Rumplestiltskin"!

KING: "Rumplestiltskin"!

ROSALIND: Oh, Father, I am so happy.

MILLER: I also found out why he wanted a child.

ROSALIND: Why?

MILLER: Because he is a lonely little old man who hasn't anyone to care about him. He needs someone to love.

ROSALIND: Oh, that poor little fellow.

(Sound effects for RUMPLSTILKSKIN's appearance stage left.)

RUMPLE: And so I am here to collect my part of the bargain. Are you ready to try to guess my name?

ROSALIND: Oh, yes. I'm ready. Ahh—is it—"Pifflelsnitzle"?

RUMPLE: *(Laughing.)* No—no—no—no! Try again.

ROSALIND: Is it—"Bickybackybumbum"?

RUMPLE: No, no, no, it isn't. You might as well give up.

ROSALIND: Is it "Rumplestiltskin"?

RUMPLE: What? You know! You know my name! I never thought you'd ever guess it. Oh— oh—oh—he is such a beautiful baby. *(Goes to crib and looks at baby.)* I guess he will be better off with his mother after all. *(Turns to leave.)*

KING: Wait! Wait! *(Clears his throat.)* We really are grateful to you for all you've done— with the straw and all. And—I was wondering if you would be our son's royal godfather.

RUMPLE: Royal godfather?

KING: He doesn't have any godparents—and there wouldn't be any work involved. And you could visit him any time you liked. *(He turns to ROSALIND. She nods.)*

RUMPLE: A godfather? Me, a godfather! Godfather Rumplestiltskin. Oh, I like that.

KING: Good. It's settled then.

MILLER: You could stay with me at the mill. It's kind of empty around there since my daughter left.

ROSALIND: Oh, what a good idea, Father.

MILLER: I'll show you the mill. *(They shake hands, bow, and exeunt stage left.)* Say, Rump, do you have any experience changing wheat into diamonds? *(Laughs.)*

TRANSITIONAL MUSIC

            (KING and ROSALIND look at the baby, embrace, and exeunt.)

NARRATOR: From that day on, the royal godfather saw to it that the royal treasury was never poor again. King Reginald and Queen Rosalind had many more children who, of course, needed godfathers. And they all lived happily ever after.

            (Cast takes their bows.)

FINALE

Production Notes

Royal records—A box or a podium can hold the book of records.

Mill—   A mill can be fashioned from a piece of thin plywood with a circular piece loosely bolted to it for the easy rotation of the mill.

Spinning wheel—Sometimes one is lucky enough to find a spinning wheel lamp or a child's toy. Otherwise, one can be built using a block of wood as a base. A wood support can be mounted on the back of the block, extending three or four inches above it. A wheel can be loosely bolted to the top of the support. A coat hanger control can be attached to the edge of the wheel to allow the wheel to be rotated. A distaff can be made by inserting a short piece of 1/4-inch dowel into a hole drilled in the block, topped by a bundle of raffia for the straw. By painting the block black and glueing 1/4-inch strips of wood for legs, the spinning wheel looks real to the audience.

Straw-into-gold—This procedure need not be complicated. It can be done in a variety of ways. One can simply slowly exchange the straw for the gold. Or a wooden circle with gold on one half and straw on the other can be attached to the playboard and rotated. Any number of magical lighting effects could be incorporated. Whatever the technique, some kind of magical music or sound should accompany the procedure.

The Swineherd

by Jean M. Mattson

Hans Christian Anderson's stories have been translated into many languages because he managed to appeal to children with his fantasies and his understanding of their world, while at the same time reaching adults with his shrewd observances and meangingful ironies. Such is true in this story.

CHARACTERS	**PROPS**	**SET PIECES**
Prime Minister	Watering can	Prince's castle
Prince Ambrose	Birdcage with cover with	Emperors castle
Princess Drusilla	nightingale inside	Pigpen
Sybil, her lady-in waiting	Rose tree	Woods
Emperor, Drusilla's father	Single rose	
Servant	Casket or chest	
Two pigs	Suitcase or satchel	
Narrator's voice		

The five scenes in this play include the inside of the prince's castle, the inside of the emperor's castle, the outside of the pigsty, and a scene in the forest. The play has been written to be performed by three puppeteers. The number of ladies-in-waiting in the original story has been decreased to one. One silver casket is included instead of two.

SCENE I: THE CASTLE OF PRINCE AMBROSE. A ROSE TREE IS ON STAGE RIGHT AND A COVERED BIRDCAGE IS ON STAGE LEFT.

INTRODUCTORY MUSIC

NARRATOR: There once was a Prince Ambrose, who ruled the small kingdom of Argonne. One day he called his prime minister to him. *(PRINCE enters and waters flowers.)*

PRIME MINISTER: You sent for me, your majesty?

PRINCE: Yes, Dudley. I'm getting older. It's time for me to marry.

PRIME MINISTER: That should be no problem, your majesty.

PRINCE: But who? That's the problem.

PRIME MINISTER: Everyone has heard of you, and there are a hundred girls who would say, "Yes, and thank you very much," if you proposed to them.

PRINCE: But I don't want to marry just any girl.

PRIME MINISTER: Of course not, your majesty. Naturally, she must be special.

PRINCE: Well, actually, I have in mind the emperor's daughter.

PRIME MINISTER: Oh, the Princess Drusilla?

PRINCE: Yes. Her father is a great emperor.

PRIME MINISTER: Hmmm. Yes, good choice. And I hear she's quite pretty.

PRINCE: Yes. But will she have me? I am the prince, yes, but my kingdom is so small.

PRIME MINISTER: Perhaps if you sent some gifts.

PRINCE: Yes, that might help, Dudley, if it were something very special.

PRIME MINISTER: Flowers, perhaps? Ladies love flowers.

PRINCE: Yes. *(Looks at rose tree.)* Yes. Just the thing! I will send her a rose from my father's wonderful rose tree. It blooms only once every five years and it's about that time, is it not, Dudley?

PRIME MINISTER: Yes. *(Approaches tree.)* Yes, indeed. *(Bloom pops up.)* It's said that anyone who smells it will forget all his sorrow and troubles.

PRINCE: Well, I doubt if the princess has much sorrow or trouble. *(Looks at the cage.)* Ahh—yes. I'll send her my nightingale too. Dudley! *(He takes the cover off the cage and the nightingale sings.)* Oh, listen. My nightingale will surely impress her.

PRIME MINISTER: Yes, Sire.

PRINCE: It shall be my special messenger. Bring me a silver casket for the rose and the nightingale. You shall take them to the emperor's castle, along with my proposal of marriage. *(PRIME MINISTER bows and leaves, followed by PRINCE.)*

TRANSITIONAL MUSIC

SCENE II: **THE GREAT HALL IN THE EMPEROR'S CASTLE. ROYAL BANNERS HANG ON THE WALLS. A BENCH ON STAGE LEFT.**

(The PRINCESS and SYBIL enter.)

PRINCESS: What shall we play now, Sybil? I get so tired playing house. That's all we ever play. *(She throws herself on bench.)* Can't you think of something else?

SYBIL: But, milady—

PRINCESS: I think we should have a royal game maker who would come up with a new game every week. That would be nice? *(Pause.)* Sybil! Wouldn't it?

SYBIL: Yes, Princess—but—*(Disgustedly.)*

PRINCESS: I thought I left my tennis racket here. *(Looks for it on stage left.)* Oh, well. Maybe we could throw darts—or I guess I could ride my pony or—

SYBIL: But, Princess—

PRINCESS: What is it, Sybil? *(Impatiently.)*

SYBIL: It's time for your piano lesson, your grace.

PRINCESS: Oh, piffle? Boring! Boring! Boring! Boring! *(As she marches off, Sybil shakes her head and follows.)*

EMPEROR: *(Enters stage right.)* Show the prime minister in.

SERVANT'S VOICE: Yes, your majesty. *(The emperor paces as he waits.)*

SERVANT'S VOICE: The prime minister of Argonne.

(PRIME MINISTER enters stage right. Servant brings in casket and exits.)

EMPEROR: So, you come from Argonne?

PRIME MINISTER: *(Bows.)* Yes, I come as an emissary for Prince Ambrose, who wishes to ask for your daughter's hand in marriage. I have brought gifts and I await your pleasure.

EMPEROR: I welcome you to the kingdom. I have summoned my daughter. Drusilla, my dear. Drusilla!

PRINCESS: What do you want, Father? *(DRUSILLA and SYBIL enter stage left. DRUSILLA looks at PRIME MINISTER and speaks rudely.)* Who are you?

EMPEROR: This is the prime minister of Argonne at your service. *(He bows.)* Prince Ambrose of Argonne is asking for your hand in marriage, my dear.

PRINCESS: Well—I don't know . . .

PRIME MINISTER: Prince Ambrose sends his warmest regards. I bring tokens of his esteem. *(Opens the casket.)*

PRINCESS: Oh, you have some presents for me? *(Clapping her hands and jumping for joy. He nods and takes rose out of casket.)* Oh, how exciting. I hope one of them is a pretty little kitten.

PRIME MINISTER: Prince Ambrose sends this rare and exotic rose as a symbol of his intentions.

SYBIL: *(Looks at rose.)* A rose. Oh, my, how beautiful! *(Takes rose and smells it)* And it smells so sweet.

PRINCESS: Is it made of gold? Is it made of rubies? *(Takes the rose.)* Oh—why, it's —it's real. It's just an old real rose. *(Tosses it.)* Who'd want that? Right, Sybil?

SYBIL :   Oh—yes. *(Unconvincingly.)* Who'd want an old real rose? *(Flat and unfeeling.)*

EMPEROR: Ahh. But—my dear—.

PRINCESS: Didn't he send anything else?

(PRIME MINISTER takes out nightingale and places it on playboard.)

PRINCESS: Ohhh. A bird.

(Nightingale sings.)

SYBIL: Oh, superb! Charming! It reminds me of a music box.

EMPEROR: Yes. I can't believe it's real.

PRINCESS: Wait a minute. You don't mean that's a real bird? *(Looks at bird.)*

PRIME MINISTER: Indeed, it is a real bird. The finest specimen in captivity.

PRINCESS: *(With disgust.)* Take it away. It's only a stinky, messy old bag of feathers! *(Looks at SYBIL.)* Right, Sybil?

SYBIL: Ahhh—yes. An old, stinky, messy old bag of feathers. *(Unfeeling. She does not agree with the PRINCESS.)*

PRINCESS: And tell your prince I won't marry him. And if he comes here, I won't even see him. So there. *(Flounces out.)*

SYBIL: So there! *(Apologetically. Unhappily exits.)*

EMPEROR: But—my dear—

(EMPEROR shrugs and exits, followed by PRIME MINISTER.)

TRANSITIONAL MUSIC

SCENE III: PRINCE'S CASTLE.

(PRINCE enters stage left. PRIME MINISTER enters stage right with birdcage.)

PRINCE: I can't believe that an emperor's daughter would behave that way.

PRIME MINISTER: I'm sorry, your grace, but I reported truly.

PRINCE: Yes, I'm sure you did. I'm sure you did. But perhaps she was having a bad day. Or maybe she wasn't feeling well.

PRIME MINISTER: Perhaps.

PRINCE: It's puzzling. I've got to find out more about her. I think I'll have to visit the emperor's castle myself.

PRIME MINISTER: Is that wise, Sire?

PRINCE: I'll go in disguise.

PRIME MINISTER: Disguise?

PRINCE: Yes. I'll put shoe polish on my face and get some old clothes.

PRIME MINISTER: But you might be in danger. No one will know you're a prince.

PRINCE: Exactly. That's exactly what I want.

PRIME MINISTER: But—

PRINCE: There's no other way. I'll go to the castle and try to find work. As a peasant, I'll learn more about the princess in three days than a prince could in a year. Come, help me find some rag of a cloak to wear. *(They exeunt.)*

TRANSITIONAL MUSIC

SCENE IV: PIGPEN. THERE ARE TREES ON STAGE RIGHT. A PIGPEN AND FENCE ON STAGE LEFT.

(PIGS are rooting about.)

PRINCE :   *(In old hat and cloak. He enters stage left and approaches pig pen.)* Here piggie, here piggie. *(Pigs come, snorting.)* I want you all to know that I am the royal swineherd. Now, a swineherd is supposed to care for the swine—and that is what you are, my little piggies. So you will be my companions for a while. *(Pigs squeal.)* I didn't plan on ending up in a pigpen. But I guess I could do worse. Now, besides taking care of you, I have things to do. Help me think of something that will attract our little princess. Come. Into the pigsty!

(PRINCE exits followed by pigs.)

TRANSITIONAL MUSIC

(PRINCE enters with pot followed by the pigs.)

PRINCE: Well, that took more time than I expected, but perhaps this will be better than a rose. *(Pigs answer. PRINCE puts pot down.)* This may look like an ordinary pretty little pot with bells around it. *(Pigs look and answer.)* No, my little porcine playmates, this is a very special pot indeed. *(Pigs squeal.)* Listen.

(Pot plays once through and then softly.)

PRINCESS: *(Offstage.)* Listen. I hear something. Come on, Sybil.

SYBIL: But that's the pigpen, your highness.

PRINCESS: I know, Sybil. *(With disdain.)* Listen. *(Enters la-la-la's to the pot's tune, "Ach, lieber, Augustine.")* That's a song I can play on the piano—with one finger. *(Looks at swineherd.)* Why, it must be the swineherd playing. How odd, an educated swineherd. Go and find out what instrument he is playing, Sybil. Be careful where you step. It *is* a pigpen. *(SYBIL goes to PRINCE.)*

MUSIC FADES

SYBIL: Pardon me, what is that you are playing?

PRINCE: It is my little pot that's playing. You see the tiny bells?

SYBIL: Oh, yes. *(Returns to PRINCESS.)* It is the little pot that was playing.

(PRINCESS approaches PRINCE and "oo's" and "ah's.")

PRINCE: And a special pot it is. Put your finger in the steam and you can smell what is cooking on any stove in town.

PRINCESS: Any stove in town? Really? *(Remembers she's a PRINCESS.)* How very interesting. *(Coolly walks away as if uninterested. Beckons to SYBIL.)* Sybil, ask him how much he wants for his pot.

SYBIL: *(Approaches PRINCE.)* How much do you want for your pot?

PRINCE: I want ten kisses from the princess.

SYBIL: Well, I never!

PRINCE: I won't settle for less. *(SYBIL returns to PRINCESS.)*

PRINCESS: Well, Sybil, what does he say?

SYBIL: Oh, I can't repeat it. It's too shocking.!

PRINCESS: Then whisper it to me. *(She does.)* Oh, how naughty! The nerve! *(She turns away, then stops and listens as pot plays again.)* Ask him if he will take ten kisses from my lady-in-waiting instead.

SYBIL: What! *(In horror.)*

PRINCESS: Sybil, go ask him!

SYBIL: *(Goes back to PRINCE.)* Ahhhh. *(Pot music stops.)* You don't want to take ten kisses from me, do you? *(Shaking her head, hoping he will say "No.")*

PRINCE: No, thank you.

LADY: Oh, thank heaven.

PRINCE: Ten kisses from the princess or I keep my pot.

SYBIL: *(Returns to PRINCESS saying happily.)* Only from you, your highness.

PRINCESS: Oh, this is most embarrassing. But I do want that pot. *(Deliberates, then decides.)* Sybil, stand guard in case anyone comes.

SYBIL: *(Looking both ways.)* Not a soul in sight.

PRINCESS: Don't think I'm going to enjoy this. *(Motions to PRINCE, who comes. She has to force herself to do it.)*

PRINCESS: One. *(Kiss.)* Two *(Kiss.)* *(etc.)* three—four—five—six—seven—eight—nine—ten.

PRINCE: Madam, your pot. *(Gesturing toward pot. She turns away with nose in the air.)*

PRINCESS:` Sybil! *(SYBIL brings pot to PRINCESS.)*

PRINCESS: Oh, what fun. Tonight we'll know who's having pickled kumquats and blackbird pie for supper. But don't you breathe one word of this, Sybil. Remember, I am the princess!

SYBIL: *(Loudly.)* Ah—yes. *(Under her breath.)* The Heavens preserve us! *(Loudly.)* I won't say a word.

(SYBIL and PRINCESS exeunt.)

PRINCE: *(Pigs snort.)* Well, my little piggies, I am finding out something about our princess all right, but I have more ideas to present to her highness. I must get busy. *(Exits.)*

TRANSITIONAL MUSIC

(PRINCE returns with rattle.)

PRINCE: Behold, a rattle. It looks like an ordinary rattle, doesn't it? But you won't believe what it can do. Listen. *(Pigs jump up and down and squeal then dance to music. PRINCE twirls rattle.)*

POLKA MUSIC OF THE RATTLE. LOUD AND THEN SOFT UNDER VOICES

PRINCESS: *(Offstage.)* Come on, Sybil. Maybe he has something else now. Listen! More music, lovely music. *(Enters with SYBIL)* Ask him the price of his instrument. But mind you, no more kissing!

SYBIL: *(Approaches PRINCE.)* The princess would like to purchase your instrument.

MUSIC FADES

PRINCE: For one hundred kisses, milady! *(SYBIL gasps.)*

PRINCESS: *(As SYBIL returns to DRUSILLA.)* Well?

SYBIL: One hundred kisses!

PRINCESS: Ridiculous! He must be mad! *(She turns away.)*

PRINCE: When you twirl the rattle, it will play all the dances ever composed—polkas, waltzes, jigs, and minuets. *(Persuasively.)*

WALTZ RATTLE MUSIC

PRINCESS: *(Thinking.)* But, after all, an emperor's daughter should patronize the arts. Right, Sybil? *(She nods.)* And I am the emperor's daughter. Right, Sybil?

SYBIL: Ahh—yes. *(Under her breath.)* How could I forget it?

PRINCESS: *(Turns to Sybil.)* Tell him he can have ten kisses like yesterday, but the rest from you.

SYBIL: I don't want to kiss a pigkeeper!

PRINCESS: Nonsense! If I can kiss him, so can you. A lady-in-waiting is kept around to handle details just like this.

PRINCE: *(Calling.)* One hundred kisses or I keep the rattle!

PRINCESS: Revolting! He belongs with the pigs! *(Pause.)* But—I want that rattle. Check the path, Sybil. *(SYBIL does so.)*

SYBIL: It's clear. *(PRINCE grasps PRINCESS and the kissing begins.)*

PRINCESS: One. *(Kiss.)* Two. *(Kiss, etc.)* Three—four—five—six—seven—eight—nine—ten—

MUSIC FADES IN AND THEN OUT

(Pause in counting as music swells, then counting continues as music fades.) . . . seventy eight, *(Kiss.)* seventy nine. *(Kiss, etc.)* Eighty—eighty one—eighty two—eighty three—eighty four—eighty five—eighty six . . .

EMPEROR: *(Offstage as counting continues.)* What is going on here? I couldn't tell from the balcony. That lady-in-waiting seems to be up to something. *(He enters and sees the kissing.)* Ohhh. What's this? *(Looks more closely.)* I can't believe my eyes. *(He sputters with fury.)* My daughter! With the pigs. I've given her everything! And look at her! You are no longer my daughter. Out! Do you hear? Out! Oh, the smirch. Oh, the shame. The embarrassment! Out! Out! Out of my kingdom and never return. *(All scuttle out. EMPEROR regains his composure.)* Oh, what a royal disgrace! It will take me many days to regain my royal equanimity! *(Exits.)*

TRANSITIONAL MUSIC

SCENE V: FOREST SCENE.

(PRINCESS enters, followed by Sybil, who is carrying a suitcase.)

PRINCESS: *(Crying.)* Oh, poor miserable me. My own father driving me out of my own home. That horrid swineherd! *(Looks at SYBIL.)* It's all your fault for letting me kiss him! You should do something!

SYBIL: Right. I will do something. I'm leaving! *(Slams down suitcase and exits.)*

PRINCESS: *(Crying)* Sybilllll! Everything is going wrong. *(Drapes herself over suitcase.)* If only I had married that prince. Oh, I am so unhappy. *(Cries. The PRINCE enters in his princely robes. PRINCESS sees him gets up and curtsies.)* Oh, there you are. The prince who sent—ahhh—that *gorgeous* rose and that—ah—*divine* nightingale. Ahh, you see,—aaah—I've changed my mind. I've decided to marry you after all.

PRINCE: Well, I'm sorry, Drusilla, but I have also changed my mind.

PRINCESS: What?

PRINCE: You did not want an honorable prince.

PRINCESS: But—well—I—

PRINCE: You did not appreciate an exquisite rose.

PRINCE: But—you see—

PRINCE: You scorned the flawless song of the nightingale.

PRINCESS: But—I didn't—

PRINCE: *But*—you could kiss a dirty, insolent swineherd for the sake of a toy. Farewell, my frivolous princess! *(Starts to leave, then turns.)* And good-bye! *(Exits. Drusilla howls loudly, throwing herself onto the suitcase.)*

SOFT TRANSITIONAL MUSIC UNDER NARRATOR

NARRATOR'S VOICE: Disappointed but enlightened, the prince returned to his own kingdom. There, he finally found a princess whose values were worthy of a throne. *(A pig enters and nudges her. She sees the pig and howls again as she exits. Pig shakes his head as he exits.)* We know that Princess Drusilla eventually learned from her experience and one day returned to her father's castle, a wiser and more kindly person.

MUSIC SWELLS TO FINALE

Production Notes

An effort was made to keep the action going while incorporating as many of Hans Christian Anderson's details as possible.

The pigs can be a fun part of the show by responding to the prince, sitting, dancing, and so on.

Bird cage— The bird cage was the major production problem in this play. We bought a wicker bird cage, available in many craft stores, installed a bird, and placed it on a pedestal with a gold lamé cage cover. The covered cage creates audience interest. The prince uncovers the cage when he suggests sending this bird as a gift, creating some legitimate stage business for the puppet. Unless two cages are used, the pedestal should be equipped with an indentation into which the cage fits (Velcro, in addition, will make it more secure), so that the cage can be detached and brought to the princess in the next scene.

Silver casket—The casket, of course, should be a three-sided box with a lid that is large enough to seem to accommodate the bird cage.

Optional set pieces—Other flowers that PRINCE can pick and/or water with watering can to create stage business.

Trashcan Neighbor

by Jean M. Mattson

CHARACTERS
Stanley Martin
Man on the Street
Woman I
Woman II
Dog
Policeman
Minister
Cliff—a garbage collector
George Freeman—an
    apartment house operator
Offstage Voice

PROPS
Suitcase
Garbage cans
Bags of garbage
Garbage truck

SET PIECES
Civic Haven Shelter
St. Christopher's Mission
Park bench
Desk

This is a modern adaptation of the Biblical story, "The Good Samaritan." It was developed for a puppetry workshop for church leaders. It has four scenes with four simple sets, three streets, and an office. It can be performed with two puppeteers.

SCENE I: A STREET.

INTRODUCTORY MUSIC

(STANLEY MARTIN enters with a suitcase, puts it down, looks around, and shakes his head. MAN enters stage left.)

STANLEY: Pardon me, but could you tell me where Franklin Street is?

MAN: Sure. It's two blocks down this street and to your left.

STANLEY: Thanks.

MAN: You're new in town?

STANLEY: Yeah.

MAN: You looking for your hotel?

STANLEY: Well, not exactly. *(MAN looks at his suticase and then back to STANLEY.)* Well, you see, I was staying at the Meadowbrook Hotel until this morning. My construction job was supposed to start Monday—but the permits didn't come through and—and then—then—well—

MAN: You ran out of money.

STANLEY: How did you know?

MAN: Lots of people are in the same fix around here. Hey, are you looking for the Civic Haven Shelter, by any chance?

STANLEY: Ahh, yes, I think that was the name. Somebody told me that they—

MAN: Look, that's a good place. Stayed there myself a couple of times. But it fills up early when it gets cold—and its going to be below freezin' tonight. If you're headed there, fellow, you'd better get a move on.

STANLEY: Oh, thanks. *(Picks up suitcase and exits stage left.)*

MAN: Two blocks down. You'll see the sign. *(MAN looks after him, shakes his head, and exits stage right.)*

TRANSITIONAL MUSIC

SCENE II: **A STREET. THE BUILDING ON STAGE LEFT HAS A SIGN, "CIVIC HAVEN."**

(STANLEY enters stage right, crosses stage and enters building.)

VOICE: Sorry, Mister, we're full up.

STANLEY: *(Offstage.)* But someone told me—

VOICE: Try the St. Christopher Mission. Three blocks west on Main. They might have something left.

STANLEY: Thanks. *(He enters stage left slowly and drags across the stage, exiting stage right.)*

TRANSITIONAL MUSIC

SCENE III: **A STREET. BUILDING ON STAGE RIGHT HAS SIGN, "ST. CHRISTOPHER MISSION." ON STAGE LEFT ARE SEVERAL GARBAGE CANS AND PLASTIC BAGS. A BENCH IS ON STAGE RIGHT.**

(STANLEY enters stage left with suitcase, crosses to building, and enters it.)

VOICE: Sorry, can't help you tonight. No beds left since right after lunch. You have to get here early, Bud.

(Stanley comes out of the building.)

VOICE: *(Calling after him.)* Say, you can come back for breakfast at 7:00.

(STANLEY stops, looks back, looks around, and trudges over to the bench on stage right. He puts suitcase down, sits, looks around, shivers, and lies down. Two women enter stage left talking.)

WOMAN I: *(Seeing STANLEY.)* Would you look at that. Isn't that the limit? You'd think this street was a bedroom!

WOMAN II: This neighborhood is getting to be a disgrace. It's bad enough to have *shelters* around here for the reprobates—but to see them sleeping on the streets—Ughhh! . .

WOMAN I: There ought to be a law!

WOMAN II: I wish our office would move to another building further uptown.

WOMAN I: Yeah, or else I'm going to start looking for another job. *(Looks again at Stanley.)* Humph!

WOMAN II: Come on, we'll be late for the bus. *(Exeunt stage right.)*

POLICEMAN: *(Enters stage left, sees STANLEY, walks over, and pokes him.)* Hey, there. Can't have no loitering on the streets. You have to go to one of those shelters around here.

STANLEY: They're full. I've tried several and . . .

POLICEMAN: I'm sorry, but you can't stay here. If you're still here when I come back this way again, I'll have to book ya.

STANLEY: But I don't know . . .

POLICEMAN: Look. You've gotta move. Understand? *(Waits for an answer. STANLEY finally nods.)* I'm sorry, but I gotta do my duty. *(POLICEMAN exits stage left. STANLEY sits quietly for a moment. A DOG enters stage left, stops, sees STANLEY, goes over to him, and whines.)*

STANLEY: Well, hello, there, pooch. *(DOG whines.)* Oh, you don't have any place to go either, huh? *(DOG barks.)* And you're cold and lonesome too. *(DOG whines.)* Yeah, I know. I'm tired too. *(DOG puts his head on STANLEY'S lap and STANLEY pets him.)* You're hungry too, I suppose. *(DOG whines.)* I know just how you feel. But I can't help you, pooch. *(DOG growls.)* Well, we can't stay here, that's for sure. *(Gets up, picks up suitcase, and starts toward stage left. He sees garbage cans, stops, looks, and goes over to them. He puts his suitcase down, looks at cans and at his suitcase. Then he puts his suitcase across the two cans.)* How's that, pooch? The royal suite. Maybe we can keep each other warm, huh? It's out of the wind anyway, and nobody'll see us here. *(DOG barks and goes under suitcase. STANLEY crawls under.)* There. It could be worse. Come on, now. Quiet down.

             (MINISTER enters stage left. He sees STANLEY and goes over to look.)

MINISTER: Well, that poor soul—sleeping in a trash heap. What is this world coming to? *(Looks around at the situation.)* Oh, dear. I suppose all the shelters are full by this time of the night. I'll certainly put him on my prayer list tonight. *(Exits stage right, shaking his head. He looks back once before he disappears.)* Such a shame.

             (Lights dim.)

TRANSITIONAL MUSIC

> *(Lights go up. Faint sound of truck increases in volume. Garbage truck enters upstage left and stops center stage. CLIFF comes around truck and picks up a plastic bag and throws it into the truck. DOG whines and barks as CLIFF takes suitcase off the top.)*

STANLEY: *(Jumping up.)* Hey, wait a minute. You can't take my suitcase!

CLIFF: It's garbage isn't it?

STANLEY: You just don't know a roof when you see it.

CLIFF: A roof? Are you kidding?

STANLEY: What are you doing collecting garbage at this time of the day anyway?

CLIFF: Holiday last week has us working overtime. What are you doing sleeping here? There are shelters, you know.

STANLEY: Yeah, well, I tried 'em They're full.

CLIFF: And you're broke?

STANLEY: Yes. And it's cold and this was out of the wind. You don't think I wanted to bed down by a garbage can, do you? I thought I had enough money to last me when I came to town for a job with Acme Construction, but something got fouled up—the permits didn't come through, I guess—and they couldn't put me on until next week.

CLIFF: That's tough. You are in a fix all right.

STANLEY: Yeah, I guess I am. Come on, pooch. We'll find another cozy spot to hole up in. *(DOG whines and STANLEY picks up his suitcase and starts off.)*

CLIFF: Now, wait a minute. It's been cold, but it's going to be below zero tonight. You've got to get inside somewhere.

STANLEY: It would be nice. I'll work on it. I'll get to a shelter early tomorrow. *(Starts off again.)*

CLIFF: You know, my cousin has a little apartment building up the street a ways. *(Thinks.)* 'N he owes me one. He's got a furnace room that has an old beat-up couch in it. Maybe he'd let you use it for a couple of days. It's ain't much, but—hey—it beats this place, huh? How about it? You might even do a couple of chores for him.

STANLEY: *(DOG whines.)* You think he'd let a dog in too?

CLIFF: *(Looks at DOG and laughs.)* Like I said—he owes me one. Come on. Let's get this trash in the truck and we'll get over there. *(They put garbage in the truck.)* What's your name, anyway?

STANLEY: Stanley Martin.

CLIFF: I'm Cliff. *(Looks around.)* That's does it, O.K., Stanley, let's go. *(They get into truck, which loudly exits.)*

TRANSITIONAL MUSIC

SCENE IV: COUSIN'S APARTMENT BUILDING. A DESK IS ON STAGE LEFT WITH A WALL BEHIND IT.

(GEORGE is sitting at the desk. CLIFF enters stage right and approaches desk.)

GEORGE: Oh, hi, Cliff. How are you? *(Rises and shakes hands.)*

CLIFF: I'm just fine, and I'm here to remind you that I once saved your neck over at the sanitation department.

GEORGE: Yeah, I remember. So what?

CLIFF: Well, I've got a little favor to ask you. There's a fellow outside who's down on his luck and I was wondering if he could use that couch in your furnace room for a few days.

GEORGE: Where did you find him?

CLIFF: On my route. He was freezin'.

GEORGE: Well, I don't know if—

CLIFF: His job will be coming through next week at Acme Construction. Now, how about that room?

GEORGE: Well, I guess he wouldn't be hurtin' anything down there. Maybe he could even do a few things around here.

CLIFF: I warned him. *(Pause.)* Well?

GEORGE: Sure, O.K.

CLIFF: Good. *(Turns to call.)* Come on in, Stanley. *(STANLEY and the DOG enter.)* This is my cousin, George Freeman. George, Stanley Martin. *(They greet each other.)* He says he'll let you use the room until your job gets started.

STANLEY: Hey, that's wonderful.

GEORGE: The furnace room is down the hall—last door on the right. You go on down. I'll be with you in a minute.

STANLEY: Thank you. *(Exits stage left behind wall with dog following.)*

GEORGE: *(Watches them leave.)* Cliff, you didn't tell me about the dog. *(Looks at CLIFF.)*

CLIFF: Oh, he'll love it down there. Look. Here's ten bucks. See that he gets something to eat, will you? I'll check back with you later.

GEORGE: *(As CLIFF turns to go.)* Hey, Cliff. I dunno, but I'm a thinkin' that *now* you owe *me* one.

CLIFF: Maybe you're right. See you later.

FINAL MUSIC

Production Notes

There are no outstanding production problems in this play. The truck can be a two-dimensional cardboard cut-out mounted on a stick with fabric matching the backdrop glued on the bottom to mask the stick and the hand. Garbage cans can be bought at craft stores or made of coffee cans with built-up paper maché lids.

The Unwanted Guest

by Jean M. Mattson

CHARACTERS
Sticks
Rabbit
Frog
Jackal
Lion
Elephant
Caterpillar
Narrator's voice

PROPS
Sticks

SOUND EFFECTS
Different drum beat rhythm
for each animal as it
enters and exits

SET PIECES
An African house
Trees
A rock

This is a simple folktale from the African Masai tribe. It has one set and one scene and is written for two puppeteers.

SCENE I: **THE WILDS OF AFRICA. ON STAGE LEFT IS AN AFRICAN HOUSE MADE OF TWIGS WITH A THATCH ROOF AND A HANGING CLOTH DOOR. ON STAGE RIGHT ARE TREES AND A ROCK.**

INTRODUCTORY AFRICAN DRUM MUSIC

> *(RABBIT enters and is busy as if tying twigs on the side of the house. He checks it on all sides and adjusts the cloth door.*

NARRATOR VOICE: *(During RABBIT's activity.)* Once upon a time in the wilds of Africa, there lived a rabbit who decided to build himself a house. He worked long and hard and the house was finally finished.

> *(RABBIT dusts off his hands as FROG enters stage right.)*

RABBIT: Whew, that was a lot of work.

FROG: Yes, it was. Why do you want to wear yourself out like that, Rabbit?

RABBIT: Frog, some of us are hard workers and we accomplish things. *(Insultingly.)* And some of us are lazy and content to just sit around on lily pads all day. Well, that made me hungry. I'm off to find some lunch. *(Exits stage left.)*

FROG: That rabbit isn't very nice sometimes. Why should I build a house? Lily pads are perfectly all right for frogs. *(He hops over to the rock on stage right and sits on it. (FROG watches as CATERPILLAR enters stage right and proceeds slowly to RABBIT's house. He looks inside, then looks both ways to see if anyone is watching, nods, and disappears inside the house.)*

RABBIT: *(RABBIT enters stage left.)* Now I feel better. *(Looks at tracks.)* Hey, wait a minute. What are these funny tracks doing here? They go right into my house. *(Excitedly.)* Some great huge creature must be in my house. Ohhh. Hey, who's inside my house?

CATERPILLAR: *(Roaring from inside house, making the cloth on the door flutter.)* I am the giant of the jungle. I squash the rhinoceros and I stomp the elephant into dust.

RABBIT: What are you doing in there?

CATERPILLAR: I am going to live here.

RABBIT: You can't do that. You're in the wrong house. That's *my* house.

CATERPILLAR: Go away or I will squash you like a peanut.

RABBIT: He sounds as if he really means it. Oh, what should I do?

FROG: *(Hops over to RABBIT.)* Maybe I can help.

RABBIT: Now just what could a little thing like you do here? Besides, the last time I listened to you, I ended up in the water.

FROG: Well, if that's the way you feel about it.

RABBIT: That's the way I feel about it. *(FROG hops back to the rock and RABBIT paces back and forth.)* How can I get that thing out of my house. *(Frantically.)* I need my home. *(JACKAL enters stage right.)* Oh, Jackal, maybe you can help me. Some strange, awful animal is in my house and won't come out.

JACKAL: Somebody's in your new house?

RABBIT: Yes, and he says he's going to live there. Look at these huge tracks. *(JACKAL looks.)* Oh, I know how clever you jackals are. Please help me get him out.

JACKAL: All right. *(Loudly.)* Whoever you are, come out of Rabbit's house!

CATERPILLAR: I am the giant of the jungle. I squash the rhinoceros and I stomp the elephant into dust. Now, go away or I will squash you like a peanut.

JACKAL: He sounds ferocious all right.

RABBIT: What can we do? What can we do?

JACKAL: I know. We'll pile up some sticks around the house and burn him out.

RABBIT: Burn him out? Won't that burn my house too?

JACKAL; You want to get rid of him, don't you?

RABBIT: *(Upset.)* What good will it do if I don't have a house?

JACKAL: Well, suit yourself. *(JACKAL exits stage left.)*

RABBIT: A lot of help he was—wanting to burn my beautiful house down. *(LION enters stage left.)* Oh, Lion, you're the king of the jungle. You'll be able to help me.

LION: Help you do what, Rabbit?

RABBIT: Some terrible creature has moved into my new house. Help me get him out.

LION: Why not. *(Loudly.)* Who is it that's inside Rabbit's house?

CATERPILLAR: I am the giant of the jungle. I squash the rhinoceros and I stomp the elephant into dust.

LION: The king of the jungle speaks. Leave Rabbit's house at once.

CATERPILLAR: Go away, or I will squash you like a peanut.

LION: You will not. I will claw you and bite you to bits. *(Roars.)*

CATERPILLAR: Then come in and try it.

RABBIT: *(When LION doesn't move.) Well?*

LION: You don't expect me to poke my head through that door with that horrible creature inside, do you? Humph! You can get him out yourself, Rabbit. *(Exits stage right.)*

RABBIT: Oh, if the king of the jungle can't help me, who can?

ELEPHANT: *(Enters stage right.)* Hello there, Rabbit. Haven't you finished your house yet?

RABBIT: Oh, Elephant. Yes, I finished it. And now my brand-new house has a ferocious animal inside who won't come out. You are the biggest animal in the bush. Will you help me?

ELEPHANT: I think I can make him leave. *(Loudly.)* You who are in Rabbit's house.

CATERPILLAR: I am the giant of the jungle. I squash the rhinoceros and I stomp the elephant into dust.

ELEPHANT: We'll just see about that. Get out of Rabbit's house.

CATERPILLAR: I will squash you like a peanut if you don't go away.

ELEPHANT: Well, I do some squashing myself. *(Moves toward the house.)* I'll show you.

RABBIT: No—no—no. Don't squash my house.

ELEPHANT: You can build another one.

RABBIT: You don't know how much work it is to build a house. I don't want it squashed.

ELEPHANT: Then you figure it out. And don't say I didn't try to help. *(Exits stage left.)*

RABBIT: Oh, whatever am I going to do? My nice little house that I worked so hard on. Oh—

FROG: *(Hops over to RABBIT.)* Rabbit.

RABBIT: *(Rudely.)* Oh, Frog, what do you want? Can't you see I'm in no mood for chit-chat?

FROG: I really think I might be able to help.

RABBIT: What can a frog do that a lion can't? Huh? Huh? Don't be silly.

FROG: Well, do you want me to try?

RABBIT: I suppose so. What have I got to lose—except my house. *(Ends with a wail.)*

FROG: *(Hops over to the house.)* Watch this. You, the giant of the jungle.

CATERPILLAR: I squash the rhinoceros and I stomp the elephant into dust, and I will squash you like a peanut if you don't go away.

FROG: I think not. I am the Green Monster. A leaper and a croaker. I swallow dragons— (dragon flies, that is) and I will swallow you. Here I come!

CATERPILLAR: No—no—no. Don't swallow me. I'll come out. *(Crawls out of house.)* I am only a caterpillar, see? I won't hurt you. I was only joking.

FROG: Well, so was I. You are the last thing I would want to swallow.

RABBIT: A caterpillar! You couldn't squash anything.

CATERPILLAR: It was a pretty good joke, though, wasn't it? *(Crawls away, chuckling.)*

RABBIT: You creepy thing, you. *(Watches CATERPILLAR disappear.)* I feel rather foolish. *(Turns to FROG.)* How did you know it was only a caterpillar?

FROG: Sitting on lily pads makes one wise, Rabbit. You should try it some time.

(FROG hops off stage right. RABBIT watches him go, thinks, looks after him again, shakes his head, shrugs, and exits into his house.)

FINAL MUSIC

Production Notes

There are no outstanding production problems in this play. It should be emphasized, however, that the use of imaginative sound effects and rhythms for the various animals will greatly enhance their personalities.

Why the Bear Has a Stumpy Tail

by Jean M. Mattson

Based on an old Norwegian folktale.

CHARACTERS
Bear
Goat
Elk
Fox
Narrator's voice

PROPS
Large snowball for snowman
Snowball for snowman head
Branch
Bucket
String of fish
Pick

SET PIECES
Trees and bushes

A simple production with one set and one scene. It can be performed by two puppeteers.

SCENE I: A FOREST. TREES AND BUSHES. THERE IS A SMALL POND CENTER STAGE.

INTRODUCTORY MUSIC

> *(BEAR enters stage left, proudly swinging his long beautiful tail as he skates.)*

NARRATOR'S VOICE: A long time ago when all bears had long tails, there was a bear whose tail was his pride and joy. *(BEAR swishes his tail.)* How he loved that tail! *(BEAR kisses his tail.)* One winter day, as he was skating on the frozen pond—

MUSIC FADES

> *(GOAT skates in stage left.)*

BEAR: Oh, hi, Goat.

GOAT: Hi, Bear.

BEAR: Didn't know you skated.

GOAT: Just trying out my new skates.

BEAR: Well, you're lucky I'm here because I'm one of the best skaters in the whole forest. I have broad paws which give me a firm grip on the ice—and then my tail gives me balance. Too bad you don't have a tail like mine. But I can maybe teach you to be a good skater anyway.

GOAT: Oh, I don't want to be a good skater, Bear. I just want to have a little fun. *(Starts to skate. BEAR grabs GOAT's scarf, causing GOAT to skitter around and almost fall.)*

BEAR: Now listen, Goat, you might as well be as good a skater as you can be. And to do that you should listen to someone who knows what he's talking about—me.

GOAT: Oh, Bear—I—

BEAR: First, you've got to watch your posture. Head up. *(Pushes GOAT's head.)* Back straight. *(Pushes GOAT's back.)* Then your rhythm is important. Watch closely. *(Begins to skate.)* 1-2-3. 1-2-3. Just like this. *(BEAR twirls and circles. GOAT shakes his head and skates off stage left. Bear finally realizes GOAT is no longer there.)* Goat? *(Looks around.)* Goat? Now where did he go, anyway? *(Shrugs.)* Too bad. His loss. *(BEAR continues to dip and glide.)*

(ELK enters stage right rolling big snowball. BEAR watches him as he rolls another smaller one and places it on top, then another for the head, which has eyes, nose, and ears.)

BEAR: Hi, Elk. What are you doing?

ELK: I'm making a snowman. All the kids on the farm make them, so I thought I'd try it.

BEAR: Oh, yeah. I've done that dozens of times. Only I make snow bears. That's what you should do—make a snow bear.

ELK: Now, why should I do that?

BEAR: Why shouldn't you? A fitting monument to one of the forest's finest specimens.

ELK: Bear, you are too much.

BEAR: *(Looks at snowman.)* You'll just need to change those ears. *(ELK exits stage left.)* Hey, where you going? Hmm. He's sure hard to get along with. *(Looks at snowman.)* Let's make you a snow bear. And to do that, you need a tail. *(Skates around and finds a branch, which he sticks on the snowman)* There. It's not soft and silky like mine. But it's the best I can do. *(BEAR skates off stage right. FOX enters with bucket and pick, which he puts down close to center stage. He chips a hole in the ice with his pick as he sing-songs.)*

FOX: How I like to fish, winter or spring
A branch for a pole, and a hook and a string.
I sit on the bank when it's balmy and nice.
When it's winter and cold, I fish through the ice.
There. That's a big enough hole I think.
(ELK and GOAT enter stage left.)

ELK: Saw you coming over here with your bucket, Fox. How are you doing?

FOX: Had some good luck around the bend, I thought I'd try over here too. It's a good fishing spot in the summer.

GOAT: How do you keep that hole open? Seems like your fish line would freeze right in there solid.

FOX: Oh, you have to keep chipping it out all the time. And you keep your line bobbing up and down. That keeps it from freezing. Lots of work, but it's worth it. I have a good time ice fishing.

GOAT: We were having a good time too, both of us, skating and making snowmen, until Bear came along.

ELK: I just hate to see that Bear coming anymore. All he can talk about is himself.

GOAT: *And* his tail!

ELK: *(He sees snowbear.)* Oh, look, he even put a tail on my snowman. That really makes me mad.

FOX: I think everyone hates to see him coming, Elk. All because of his stupid pride and that ridiculous tail.

ELK: *(Hears BEAR singing.)* Oh, here he comes. Too bad! Your good fishing is over, Fox.

GOAT: Oh, I just can't stay and listen to any more of Bear's bragging. I'll see you later.

ELK: Me too. *(Exeunt stage left.)*

FOX: *(Thinks as he looks at hole and then at BEAR as he nears.)* Well, if Bear bothers me, I'll show him. I'll fix him and his tail.

BEAR: *(Enters right.)* Well, if it isn't my old friend, Fox. And look at that nice hole you've chopped there.

FOX: Careful, there, Bear. Careful. *(BEAR steps into his hole.)*

BEAR: Oh, sorry. Didn't mean to disturb your line.

FOX: Just stay away, Bear. Stay away!

BEAR: I knew you were fishing by the way you were concentrating.

FOX: Yes, you've got to concentrate to fish, and you need peace and quiet. *(Insinuatingly.)*

BEAR: I know that. I'm a fisherman from way back.

FOX: Good. Good. *(Turns back to hole.)*

BEAR: Yeah, I've fished in all the rivers, streams, lakes, bays, and even the puddles. *(Laughs.)* Get that? Even the puddles. *(Laughs again.)*

FOX: *(Aggravated.)* Yes, Bear.

BEAR: I've caught just about every kind of fish there is too—trout, bass, smelt, pike, perch, goldfish, and whales. Yeah. Yeah. I know all about fishing equipment too. If you want to know anything about anything, just ask me. I know a stringer from a sinker, you bet. Hey, have you caught any fish?

FOX: Oh, what's the use. Yes, Bear, I got some fish, over at the other lake where I had *peace* and *quiet*. *(Pulls string of fish out of the bucket.)*

BEAR: Hey, that's some catch. How did you do that? What kind of bait did you use? Come on, you can tell me. *(Pokes him in the ribs.)* I'm your friend, the bear with the most beautiful tail in the world. Come on. *(Cajolingly.)*

FOX: Ahhh. *(Getting an idea.)* Well—yes, I'll tell you, Bear. Since you're such a good fisherman.

BEAR: Good! Good!

FOX: I caught those fish . . . *(Looks around to be sure no one is listening.)*

BEAR: Yeah, yeah?

FOX: . . . with my *tail.*

BEAR: With your *tail?*

FOX: Shhhhhh! Yes, my tail.

BEAR: You know, I always thought that might work, but I never got around to trying it somehow.

FOX: Sure, Bear, sure. Ahh, why don't you try it now? You can use my hole here.

BEAR: Oh, that's mighty decent of you *(Looks in hole.),* but I hate to put my tail in the—

FOX: If I caught this many fish with my so-called second-rate tail, think what you could do with what you've got back there.

BEAR: *(Looks at his tail.)* Ahhh, yes. You're right. What do I do?

FOX: Well, you just put your tail right down into the hole here. Sit down. *(Pushes BEAR down and his tail in the hole. BEAR jumps yelling.)* What's the matter?

BEAR: It's cold, that's what's the matter. That's ice water down there.

FOX: Well, of course. That's what makes the fish so good to eat. You'll get used to it. And it'll be worth every shiver. Now sit down and put your tail in. *(BEAR does so "ooing.")* You got it in? Good. Good.

BEAR: And I just sit here?

FOX: That's right—quietly. And don't move. It'll scare the fish. Now, your tail may sting a little after a bit, but don't let that bother you. That's the fish biting.

BEAR: Oh, O.K.

FOX: I'll be back after a while and help you count the fish. *(Takes bucket and exits, laughing.)*

BEAR: Oh, boy. Fish for dinner. I can hardly wait to pull them up. Sure glad I got this idea. Hmmm. It's beginning to sting. That means they're biting already.

             (ELK and GOAT enter stage left.)

GOAT: Fox told us what a marvelous thing you're doing with your tail.

BEAR: Oh, yes, my tail becomes more valuable ever day. In addition to its beauty, it can now provide me with not only fun and games but also food. I shall soon pull up a catch the likes of which you have never seen.

GOAT: How do you know when you've caught some?

BEAR: When it stings. And it's stinging like crazy now—just like crazy. Oh, what a tail I've got.

ELK: Well, good luck. We'll come back later and see all the fish, won't we, Goat?

GOAT: Yeah, good luck. *(They exeunt, laughing.)*

BEAR: Oh, it's really stinging now. It must be time to pull it out. *(Tries.)* Oh, oh, it must be stuck. Oh, dear. *(He pulls hard again and again until he's finally loose and he sprawls on the ice.)* Ohh. I'm so stiff from sitting on that cold ice, I can hardly move. *(Finally stands up and is able to look behind.)* Oh, I don't have any fish. Wait a minute. *(Screams.)* I don't have any tail! *(Hysterically.)* My lovely tail! It's gone! Where did it go? The hole. *(Looks.)* It's frozen in the ice. Oh, my lovely tail. It's pulled right off. My beautiful, graceful, luxurious, shiny, sleek tail. How can I face my friends without my lovely tail? *(Looks.)* All I have left is a stub, a stump. I'm ruined. *(Looks.)* Well—maybe that stump isn't so bad. *(Looks and walks.)* Well, ahhhh *(Modestly.)*, it's really kind of cute. *(Looks.)* Yeah, it is. *(Prances.)* Yes, it's really rather a cute little stubby tail—if I do say so myself.

             (ELK, GOAT, and FOX enter stage left.)

ALL: How'd you do? Catch anything? Having good luck?

BEAR: Well, no. I didn't catch any fish. *(They react, "Too bad," etc.)* And on top of that, I lost my beautiful long tail. Caught there in the ice. Pulled right off. *(They sympathize.)* But, you know, I've got something else.

ALL: What do you mean? Something else? *(Etc.)*

BEAR: Well, I hope you guys won't be too disappointed if I don't play with you this afternoon. I've got to go and show everybody this new development.

ALL: New development?

BEAR: Listen to this. I have now got the most adorable, darling, precious little tail you ever saw. Take a look. *(Wiggles his tail.)* Cute little stub of a tail, huh? Perky, tricky little stump! Cutest little tail in the whole darn forest. I should say. *(BEAR prances off stage right continuing to expound. The animals watch him exit.)*

FOX: It didn't help a bit. Now he's got the cutest *little* tail in the whole darn forest.

ALL: Oh, noooooooo.

FINALE

VOICE: *(Voice-over.)* Bear never changed, and the forest animals learned to be charitable toward him and his attitudes, but from that day on, so the story goes, bears have had very short stubby tails.

Production Notes

Snowball— A styrofoam ball with a dowel or stick embedded in it as a control makes a great snowball that can be rolled out onto the stage. It should be secured in some way on the playboard so another snowball can be mounted on it. The stick can be clipped onto the playboard or the snow can be seated in a cardboard snowbank.

Bear's tail— A bushy tail can be made with a pocket on the end that fits over and is pinned to Bear's little stubby tail. Velcro also can be used to attach the tail to Bear's body. The sound of it being ripped off would be appropriate when his tail comes off in the ice.

String of fish—The string of fish can be more easily manipulated if they are attached to a small dowel.

Zap Happy

by Betsy Tobin, Paul Nelson, and Jean M. Mattson

An original play about electrical safety.

CHARACTERS
Ginger Lee—a fifth-grade girl
Hap Hazard—a middle-aged man,
    Ginger's neighbor
Nurse Penny Cillin
Noah Lott—a fifth-grade boy
Alec Smart—a fifth-grade boy
Miss Peabody—principal of
    Seymour Recess Elementary
    School
Herb—Alec's cat
Voice of disc jockey

PROP
Book
Pamphlet
Telephone
Kite
Bundle of wood
Super lunch box
Rod of amber
Hap Hazard on gurney

SET PIECES
Street with tree and
    power poles
Yard with tree to climb
Substation with fence
School stage

SOUND EFFECTS
Crackle and hissing
Siren
Thunder
Explosion

Seattle Puppetory Theatre was commissioned by Seattle City Light to write and produce this play to teach electrical safety to the children in the elementary schools of Seattle. It was written to be performed by two puppeteers. It has four sets and six scenes.

INTRODUCTORY MUSIC

> *(Small table to left of stage with a lamp that lights a radio. Lights out on blank stage.)*

MUSIC FADES

VOICE: Hey, that was a really hot tune by a number one band, and now the last item on our Local Coming Events Calendar. At two o'clock this Friday at the Seymour Recess Elementary School there will be a panel discussion on electricity with student presentations. The public is invited to attend. And now, more music on K-O-R-N.

> *(Song begins and fades out. Radio light fades as lights go up on blank stage. GINGER LEE enters in a state of exasperation. She paces back and forth.)*

GINGER: Hi, I'm Ginger Lee and I'm one of three students who's been asked to make a presentation on electricity at my school on Friday—that's Seymour Recess School—and I just can't think of anything. I've got my encyclopedia here—maybe it'll give me some ideas. *(Brings up a book and turns the pages.)* Let's see. Elastic, elec—oh, here it is. "Electricity. Electricity is a form of powerful energy looking for a place to go that travels through wires to homes, schools, offices, and factories to do many things." Well, that doesn't help me much. *(Puts book away.)* Maybe I should look in that little pamphlet I had. Where is that anyway? *(Looks and finds it.)* Oh, here it is. It's called "Electrical Safety from A to Zap" Let's see. "Think 'Zap' when you fly kites or model airplanes around electric lines." Hmm. "Think 'Zap' when you play with electrical appliances, especially near water." Like in a bathtub. Say, that might be a good idea for my presentation. Oh, no. I don't think I want to take a bath in front of the whole school. Oh, I'll just never think of anything. *(Rolls on the floor, hits head on the stage, and thinks. Phone rings.)* Oh, now the phone. I'm coming. I'm coming. *(GINGER answers the phone.)* Oh, hello. Hi, Noah. Have you got your project yet? You do? You are? You have? You did? Oh, yeah. Bye. *(Hangs up.)* Wouldn't you know. Noah has his project all planned. I'll be the only one who doesn't have a presentation. I'll be laughed right out of school. Just think, a washout at age ten! Ohhhhhhh! *(Ginger exits.)*

LIGHTS DIM ON MAIN STAGE. LIGHT ON RADIO UP. RADIO FADES IN. THE MUSICAL NUMBER ENDS

VOICE: And now, here's K-O-R-N weather. It's sixty-five degrees in beautiful downtown *(Insert name of city.)* Quite a breeze blowing out there, and it's a fine day for sailing. By the way, this is Rats Roberts telling you all to go fly a kite. But first, how about listening to this hot new tune by Peppin called "Crunchy Piano."

MUSIC UP AND FADES. LIGHT ON RADIO FADES AS LIGHTS GO UP ON MAIN STAGE

SCENE II: **A STREET. UTILITY POLES ON STAGE LEFT WITH WIRES LEADING TO A TREE ON STAGE RIGHT.**

(HAP HAZARD enters stage right with kite.)

HAZARD: Hap Hazard here, world champion kite flyer! *(Hazard runs across the stage pulling a kite, which does not go up. He runs back across. He runs halfway across again and looks up in the air. To audience.)* Is it up yet? Is it up yet? No? *(To kite on the ground.)* Listen, kite, if you don't go up, you'll end up in the bottom of my bird cage. *(Kite goes up immediately, swooping through the air.)* That's more like it.

(GINGER LEE enters stage right and watches HAP HAZARD fly his kite.)

GINGER: Hi, Mr. Hazard. Can you help me with my school project on electricity?

HAZARD: Please don't bother me now, kid. I'm busy.

GINGER: Are you flying a kite?

HAZARD: No, I'm cooking spaghetti. Of course, I'm flying a kite. Now don't bother me.

(Kite flies close to wires.)

GINGER: Well, excuse me, Mr. Hazard, but I read somewhere that it's very dangerous to fly kites close to power lines. You should think "Zap."

HAZARD: Zap, shnap! Leave me alone, kid. Can't you see I'm having fun?

(GINGER watches, shaking her head. Kite flies into wires. There is a big flash, a loud crackle, and a puff of smoke. HAZARD collapses, shocked.)

GINGER: Oh, oh.

SOUND OF SIREN

PENNY: *(PENNY CILLIN swoops in stage right.)* Nurse Penny Cillin on the job. *(Examines situation.)* Why, this man has been zapped!

GINGER: He was flying his kite, and it went too close to the power lines. I told him—I told him—

PENNY: *(In a clipped authoritative voice.)* Don't touch that kite! Call your electric power company. *(Or use the name of your local power company.)*

GINGER: Oh, O.K. *(GINGER exits stage right. Penny picks up Hazard and carries him off stage right.)*

SOUND OF SIREN. LIGHTS FADE ON MAIN STAGE. MUSIC FADES IN. LIGHT ON RADIO UP. SONG ENDS

VOICE: Here's a special news bulletin. Mr. Hap Hazard, a highly respected citizen out in the north end, was seriously injured today flying his kite too near the power lines. Nurse Penny Cillin of the Department of Health says that this should be a warning to all you kite flyers out there. And now, the weather. Storm off the coast. Small craft warnings. 90% chance of rain. Thunder and lightning storms expected. And now back to more K-O-R-N.

MUSIC UP. LIGHT ON RADIO FADES. LIGHTS UP ON MAIN STAGE. MUSIC FADES

SCENE III: A YARD. A TREE IS UP STAGE.

             (HAP HAZARD enters stage right with arm in a sling, carrying a bundle of wood and tools. He attaches bundle to rope in tree and examines the tree.)

HAZARD: Hap Hazard, master builder. I'll just give it the old "one-two." One, two, three, four.

             (Grunts and groans as he climbs the tree. He disappears into the leaves and appears in the tree looking down at the wood. He nods and pulls the wood up.) Heave—ho! Heave—ho! Heave—ho!

             (GINGER LEE enters in yellow rain slicker, singing a song. She hears HAP HAZARD hammering. He yelps in pain as he hits his finger. GINGER giggles, then approaches the tree.)

GINGER: Hi, Mr. Hazard. Are you building a tree house?

HAZARD: *(Peeks out of the leaves.)* No, I'm taking tap dancing lessons. Of course, I'm building a tree house, so I'll have my own private place. No kids allowed!

GINGER: Well, Mr. Hazard, I'm still working on my presentation on electricity. Can you help me now?

HAZARD: *(Disappears.)* Uh, nope. Uh-huh! *(Continues to hammer.)*

GINGER: Oh. *(Sound of thunder.)* Excuse me, Mr. Hazard, but it's raining. *(Appears.)*

HAZARD: *(Looks up at the sky.)* I know it's raining. *(Disappears.)*

GINGER: Well, according to the booklet I read, you're not supposed to play in trees near wires. Especially in the rain!

HAZARD: *(Looks down.)* Look, kid, you don't have to tell me anything about—

(Thunder. Lightning strikes tree with a flash. HAP HAZARD falls out of tree. GINGER Looks on.)

GINGER: Oh, oh.

SOUND OF SIREN

PENNY: *(Enters and surveys the situation.)* Zapped again!

GINGER: I told him not to play in the tree so close to the power lines. I told him—

PENNY: Well, he should have listened to you-know-who.

GINGER: The electric power company. *(Insert name of local company.)*

(PENNY picks up Hazard and rushes off stage right.)

SOUND OF SIREN. LIGHTS FADE ON MAIN STAGE. MUSIC UP. LIGHT ON RADIO UP. SONG ENDS

VOICE: K-O-R-N News Bulletin. We have one casualty to report from today's thunderstorm. Mr. Hap Hazard, released only this morning from General Hospital, was rushed back to the emergency room for severe head wounds suffered when lightning struck the tree he was playing in. Stay tuned to K-O-R-N for more news updates. Now, back to some Korny music—

MUSIC ON. RADIO LIGHT DIMS. SONG FADES AS LIGHTS GO UP ON MAIN STAGE

SCENE IV: SUBSTATION. A FENCE HAS A "DANGER HIGH VOLTAGE" SIGN.

(HAZARD enters stage left with head and body bandaged. He is limping.)

HAZARD: Hap Hazard, wounded in action.

GINGER: *(Offstage.)* Hi, Mr. Hazard. It's me.

HAZARD: That kid again. That little brat is beginning to bother me. *(Sees substation.)* Oh, I'll just sneak in here and ditch her. *(Crawls over fence, groaning. GINGER enters stage right.)* I'm still working on my electrical project. Can't you help me now? Mr. Hazard—Mr. Hazard—Yoo hoo! Mr. Hazard, is that you hiding behind that fence?

HAZARD: No, it's a talking power line pole. Of course, it's me hiding behind the fence.

GINGER: Oh, Mr. Hazard, you're not supposed to be playing in substations. Didn't you see the sign? It says "Danger High Voltage."

HAZARD: I don't want to hear anything about voltage.

GINGER: Oh, but, Mr. Hazard, it's dangerous in there.

HAZARD: I don't want to hear anything about it, you hear?

GINGER: Be careful. There are transformers back there.

HAZARD: Leave me alone, Kid. I don't care! I don't care! I don't care! I don't carrrrr—

EXPLOSION. LIGHTS FLASH

(HAZARD'S voice trails off as he falls.)

GINGER: Oh, oh.

SOUND OF SIREN

(PENNY CILLIN enters stage right and looks at HAZARD.)

PENNY: This man is absolutely zap-happy!

GINGER: Oh, I told him. I told him he shouldn't be behind the fence. I told him—

PENNY: Oh, he needs a lot of help. Come on. We'll need help to get him out of there.

(They exeunt stage right.)

SOUND OF SIREN. LIGHTS DIM ON MAIN STAGE. LIGHT ON RADIO UP. RADIO FADES UP

VOICE: KORN news time is half past a freckle. The power was out in the north end of town today for five hours while workmen repaired considerable damage done to the substation. Homes in the area have been without lights since this morning. You're listening to K-O-R-N, and we'd like to remind you that tomorrow's the day for the panel discussion on electricity with student presentations. Everyone is urged to attend. That's two o'clock at Seymour Recess Elementary School. And now for more KORN music.

MUSIC UP AND FADES. LIGHT ON RADIO FADES. LIGHTS UP ON MAIN STAGE

SCENE V: **PLAYGROUND.**

(NOAH and ALEC enter.)

ALEC: My project's gonna be the best.

NOAH: Mine's better. It's an invention and I'm the inventor.

ALEC: Mine's still better.

NOAH: Uh-uh. My dad says that mine is gonna change things.

ALEC: Uh-huh. *(Pushes NOAH.)*

NOAH: Uh-uh! *(Shoves ALEC.)*

ALEC: Uh-huh. *(More pushing and shoving.)*

NOAH: Uh-uh!

(A short fight ends up with them rolling on the stage with groans and shrieks.)

ALEC: Draw. *(They stop fighting. ALEC gets up.)* Are you O.K.?

NOAH: Uh, well, I think so. *(Gets up)*

ALEC: Well, you know, at least they'll both be better than Ginger's. *(NOAH nods his head.)* She doesn't have anything. *(They giggle.)* Come on, I'll show you mine. It's gonna be the best.

NOAH: No, it isn't. *(They exeunt as voices trail off.)*

TRANSITIONAL MUSIC

SCENE VI: STAGE AT SEYMOUR RECESS ELEMENTARY SCHOOL WITH A PODIUM ON STAGE LEFT AND AN AMERICAN FLAG ON STAGE RIGHT.

(MISS PEABODY enters.)

Miss Peabody instructs her class in *Zap Happy*. Puppet by Nick LeFeuvre.

PEABODY: To conclude our program today, we have presentations on electricity given by the students here at Seymour Recess Elementary School. The first will be given by Noah Lott. Noah.

NOAH: *(Enters stage right and clears his throat.)* Thank you, Miss Principal, Miss Peabody. *(MISS PEABODY exits.)* Electricity can be very useful. It can make things easier. My invention can make things easier. My father says that my invention could revolutionize the whole school system. He's very proud of me, and I know that you will be too. And now for my invention. *(Exits and returns with large lunch box.)* Have you ever wished that noontime was a time of excitement? Have you ever dreamed that 12 o'clock was full of fun, zip, and zingy? Well, if you have—what you need is my invention, Noah's Automatic Lunch Box. It will peel your orange, salt your egg, and wipe your mouth. In other words, it will put punch into your lunch! And all you have to do is push the button—which I will do now.

           (NOAH pushes the button and the lunch box rattles and jumps around the stage, opens and shuts with loud noises, flashes, and explodes with confetti streamers. Bell rings and bubbles float up from the lunch box. NOAH is

shocked and stammers.) Well, my invention needs a little work—but you get the idea. *(NOAH exits hurriedly stage right, taking his lunch box with him.)*

PEABODY: *(Enters stage left puzzled and embarrassed.)* Ahhh. Thank you, Noah. Well—our next presentation will be given by Alec Smart. Alec.

ALEC: *(Enters stage right.)* Boy, that one really backfired. *(Giggles, then notices MISS PEABODY.)*

PEABODY: Alec! *(Looks disapprovingly at ALEC as she exits stage left.)*

ALEC: Oh, excuse me, Miss Peabody. *(Looks at audience and bows.)* Sometimes you need electricity and there's no plugs available, so you have to make your own. And for my presentation, that's what I'm going to do—right here now. First, you need some fur. So I brought my cat, Herb. He's got some. Herb—come here, Herb. Come on, boy. Herb? *(Exits stage right. Heard offstage.)* Come on, Herb, would you get your tail up there. *(Enters with HERB who looks around and rubs up against ALEC.)* Then you need a rod of amber, and I brought one of those, too. Now, Herb, you stay, boy—*(Exits and returns with rod. HERB meows.)* Then you have to rub the fur, well, in this case, the cat. Here, I'll show you. *(HERB meows.)* Any minute now you'll see the sparks. Come on, Herb. Do it. *(HERB hisses and backs away. ALEC drops the rod of amber. HERB leaps after him and chases ALEC offstage right. ALEC exits screaming.)*

PEABODY: Thank you, Alec. Oh, dear. Well, our third and final presentation will be given by Ginger Lee, who will speak to us on a very important subject. Ginger.

(GINGER enters stage right as MISS PEABODY exits stage left.)

GINGER: Thank you. In my research, I learned that electricity can be very dangerous if you do foolish things. So, do not fly kites near power lines. Do not play in trees near power lines, especially in the rain. And never, never, *never* play inside substations. And now, my presentation—an example of what electricity can do to you if you're not careful around it.

SOUND OF SIREN

(NURSE PENNY CILLIN enters stage right pushing HAP HAZARD in on a gurney. HAZARD is covered from head to toe with bandages. Only his eyes are visible.) Ladies and gentlemen, Mr. Hap Hazard. *(HAZARD groans.)* A living example. *(HAZARD lifts his head and looks at audience, nods, and sinks back.)*

PENNY: Well, just barely. *(HAZARD groans again as NURSE PENNY CILLIN exits stage right with the gurney.)*

SOUND OF SIREN

GINGER: Thank you very much. Now remember, everybody, if your kite gets caught in the wires, if you see a fallen wire, if your baseball goes over the fence, who are you going to call?

ALL: Your electric power company! *(The name of your local power company.)*

GINGER: That's right. Thank you. *(Exits stage right.)*

LIGHTS DOWN ON MAIN STAGE. LIGHT ON RADIO UP. MUSIC UP

VOICE: *(Over music.)* This program was brought to you by *(The name of the Sponsor.)* *(The name of the performing company)* thanks you for tuning in to K-O-R-N.

MUSIC SWELLS INTO FINALE

Production Notes

Alec's lunch box—A rod on the lid of a lunch box can open and close it. Poppers make noise and confetti. A bright flashlight for flashes, a whistle and bubbles complete the erratic actions of Alec's invention.

Puff of smoke—Powder can be used in a small funnel with a nylon or cheesecloth cover and a rubber hose attached.

Tree—A plywood tree behind a high fence works for Hazard's climbing. A hole can be cut in the upper tree and the whole tree covered with felt leaves.

Kite—A tagboard kite can be mounted on a wire.

Appendix

Manipulation Charts

The following pages include manipulation charts for several of the plays in the book. The charts are merely suggestions for performing the plays, offered to help beginning puppeteers. The left-hand and right-hand positions, no doubt, will be modified according to the type of stage, the type of puppet, the location of the set pieces, the number of puppeteers available, and personal preferences. (These plays were originally performed using a stand-up stage.)

The two-person plays were originally performed by two experienced puppeteers who were used to working together. For beginners, to assure smooth performances, an additional puppeteer or two can be a big help.

In some cases stick (or rod) puppets may be used in these plays. It is noted when their use is mandatory.

For more information about the manipulation charts, please contact the Seattle Puppetory Theatre, 13002 10th Ave., N.W., Seattle, Washington 98177, or send an E-mail message to the author at jmariematt@aol.com.

The Frog Prince
Manipulation Chart for One Puppeteer

LEFT HAND		RIGHT HAND
	PRESET Bare Stage.	
	SCENE I	WITCH
BETWEEN SCENES: UP PRINCE'S CASTLE.		
PRINCE	**SCENE II**	WITCH
BETWEEN SCENES: DOWN CASTLE. UP TREES.		
FROG	**SCENE III**	WOMEN
BETWEEN SCENES: UP WELL.		
FROG / BALL / KING / BALL / FROG / KING / FROG / PRINCE	**SCENE IV**	GRANOLA

ADDITIONAL SUGGESTIONS
1. The Frog must be a stick puppet.
2. The left hand has the King or Prince on while manipulating the Frog and the Ball.
3. When the Frog brings the Ball out of the well, the Ball appears and is taken by Granola, and then the Frog appears.
4. Puppeteer changes from King to Prince while Granola is deciding to kiss the Frog.

The Ant and the Grasshopper
Manipulation Chart for One Puppeteer

LEFT HAND		RIGHT HAND
	PRESET Outside Ant's House.	
HOPPER	**SCENE I**	ANT
BETWEEN SCENES: UP Snow.		
HOPPER	**SCENE II**	ANT

ADDITIONAL SUGGESTION
1. Ant can carry a bag for wheat on his back.

The Lion and the Mouse
Manipulation Chart for One Puppeteer

LEFT HAND		RIGHT HAND
	PRESET UP Jungle.	
MOUSE	**SCENE I**	LION
MOUSE	**SCENE II**	LION

ADDITIONAL SUGGESTIONS
1. With hand puppets, there is no problem for the Mouse to remove net from Lion.
2. With stick puppets, the puppeteer can hold the Mouse in his left hand, behind the Lion, as right hand removes the net.

Christmas Constellation

Manipulation Chart for Two Puppeteers

PUPPETEER I

	LEFT HAND	RIGHT HAND
SCENE I	CONOVER	HILL
	BOY	SIMMS
	DOG	
	HILL	
SCENE II	DAVEY	
	CONOVER	
	HILL	

PUPPETEER II

	LEFT HAND	RIGHT HAND
PRESET — Street Scene.		SIMMS
SCENE I	ELLEN	DAVEY
	DOG	DOCTOR
SCENE II	DOG	ELLEN
	DOCTOR	SIMMS

BETWEEN SCENES — DOWN Street. UP Bedroom.

SEGUE TO DREAM AND RETURN

ADDITIONAL SUGGESTIONS

1. For easy manipulation, the DOG can be a stick rather than a hand puppet.
2. OPTIONAL. After several performances the children in the audience let us know they wanted ELLEN and DAVEY to see their Christmas gifts. So, in subsequent performances, during the final VOICE-OVER, the children awake, see their gifts, and hug each other. FATHER enters, receives his cookies and hugs, and then all take a bow and exeunt.

Gold Nugget Champ

Manipulation Chart for Two Puppeteers

Scene	PUPPETEER I LEFT HAND	PUPPETEER I RIGHT HAND	PUPPETEER II LEFT HAND	PUPPETEER II RIGHT HAND
PRESET Front Yard.	DOG / MRS. CRAWFORD	JEREMY	DOG (during stick throwing) / MR. CRAWFORD	SAM
SCENE I	JEREMY	MR. CRAWFORD		MRS. CRAWFORD
BETWEEN SCENES: DOWN YARD. UP LIVING ROOM.				
SCENE II	CUSTOMER	JEREMY		
BETWEEN SCENES: DOWN LIVING ROOM. UP STREET.				
SCENE III			DOG SLED AND DRIVER	MR. BERRY / MR. BERRY
BETWEEN SCENES: DOWN STREET. UP Ship.				
SCENE IV	PASSENGER	SAM	DOG	DOG OWNER
BETWEEN SCENES: DOWN SHIP. UP LIVING ROOM.				
SCENE V	SAM	JEREMY	DOG	MRS. CRAWFORD

ADDITIONAL SUGGESTION DOG should be a stick puppet. Throwing stick can be on a wire, or multiple sticks thrown and attached to dog's mouth.

Rumplestiltskin

Manipulation Chart for Two Puppeteers

PUPPETEER I		SCENE	PUPPETEER II	
LEFT HAND	RIGHT HAND		LEFT HAND	RIGHT HAND
		PRESET Castle with Table and Records.		
	QUEEN	**SCENE I**		KING
		BETWEEN SCENES DOWN CASTLE. UP MILL.		
ROSALIND	MILLER	**SCENE II**	KING	
		BETWEEN SCENES DOWN MILL. UP CASTLE WITH SPINNING WHEEL.		
ROSALIND	KING / MILLER	**SCENE III**	RUMPLESTILTSKIN / KING	QUEEN
		BETWEEN SCENES DOWN SPINNING WHEEL. UP CRADLE.		
MILLER	ROSALIND with baby	**SCENE IV**	RUMPLESTILTSKIN	
		BETWEEN SCENES DOWN CASTLE. UP FOREST.		
	MILLER	**SCENE V**	RUMPLESTILTSKIN	
		BETWEEN SCENES DOWN FOREST. UP CASTLE.		
KING	ROSALIND with baby	**SCENE VI**	MILLER	RUMPLESTILTSKIN

Index

About the Author

Jean Mattson has had a life-long interest in theatre. She has been writing plays since elementary school and has had a number published through the years. Although sidetracked in college by a degree in chemistry, in 1972 she finally earned her M.A. in theatre arts with a focus on playwriting. Her master's thesis was a full-length play, a humorous but faithful history of the women's movement from 1820 to 1920 entitled *The Petticoat Prerogative*. It was among several of her plays produced by the University of North Dakota's Summer Theatre.

Since 1973, when she and Paul Nelson founded the Seattle Puppetory Theatre, Mattson has concentrated on puppet plays, which she writes, produces, and performs for schools, libraries, theatres, and parties. The company has toured Japan five times, as well as Mexico, Spain, Pakistan, and Canada. In 1988 the Seattle Puppetory Theatre received the coveted Citation of Excellence from the American Center of the Union Internationalle de la Marionnette. Mattson has served on the national board of the Puppeteers of America and is currently their script consultant. She is a widow with three grown children and currently lives in Seattle.

Jean Mattson and Matajaro Oda pose in Osaka in front of a billboard advertising *The Return of the Bounce.*

235